Suffering and Smiling

Suffering and Smiling

Daily Life in North Korea

Byung-Ho Chung

ROWMAN & LITTLEFIELD
Lanham • Boulder • New York • London

Published by Rowman & Littlefield
An imprint of The Rowman & Littlefield Publishing Group, Inc.
4501 Forbes Boulevard, Suite 200, Lanham, Maryland 20706
www.rowman.com

86-90 Paul Street, London EC2A 4NE

British Library Cataloguing in Publication Information Available

Library of Congress Cataloging-in-Publication Data
Names: Chung, Byung-Ho, 1955- author.
Title: Suffering and smiling : everyday life in North Korea / Byung-Ho Chung.
Description: Lanham ; Boulder ; New York ; London : Rowman & Littlefield, [2024] |
    Includes bibliographical references and index. | This book is a complete revision of
    the original Korean version for English readers.
Identifiers: LCCN 2024018333 (print) | LCCN 2024018334 (ebook) | ISBN
    9781538193846 (cloth) | ISBN 9781538193853 (epub)
Subjects: LCSH: Korea (North)—Social life and customs. | Korea (North)—Social
    conditions. | Korea (North)—History. | Korea (North)—Politics and government. |
    Chung, Byung-Ho, 1955-
Classification: LCC DS935.7776 .C49 2024 (print) | LCC DS935.7776 (ebook) | DDC
    951.93—dc23/eng/20240503
LC record available at https://lccn.loc.gov/2024018333
LC ebook record available at https://lccn.loc.gov/2024018334

To the memory of my grandmother, Oh Hyun-Kwan,
and my mother, Lee Hak-Suhn

Contents

Prologue

Suffering and smiling coexist in the everyday lives of North Koreans. The Arduous March of guerrillas led by Kim Il-Sung in the struggle against Imperial Japan has long been viewed as a symbol of great suffering that paved the way for the triumph of national independence. The widespread famine of the 1990s in North Korea was also called the Arduous March (*gonan ui haengun*). Throughout this period of national suffering, signs commanding the nation to smile were seen across the country: "March with a smile though the roads are rough!"

Unbeknownst to the outside world, the North Korea of today is undergoing a period of rapid change. To understand this process, one must understand the norms and values that shape the behavior of the people. Considered alongside one another, suffering and smiling are two concepts that can help us understand contemporary North Korean society and culture.

In the spring of 1996, I came across a picture of children with wan expressions gazing vacantly at the camera. The caption read: "North Korean children dying of hunger." This photo was the impetus for me to begin my journey as a famine relief activist. At first, I thought that a campaign against famine in the North would resemble any other disaster relief campaign and that all we would need to do in the South to help its victims would be to collect donations. The reality turned out to be far more complex. What I couldn't have known then was that the famine would transform North Korean life in fundamental ways. Nor did I suspect how deeply my own life would change.

I have visited North Korea thirteen times since I saw that picture, my first trips taking place while the famine was still raging. Images of the devastation I witnessed during my early trips are still vivid in my mind. The North Korean children I met at the time would now have matured into adults living in the era of Kim Jong-Un's reign.

As a famine relief activist dealing with North Korea, I had the rare opportunity to visit the veiled nation numerous times, meeting and negotiating with North Korean state representatives. Each of my visits to North Korea was short. Moreover, I was barred from interacting with ordinary people as they went about their daily lives, a distancing that disappointed the anthropologist in me. However, North Korea was not—and is still not—a country that anyone can visit on a whim where the traveler defines the terms of interaction. This is especially true for those of us from South Korea. My visits afforded me rare opportunities to observe a culture in action, however limited the circumstances, providing rare insights into many aspects of North Korean society, culture, and the politics of theatrics.

I have also maintained long and close relationships with people who have escaped from North Korea. In the summer and winter of 1999, I did fieldwork in China in the border areas near the Yalu and Tumen Rivers, where I met North Koreans fleeing from hunger. In 2001, I established the Hanadul School for North Korean refugee children in South Korea as an initiative aimed at healing the deep scars caused by famine and flight. Later, I organized a group home for unaccompanied refugee children. Many of them had escaped through China into Southeast Asia before finally being brought to Seoul.[1]

Due to a chilling in inter-Korean relations in the years after 2008, my plans to visit North Korea were thwarted time and again. I channeled my interest in North Korea then by coauthoring a book in English titled *North Korea: Beyond Charismatic Politics*. Published in 2012, it analyzed the politics of theatrics and hereditary power succession in North Korea.

The present book, *Suffering and Smiling: Daily Life in North Korea*, is a field report on North Korean culture based on two decades of personal observation and contact with North Koreans, both within North Korea and abroad in China and South Korea. Understanding the cultural and historical context of "suffering" and "smiling" is crucial to understanding the ongoing nuclear arms conundrum and the unresolved war in the Korean Peninsula.

~

On the morning of April 27, 2018, the press center for the inter-Korean summit then taking place suddenly erupted in cheers and applause. Thousands of reporters from across the world had been waiting for the leaders of North and South Korea, Kim Jong-Un and Moon Jae-In, to appear on the screen. The sense of anticipation was palpable as Kim finally arrived to shake hands with Moon. Then, with a single step, he crossed the Military Demarcation Line that divides the Korean Peninsula. The next moment, in a move that surprised the world, Kim gently grabbed President Moon's hand, and together they crossed over into the North and back. It looked quite playful.

The world was enthralled by the sight of the two leaders hopping back and forth across a simple concrete slab, one of the last vestiges of the Cold War, although for Koreans this was a hot war until 1953 and has never ended. Only a few months earlier, Kim Jong-Un had been a villain threatening the world with the possibility of nuclear war. At the summit, he shocked the world again, this time with an all but rogue impromptu gesture. He showed his global audience that he alone could freely cross the line separating the two Koreas. With this single gesture, Kim Jong-Un, long an international pariah, became a rising star on the world diplomatic stage. In South Korea, too, he gained newly minted popularity among young adults as a man whose talents included entertainment.

Surely, one might say, Kim could afford to be so indulgent because he wields absolute power. Indeed, in most cultures, the higher one's status, the more one can afford to be relaxed and flexible. However, during my twenty-five years of encounters with North Koreans, I have witnessed displays of similar types of individual behavior, regardless of class, age, or gender.

Many years ago, I and other members of a group of South Korean research-ers were interviewing a North Korean refugee. She had been a poet in North Korea and had defected to the South to escape the famine. Scholars specializ-ing in famine, refugees, and human rights had arranged the interview in order to learn about her experiences. By the time she arrived in South Korea, she had suffered a gamut of unspeakable experiences, including being a victim of human trafficking. When we met her, she had just been released following rigorous interrogation sessions by South Korean intelligence agents.

She was now free, but still anxious. We started the interview by asking her to tell us her name and date of birth for our records. It turned out that she was younger than her weary appearance had made her seem. To break the ice, I told her that I was quite a few years older than she was. Looking at me with pity in her eyes, she said, "You're the same age as my ex-boyfriend in Pyongyang. It saddens me to think that he must look as old as you do now." Everyone present burst out laughing. Her cavalier comment dissolved the ten-sion and instantly transformed the power relations in the room. My research assistants seemed to enjoy the situation most.

She was the refugee, the lone victim, and the subject of research in that room. Against all odds, with one spontaneous and striking statement, she had made herself into a person, a colleague, and a friend. I was moved. I real-ized then why I had so often felt awe and admiration when meeting North Koreans. To preserve one's humanity in an environment in which one must struggle simply to survive, a tightly controlled society bombarded with collective self-righteousness, one must find small cracks in the system in which to nurture one's inner strength. What improvisation and humor does in these circumstances is affirm and cultivate one's individual humanity. North Koreans are masters of such niche-digging, subversive humor.

For instance, I once watched a group therapy play put on by young North Korean refugees based on their own experiences. The play told the story of Inho, a former wandering beggar child who had been resettled in a government-subsidized apartment in Seoul. In a scene depicting a birthday celebration, he was visited by fellow refugees who had come bearing a cake. This, we learned, was his first-ever birthday cake. After singing the newly learned birthday song together, his friends told him to blow out the candle. The next moment, something unexpected happened. Inho shouted out, "No! Don't blow out the candle!" This exclamation had not been scripted, and the atmosphere in the room turned tense and awkward. He continued, "I've never felt this good before. If we were to blow out the candle, it would all be over, wouldn't it?" The auditorium erupted in laughter and applause, both from backstage and from the spectators' seats. Then, in silence, as Inho and the audience watched the candlelight slowly burn out, many in the audience wept.

While these episodes show the power of improvisation and humor in difficult circumstances, the following episodes illustrate how happiness is conceptualized and socialized in North Korea, almost to the extent of "commanding" it.

One of the scenes that are performed during the Arirang Mass Games[2] in North Korea is titled "Smile Broadly!" The preceding scene, titled "The Bright Moon of My Fatherland," portrays the (military-first) era of widespread famine in terms of darkness and moonlight. Even in such trying times, the performance informs us, the children are growing up bright and full of vitality. While school-aged children on the ground of the arena jump ropes "to grow taller," cards held by twenty thousand students in the stands form giant illustrations depicting soy milk trucks out on deliveries and a boy and girl drinking glasses of soy milk—a daily gift from the Supreme Leader. The children on the ground smile toothy grins, despite what is obviously a physically demanding performance. They then fill the entire area of the stadium with a flower-shaped mass movement, the cards held up in the stands flipping over to reveal the message: "Bloom brightly!"

"Smile Broadly!" symbolically demonstrates the power and contradiction of a theater state, one that commands and trains emotional expression in children. Children are encouraged and trained to bare their teeth and consciously smile broadly when practicing for performances or engaging in other difficult activities; this training takes place at all levels of education.

Certain psychological studies have shown that smiling, even if inauthentic, can improve one's mood. Of course, such an effect is either temporary or limited. However, the North Korean regime seeks to prove that mental strength can overcome material difficulties encountered in real life through theatrical staging.

~~~

To this day, North Korea reiterates its raison d'être by recalling the epic national liberation struggle. It loudly proclaims that, just as past revolutionaries fought a guerilla war against Japanese imperialism, it is now the "one and only" country facing off against the strongest of imperialist forces, the United States. This pride is the fundamental force sustaining the North Korean regime. International isolation and periodic threats of war make this narrative all the more viscerally real for North Koreans.

Guns and missiles are emblematic of the legitimacy of power in North Korea. According to the founding legend of the North Korean state, two pistols that Kim Il-Sung inherited from his father turned into thousands of guns that were used to arm the partisans who liberated the Korean people from the Japanese Empire. These very guns again turned into countless arms for the People's Army as it defended the nation from American imperialists. Kim Jong-Il's missiles and nuclear bombs were, collectively, a reimagined gun defending the *juche* (self-reliance) system[3] amid the collapse of international socialism. Kim Jong-Un, as heir ascendant to the helm of power, further developed his father's nuclear bombs into hydrogen bombs and his father's missiles into ICBMs. These developments shocked the world and wildly excited North Koreans. Their leader had compelled the whole world to watch their display of power and made the whole world—above all, the United States—take them seriously. From their perspective, the summit between the United States and North Korea in 2018, far from being a sign of surrender, was a testament to the success of their self-made military might.

Many countries have the ability to manufacture nuclear weapons. What is notable about North Korea is that it has actually made them. Ironically, it is because of international blockades and pressure that poverty-stricken North Korea prioritized the manufacture of weapons of mass destruction. In a prolonged state of national crisis, its resources and talents were concentrated on this project.

Guns, missiles, and nuclear bombs are central to the national identity of the guerilla state of North Korea. They are the core symbols and tools of political power. Will North Korea give them up? Can it survive without them?

Gwangmyeongseong[4] soared in the General's country
We are strong, we are strong
We are the strongest in the world!
We are the strongest in the world!

So went the lyrics of a song celebrating missile launching performed at a child-care center I visited in Pyongyang. Throughout their performance, the children smiled brightly and shouted fervently, like a battalion of victorious soldiers. I could feel the lively spirit of the "guerilla state" in the brisk gait of these scrawny children as they filed out of the room in an orderly line.

After watching my video of the children's performance, an elderly Japanese professor told me with a sigh, "During the Pacific War, Japanese children sang a similar song." When he was a schoolboy, he told me, he had pretended to beat "the demons and beasts, America and Britain," and had sung a song extolling Japan as the strongest nation in the world. As a boy, he himself had resolved to "win at any cost" and fight to the death with a bamboo spear to protect the emperor and his country. In his eyes, the kamikaze suicide bombers had been glorious national heroes. He told me that one way of understanding North Korea today was to think of the Japanese people of that era who had cheered for the emperor and the empire and had been prepared to give their lives for both.

To conclude this series of examples, the following incident, which occurred at a school for newly arrived North Korean refugee children in South Korea, illustrates the cultural pattern of negotiation for North Koreans.

I was the founding principal of the school and was known to the students as Mr. OK, a nickname I had for frequently saying "OK" to the kids. One day, a twelve-year-old student named Jucheol brought in three Hong Kong gangster movies he wanted to show in class. I refused to let him do so, explaining that the movies were too violent. He argued that South Korean TV dramas were violent too. I told him not to worry, adding that I would give him the money for the video rental so he could return them. As soon as he heard this, he jumped up and down in a wild fit of anger. "Do you think it's the money I care about?! What would they think of me at the store?" I didn't know what to do, and I told him that if he kept acting up, I would call his mother. At that, he pounced on me, shouting, "I'll rip your stomach open!" There was nothing stopping him from doing so. I held him tight in my arms, his small, thin frame rebelling against my constraint. He cried and struggled, shouting, "Who are you to give my mom a hard time?!" After a while, he asked me to let him go, and I did. He scurried off for a moment, then reappeared with his face washed. He then repeated the very same sequence of pleading, move for move. With the same expressions, he first begged, then argued, then persisted, then threw a fit, and then finally pounced on me, saying, "I'll rip your belly open!" Each time, I held him as tightly as before, letting him go when he asked. He repeated this cycle of dramatic actions without any sign of embarrassment.

At one point, one of his older classmates said to him, "Why are you messing with our teacher? He's like a father to us." The older boy swung a chair high above his head, poised to bring it down on Jucheol, saying, "I'm going to crack your skull open." Now I had to stop him too, while also trying to maintain my own composure. Another boy in the class who was watching the whole scene looked at me with pity in his eyes, simply saying, "Don't you get how he feels?"

Ultimately, we agreed to watch the least violent of the films Jucheol had brought in, followed by an educational one of my choice. At dinner that evening, he came to my table, sat next to me, and started a conversation as if nothing had happened. He then placed his dessert on my tray without a word.

A few days later, I brought in a play therapist. She asked the students to draw pictures and then talk about them. Jucheol went through the motions of scribbling something, then practically threw the paper at the therapist. He added gruffly, "What's the point of this, anyway?" The therapist took a close look at the drawing, telling Jucheol, "I know you can draw better." He looked visibly taken aback. "What, are you a mind reader or something?" His eyes shone with curiosity and innocence, like those of a little child. From then on, he never left my side at school.

~

By 2017, the intermediate-range ballistic missile (IRBM), first launched in 1998, had evolved into an intercontinental ballistic missile (ICBM), becoming the symbol of the Kim Jong-Un era. A musical group known as the Moranbong Band performed in Pyongyang to a massive crowd to celebrate the successful test launch of the new missile. The miniskirts worn by the band members reflected the changing times, as did their rock melodies and K-pop-esque choreography. The concert reached its climax with the song "Dansume!" (In a single breath!).[5] Footage of rockets blasting off played on the screen behind them as they shouted the titular lyrics. The crowd ate it up, dancing and jostling to get closer to the stage. When the missiles reached the mainland United States on the screen, pyrotechnics lit up the stage. By this time, the entire audience was on its feet, clapping, dancing, and cheering fervently.

A country with one nuclear bomb was testing the patience of a country with thousands. Nuclear war, the unthinkable, was fast becoming reality. When North Korea succeeded in building a missile that could reach the US

Figure 0.1.   In a single breath! Moranbong Band celebrates successful intercontinental ballistic missile test. Source: Uriminzokkiri

mainland, serious dialogue between the two nations started. In possession of a weapon capable of attacking the United States "in a single breath," North Korea began dreaming about reviving its collapsed economy "in a single breath" too. While dialogue is underway, the path forward will not be easy. However, as challenging as it may be, dialogue must succeed if we no longer want to witness further spectacular events that celebrate the use of such devastating weapons.

Moral righteousness, all-or-nothing brinkmanship, pride, and inflexible positions coupled with a dramatic persona—North Koreans may exhibit some or all of the above when engaged in negotiations. Jucheol, the refugee boy mentioned above, protected his pride and handled conflict in a manner strikingly similar to that of the seasoned diplomats involved in denuclearization talks. This is their cultural habitus, a social survival strategy employed not only by the leaders and the elite but shared widely by members of the population, regardless of age or class.

In October 2019, eight months after the failed Hanoi Summit between Donald Trump and Kim Jong-Un, North Korea and the United States renewed denuclearization talks in Stockholm.[6] Watching the news that the meeting broke down only hours after they began, I could not but think about my own negotiations with North Korean officials. I could envision the North Korean delegates meeting their US counterparts in a fancy hotel and repeating an endless loop of handshakes, smiles, and talk sessions followed by the inevitable eruption of conflict, the lashing out with abusive language, the breakdown of talks, and criticism of the counterpart for the breakdown.

When North Korean delegates lash out, they do so with moralistic, though not moral, arguments. Their attitude is an uncompromising one, marked by determination to achieve results "at once!" The next day, the cycle starts all over again. The insults with which North Korean diplomats lash out and the blunt remarks they make, such as saying that they'll turn Seoul into "a sea of fire" or that they'll "be ready for nuclear war," reminded me of the refugee boy Jucheol who screamed, "I'll rip your stomach open." They are desperate cries to be acknowledged and understood. Behavior embodies cultural patterns, just as languages have grammars. The world must understand the deep and abiding cultural and political dimensions of North Korean behavior if the stalemated Korean War is to end and achieve an abiding settlement.

Recently, a young couple who had been students at the Hanadul School for North Korean refugee children years earlier paid me a visit before their wedding. The bride had graduated from a US college and graduate school in Britain. With a smile, she told me, "The Americans and the British are strange. They always say that North Korea is an unpredictable country. Wouldn't you say that it is the most predictable and consistent country in the world?"

As repeatedly in the past, however, it is not up to the will of the North Korean leader alone to determine the outcome of negotiations. The decisive factors are the state of the country's relations with the other half of the divided Korea, namely South Korea; its relations with the United States, China, Japan, and Russia; and the political and economic situations in those countries. Success also depends on overcoming the obstruction of those forces that have a vested interest in maintaining tension and conflict in East Asia. There is a difficult road ahead, but one that must be taken, and the principal actors making this journey are the North Korean people and their leaders. What do they really want? What will they do? It is time that we understood who the North Koreans are.

Many North and South Koreans hope that our "divided families" will one day come together and enjoy a common future. A shared language and a common ethnic heritage have not been enough to bring this about. I wrote the Korean-language version of this book in the hope that it would encourage readers to strive for a better understanding of cultural differences on both sides of the DMZ.[7] Creating the English version has been a struggle. But I hope that these efforts may ease my worry that the dream of a unified Korea cannot be realized in a world that has trouble seeing our common humanity, a world that tends to think of us only as unpredictable, bickering siblings.

Cultural relativism is not only an ethical code in anthropology but also the most effective tool for understanding others. An anthropologist's mission is to prescribe glasses for understanding the Other without prejudice or stereotyping, no matter how strange that Other may seem at first glance. With this book, my aim is to provide a set of glasses that will allow readers to view North Korean culture not only more clearly but also more empathetically in light of its historical experience of national division and the Korean War that shows no signs of ending.

NOTES

1. Michael Paterniti, "The Flight of the Fluttering Swallows," *New York Times Magazine*, April 27, 2003, 46.
2. The Arirang Mass Games is the largest mass arts festival organized by the North Korean government. Attended by millions, the games were first held in 2002 and then almost every year until 2013. In both name and substance, the event became the "performance of the nation." The games returned for a performance titled "The Glorious Country" in 2018 when South Korean president Moon Jae-In visited Pyongyang.
3. *Juche* has a connotation of "self-reliance," "autonomy," and "independence." The concept incorporates the historical materialist ideas of Marx-Leninism but also includes a strong emphasis on the individual, the nation-state, and national sovereignty. Bruce Cumings, *Korea's Place in the Sun: A Modern History* (New York: Norton, 1997), 207, 403–4.
4. The "bright star" symbolizes Kim Jong-Il. It is also the name of the first intermediate-range missile (or satellite, as North Korea claimed), launched on August 31, 1998.
5. Outsiders' YouTube clips show the concert scene with the title "Dansume!" (In a single breath!), last modified May 6, 2013, https://www.youtube.com/watch?v=SSbYc0ojjo8.
6. David E. Sanger, "U.S. Nuclear Talks with North Korea Break Down in Hours," *New York Times*, October 5, 2019, https://www.nytimes.com/2019/10/05/us/politics/trump-north-korea-nuclear.html.
7. Byung-Ho Chung, *Gonangwa Useumui Nara: Inryuhakjaui Bukhan Iyagi* [State of suffering and smiling: An anthropologist's story on North Korea] (in Korean) (Paju: Changbi, 2020); *Jinruigaksha Ga Nojoita Kitachosen: Gunan to Hohoemi No Kuni* [North Korea observed by an anthropologist: A state of suffering and smiling] (in Japanese) (Tokyo: Seidosha, 2022).

North Korea and Neighboring Countries

RUSSIA

CHINA

Tumen
Yanji
Hunchun
Hoeryong
Musan
Mt. Baekdu
Tumen River
Tuman River
Rason
To Trans-Siberian Railway
Chongjin
Shenyang
Tonghua
Yalu River
Amnok River
Hyesan

NORTH KOREA

Yalu River
Amnok River
To Beijing
Dandong
Sinuiju
Hamhung
Railway from Pyongyang to Rason

Mt. Myohyang

East Sea (Sea of Japan)

Railway from Pyongyang to Sinuiju
Pyongsong
Pyongyang
Wonsan

Nampo
Highway
Mt. Kumgang
Demarcation Line and Demilitarized Zone

Railway from Pyongyang to Kaesong
Kaesong
Seoul
Incheon
Suwon
Pyeongtaek

Daejeon

Yellow Sea

SOUTH KOREA

Busan
Gwangju

N

0   100 kilometers
0   100 miles

Jeju
Fukuoka
JAPAN

Map 1.   North Korea and Neighboring Countries. Byung-Ho Chung

Acknowledgments

"Our Wish Is Unification!" The song, ingrained in my memory since elementary school, still holds deep meaning for this gray-haired author as I reflect on the pain endured by my grandmother and mother, who suffered from the agony of family separation. The song also evokes my uncle, who was a surgeon in Seoul, taken away by the People's Army to the North during the Korean War. We never heard from him again.

I recall a moment from my childhood when I awoke to a strange sound in the early morning darkness. My grandmother, who slept beside me, was absent from her bed. From the other side of the door, I could hear her prayers and the sound of the radio. It was the morning broadcast, which she listened to everyday hoping for news of unification and longing to be reunited with her only son. I could sense her body contorting in pain as she struggled to suppress her agony. Frightened and saddened, I cried, hugging her from behind. As she wiped her tear-stained face with her weathered hands, my grandmother smiled, a smile that seemed like a facade, and embraced me tightly.

I dedicate this book to my grandmother and mother, both of whom passed away without ever having been reunited with their only son and younger brother. Their pain of separation has been my lifelong commitment. I strive to remember and convey not only their pain but also the tears of millions of separated families.

This book is also an earnest attempt to remember and commemorate those who have died or suffered from the famine in North Korea. I express my gratitude to the humanitarian aid activists who tirelessly worked to help them, as well as the volunteers and donors who made it possible to overcome countless barriers of political division. As a researcher who witnessed the enormous calamity of a nation and an activist who participated in relief efforts, I have endeavored to faithfully record and testify to these events.

My heartfelt thanks go to the many people I met in North Korea and the refugees along the Chinese border. I could not have written this book without their generosity and the valuable lessons they imparted, tolerating the anthropologist who asked them endless questions. Unfortunately, I cannot name them individually for their safety.

To the young refugees I taught at Hanadul School, who affectionately nicknamed me "Principal Mr. OK," I honor their courage and vitality. Despite the harsh difficulties you experienced, you chose laughter and hope over brokenness. Your curious explorations, as those "who came first from the future," will undoubtedly open new possibilities. My special blessings go to Young-Ho and Bok-Keum, and their baby son Tae-An.

My gratitude also extends to everyone who contributed to the original Korean version of this book. Students of the North Korean Culture class at Hanyang University, librarians at the Ministry of Unification North Korea Archive, and graduate students Ahn Jong-Soo, Han Hyo-Joo, Im Jae-Yoon, and Park Chae-Hwan, I appreciate their assistance in searching for historical photos and literature. Special thanks to Prof. Kwon Hyeok-Beom at Daejeon University, Drs. Lee Hyang-Gyu, Choi Eun-Young, Cho Il-Dong, Kim Ki-Young, and Im Seong-Suk at the Institute of Globalization and Multicultural Studies of Hanyang University, and writer Yoon Eun-Jeong for reading the manuscript and providing valuable comments. I also appreciate Prof. Kim Kyung-Mook at Waseda University and Activist Suh Sook-Mi for their efforts to translate this book into Japanese.

In particular, my late father-in-law, Prof. Bommo Chung, ninety-five years old then, read the first draft in advance and encouraged me during lulls in the writing process. My late mentor, Prof. David W. Plath, read the first draft of the English version and provided directions for editing for English readers. He would be delighted to see this book as slim as he expected, but like my dissertation, I apologize for the delay.

This book is a complete revision of the original Korean version for English readers. I want to thank translator Lee Kyung-Hee for her persistence and sensitivity. The copy editors, Grace Payer and Don Cameron, were immensely helpful not only in tightening the content but also in clarifying meanings. My former student Jung Woo-Chang assisted in selecting photo images and maps and formatting the final manuscript. I appreciate our long friendship.

Editors at Rowman and Littlefield, Susan McEachern and Ashley Dodge, have provided abiding support throughout, and I am grateful for their enthusiasm. I also appreciate the warm and thoughtful suggestions of Profs. Tessa Morris-Suzuki and Gavan McCormick at Australia National University. For

Dr. Mark Selden, the series editor, I express my deep appreciation for meticulous editing and insightful feedback. This collaborative effort has allowed me to identify and rectify numerous areas that needed attention. I am truly grateful for his friendly guidance.

Finally, I express my gratitude to my wife, Prof. *Chung Jean-Kyung*, the first avid reader and strict editor of all my writings. For twenty-five years, we have worked together on the issues of cultural integration of South-North Korea. As a social psychologist, she has always been with me in research and practice. This book could not have been written without her love and support.

Chapter One

Commanding Happiness

WE ARE HAPPY!

"We are happy" is one of the many verbal instructions attributed to Kim Il-Sung. The banner above the kindergarten gate, its bright, multicolored letters carrying this slogan, made a lasting impression on me. I visited this kindergarten in Pyongyang, famous for its music education, in early March 2000 with a group of relief activists. As winter reluctantly gave way to spring, a chill lingered in the air. Inside, in the entrance hall, I walked past large pictures of Kim Il-Sung and Kim Jong-Il holding children in their arms, broad smiles adorning their faces.

Led by the kindergarten's director, we went upstairs to the auditorium, where children were busily preparing to sing for us. When they were ready, a girl shouted out, "We Are Happy!" in a high, ringing voice, her right palm spread across her cheek and her head tilted. The echo of her voice across the large room pierced my heart as the curtains of the small theater opened. Around thirty children appeared on stage and sang in an amazingly loud chorus. Their vocal training was evident.

Our Father who is revered by the entire nation
Ah— Ah— Our Father, the General
We will worship you higher and higher for one thousand and ten thousand years,
We will worship you.
Ah— Ah— Our Father, the General
We are so, so happy.
Brimming with happiness, brimming with happiness.

1

Figure 1.1.   We are happy! A performance at Mankyongdae Children's Palace. Byung-Ho Chung

I was utterly dumbfounded. What happiness? I knew that at that very moment, there were children dying of hunger elsewhere in the country. Even some of the children at the school, who came from relatively well-to-do Pyongyang households, were obviously undernourished.

They couldn't possibly be happy, yet here they were singing that they were. One could only conclude that the children had been taught to believe that they were happy. Or so the anticommunist education I had received in South Korea had me believe. It is easy to hold in contempt adults who manipulate innocent children into believing that they are happy. However, when one is among the people themselves, one realizes immediately that when they sing their song of happiness, both children and adults are completely genuine. This is where confusion begins. Either the North Koreans are putting on a perfect show, or they actually believe that they are happy. How could the latter be possible?

Could it be that they see and feel happiness from a different perspective? Every society has its rich and poor, and being poor does not necessarily equate to being unhappy. The United Nations (UN) has reported that people living in poorer countries, such as Bhutan, for example, score higher on happiness indices than people living in affluent South Korea and other rich, advanced countries.[1] North Korea is currently one of the poorest countries in the world, yet one would be wrong to conclude that everyone living there is unhappy.

Psychologists explain that happiness is not simply a state of painlessness. Happiness is highly subjective—it places importance on experience over possessions, relationships over competition. As cultural beings, meanings and values beyond our basic survival needs are important to humans. People feel their lives are meaningful when they are engaged in actions of value to their societies and, in the process, gain an understanding of the world and realize their purpose in life.

Still I wondered. What did the children's happiness have to do with "Our Father, the General," and why did they call their leader their father? One simple answer would be that the children had simply been trained, like parrots, to echo what they had been taught. However, there seemed to be something special about the relationship between the Supreme Leader and these children, one that was not the result of simple training by rote repetition but based on a semantic system reinforced by historical, social, and cultural experience.

According to the reigning *juche* ideology of self-reliance, the children of North Korea are the successors to the nation's anti-Japanese guerrilla fighters. As such, they are still waging a struggle for the freedom of the Korean people, who have not yet been fully liberated from imperialism. In order to achieve this goal, they are firmly united around their Supreme Leader and are willing to endure hardship. They believe that the poverty and suffering they are currently facing is due to the fact that North Korea is being choked by powerful foreign forces. They also believe that, as they are following the righteous and honorable path, they will, one day, succeed in uniting and liberating Korea. The happiness that the children sing of, in fact, may have little to do with material happiness. "We are happy" is only one of numerous mottos used in North Korea that are hard to comprehend, others including "Nothing to envy in the world," "Let us live our way," and "No North Korea, no World!" These are idealistic expressions based on their moral principles.

On the other hand, in South Korea, one of the distinctive criteria for children's happiness is whether they have the things they want. North Koreans may consider the simplicity and extreme materialism in the South strange. While some in the South may express concern about abuse in the training of the highly skilled children in the North, North Koreans may think it is in poor taste to allocate excessive resources to educational competition for children in the South.

When the chorus of children finished singing, they all ran forward and grasped the hands of their visitors from the South. Their small hands were startlingly cold. I realized that they must have been preparing for the chorus long before our arrival, their uniforms hardly sufficient to keep them warm in the unheated auditorium. When one little boy grasped me by the hand, I recall feeling embarrassed that my hand must have felt hotter than a stove to him. I took both of his hands in mine, trying to warm the boy up as much as I could, while lavishly praising him for his excellent performance. The director wanted to move on to another room, and I had to let go of the boy's hands. When I looked down at him, I saw in his eyes a hint of reluctance to let go of mine mixed with a glimmer of curiosity.

Nothing to Envy in the World

The motto "Nothing to Envy in the World" is displayed everywhere in North Korea at sites related to children. Even at an orphanage where the children were clearly suffering from severe malnourishment, I came across a large signboard with this motto hanging on the wall. What do people think when they see such a slogan, one that appears so diametrically opposed to reality? The more I saw of North Korea, the more mysterious a riddle this became. Everywhere we went, children joined hands, opened their mouths wide, and launched into cheerful songs such as the following:

The sky is high and my heart is joyful.
Let the accordion play
For people live harmoniously
In my fatherland that I love infinitely.
Our Father is our General Kim Il-Sung.
Our home is the bosom of the party.
We are all brothers and sisters.
Nothing to envy in the world.

This song came out in 1961, when the Chollima Movement, which aimed to increase production, was at its height. The British economist Joan Robinson called North Korean achievements the "Korean Miracle," reporting that North Koreans considered Kim Il-Sung to be a "messiah rather than a dictator" for having resurrected the country from the ruins of the Korean War (1950–1953) at such breakneck speed.[2]

But by the time of my visit in the year 2000, Kim Il-Sung had been dead for years, and the entire nation was suffering from the Great Famine. Yet here they were, still singing the same song from their economic heyday some forty years earlier. What did it mean? The words could no longer be viewed as descriptive but rather as imperative, a command not to envy. Now, the most dangerous criminal act was to contact the outside world and compare North Korea with it. In fact, those few who experienced the outside world and saw the clear contradiction in the song became disenchanted and embarrassed. Some of them would seek to join the ranks of refugees.

The first time I met a North Korean who felt betrayed by the words of this song was in the winter of 1999, when North Korea was in the throes of famine. A former party cadre from a rural area, he was now hiding in a mountain hut near the Tumen River on the Sino-Korean border. In a trembling voice he recalled how he, too, had hummed this song when he had been living in North Korea. When he first crossed the river into China to scavenge food for his family, he was so shocked by what he saw that his world was turned upside down. What broke his heart most was the memory of a homeless *kkotchebi* child in North Korea singing "Nothing to Envy." The boy, barefoot and clad in rags, was singing the refrain of the song repeatedly in a hoarse voice, shivering with cold at a rainy train station as he begged for sympathy from passengers waiting for a train to arrive.

When the public distribution system collapsed during the famine and trading at open-air street markets known as *jangmadang* became the last resort for families left to survive on their own, people began changing the words of this song, which was familiar to them from their earliest childhood: "Our home" was no longer "the bosom of the party" but the "*jangmadang*." Yet people still did not change the part about "Our Father." Kim Il-Sung became Kim Jong-Il, and then Kim Jong-Un as the times changed, with people expressing their discontent only through slight changes in tone.

By this time, information about the outside world was already circulating widely, albeit furtively, inside North Korea via movies, TV dramas, and music that entered the country and circulated via the *jangmadang* and contraband trade. In addition, by this time, hundreds of thousands of North Koreans, including those working in the Kaesong Industrial Zone and overseas, had experienced contact with the outside world. Many started to suspect what a poor country North Korea was in the broader scheme of the world. What were they thinking as they sang "Nothing to Envy" now? I tried once again to decipher the meaning of the song. There is no reference to material possessions or competition anywhere in its lyrics. It is a song of subjective happiness, the kind that one feels through contact with nature, art, or relationships with others. In the refrain, symbolic terms such as "father," "home," and "brothers and sisters" emphasize relationships and a sense of belonging to a family-state.

I recall once hearing a North Korean who had defected as a teenager and had been living in South Korea for almost two decades humming the song. When I asked if he was feeling homesick for the North, he said that he wasn't, adding, "But sometimes I do miss that strange happiness I felt there." He said that in the South, amid all of the material abundance, the hardest and the most painful parts of his life were those involving competition and comparison. When everyone around him worked themselves to the bone and spent money obsessively, he felt insecure, encountering discrimination and experiencing alienation in an environment characterized by boundless competition. He was also experiencing poverty, at least in a comparative sense, in the South in a way that he had rarely experienced it in the North. He was still not yet quite used to the transactional nature of interpersonal relationships in the South, from time to time, out of the blue, missing the simple sentiments reflected in phrases such as "For people live harmoniously" and "We are all brothers as sisters."

Springtime at Home

Kim Il-Sung's birthday is April 15, when spring is at its peak in Korea and seasonal flowers are in full bloom. In the official hagiographic narrative, Kim brought with him the warmth of sunlight to thaw the land frozen by Japanese colonial rule. April 15 later became known as the Day of the Sun, a spring festival celebrated as a major national holiday. In major city squares across the country, young men and women dress up in their holiday best to take part in massive dance parties and watch fireworks light up the night. Much like the spring festivals found in other cultures, it is a day for celebrating life, resurrection, and new beginnings.

At an elementary school I visited in North Korea, I watched a performance by a second-grade girl wearing the red scarf of the Youth League tied around her neck. She sang with considerable emotion, her slightly nasal voice ringing high and clear:

My home was a valley of flowers,
Blooming with peach flowers, apricot flowers, and baby azaleas.
A palace of flowers in red and blue, a village so decked out.
How I long for the time when I played there.

The child sang with longing eyes, her head tilted sideways, as if the home she so longed for was really there before her eyes; her emotion was genuine, and her gestures earnest.

At every nursery, kindergarten, and school that I visited, as well as at the Mangyongdae Children's Palace,[3] I saw children singing the same song with almost identical vocalization and gestures. Their expressions were so heartfelt that I wondered how they were able to sing about their "home" with such genuine emotion, and what picture they had in mind when singing about it.

From age three, children familiarized themselves with the "homes" (*gohyangjip*) of the three saints—Kim Il-Sung, his wife Kim Jong-Sook, and his son Kim Jong-Il—and childhood stories related to them, both visually and aurally. They also grew up learning to express what they have learned via storytelling, song, and dance. In the cultural refinement rooms of nurseries and kindergartens, mock-ups of the childhood homes of the three saints were installed. In elementary, middle, and high schools, and even in universities, the mock-ups became paintings and photo plates, and the stories of them were imbued with political and ideological significance. In contrast to the colorless and rigid environment of the regular classrooms, the mock-up homes were decorated with flowering trees, while the paintings and photos came in the florid technicolor emblematic of a "springtime home."

The Sun of the Nation

In North Korea, the red sun is the *suryeong*, or Great Leader Kim Il-Sung. He is revered as the sun not simply because he was the highest authority in the nation but also because of the emphasis on his symbolic significance; it is through Kim Il-Sung that the people found light in the dark and life amid death. The people who receive his light become the "Sun Nation."

It is not uncommon to find societies that liken their paramount leaders, such as emperors or kings, to the sun. The Egyptians did so, as did the Incas and Aztecs. Closer to our own times, the Japanese national myth held that the emperor was the direct descendant of the sun goddess. The sun is the source of life and a symbol of cosmic energy. Its brightness is often considered a symbol of civilization against barbarism.

Kim Il-Sung's life story is the central theme of all major art productions in North Korea. The stories follow the typical hero-myth structure. Hagiographic in nature, they contain the rite-of-passage narrative structure found in the hero myths of most cultures. Typically, born in ordinary circumstances, the hero leaves home early, undergoes a battery of hardships in a foreign land, and grows up to be a great person of character. In the case of Kim Il-Sung, he receives "sacred gifts" in the form of two handguns from his father, ascends the holy Mount Baekdu, and undergoes life-or-death hardships while defeating a foreign enemy (Japan) that enslaved the Korean people; then, finally, he returns home to Mangyongdae triumphant, founds the nation, and lives eternally as the sun shining on a liberated fatherland—thus establishing heaven on earth.[4]

In fact, when Kim Il-Sung died in April 1994, the country went into a three-year period of mourning, during which people offered flowers in prayer for his eternal life. Thousands of golden statues symbolizing the Sun of the Nation were erected across the country, while tens of thousands of Towers of Eternal Life were installed, each etched with the sentence: "Supreme Leader

Figure 1.2.   Father the Generalissimo is Our Eternal Sun: A tile mosaic on a Pyongyang street depicting the generalissimo, Kim Il-Sung, as the sun, the people as the sunflowers, and children as the flower buds. Byung-Ho Chung

Kim Il-Sung is forever with us." The entire marble palace that functioned as Kim Il-Sung's residence and office while he was alive was turned into a colossal marble mausoleum, now known as the Geumsusan Palace of the Sun. His corpse is embalmed and preserved in a glass vacuum and is visited by pilgrims from all over the world.

The mythical hero narrative based on Kim Il-Sung's personal life is so interwoven with events in North Korea's history that the two are inseparable. That is to say, the binary oppositions of colonialism and liberation, suffering and glory, poverty and prosperity, war and peace, subjugation and self-reliance, and subordination and autonomy are told in connection with the hero's personal life history. Thus, Kim Il-Sung is the savior who liberated the nation from slavery, the leader who built the nation from the rubble of war, a prophet who brought a vision of a bright future for the nation when it was still in darkness, and the sun that vanquished the darkness.

Juche ideology posits that Kim Il-Sung should be recognized and respected not only by North Koreans but by all the people of the world. Given that the country has been isolated, it was thus especially important to emphasize that people from all over the world visit his birthplace at Mangyongdae in Pyongyang. Foreigners are said to embark on this journey because, like the sun, Kim Il-Sung shines not only on Koreans but on all oppressed people of the world. The thatched-roof house at Mangyongdae is presented as a sacred place for people around the world still living under imperialism.

The travel itinerary for all international visitors to Pyongyang starts with a visit to the Mangyongdae home. I was taken there six times, once during each of my six visits. Each time, I observed groups of North Koreans from all walks of life, neatly dressed and waiting in long lines for their turn to enter the house. They always yielded their turns to foreign visitors. Upon such occasions, the local and foreign groups do not intermingle, stealing furtive glances at each other out of the corners of their eyes as they pass. Often, outsiders tense up when they observe the North Koreans' solemnity and orderliness, then seek to fit in with the atmosphere by taking stock of their own attire and expressions.

For the North Koreans, each of these encounters is probably an opportunity to confirm the prestige of the home and the significance of the pilgrimage by people from other parts of the world. In other words, such close encounters with foreigners are probably rare and exotic experiences that confirm the home's international status. In this regard, foreigners, including Koreans from South Korea and other parts of the world, are at the same time objects of spectacle and a tool for reconfirming North Korean people's pride.

Hymns of Love

Once we visited an elementary school in North Korea without prior arrangement—an exceptional situation. In the first classroom we set foot in, the teacher and students were caught off guard by our abrupt visit. In North Korea, people are not used to unannounced encounters. At first they seemed at a loss and were clearly uncomfortable. I looked around at the class of second graders and remembered my own time in second grade, when I struggled to memorize the multiplication table. I asked if any of the students could recite the multiplication table for me. A smart-looking girl sitting in the middle of the class with a red Youth League scarf stood up and started reciting the table in a clear ringing voice. "Five times one is five, five times two is ten, five times three is fifteen . . . five times ten is fifty!" To *my* relief, she didn't make a single mistake, and I could not help but clap enthusiastically at her adorable presentation and clear voice.

Next, I asked them to sing a song, any song. But they did not know what to sing; I had put them on the spot. The guide said we should leave now. But this was a rare opportunity, and I could not let it pass like that. Cautiously I asked, "Shall I sing a children's song from the South while you pick your song?" Everyone was surprised at this out-of-the-blue suggestion and looked at my guide with wide eyes. The principal was standing nearby the whole time and, in the confusion of the moment, she shouted, "Let's give him a hand!"

I chose a children's song about making friends all over the world. I was used to singing this song, along with miming its rhythmic actions, with children at the nursery cooperative I had founded in Seoul. In front of the class, I sang the song the same way, moving my entire body, stretching my two arms to make the round shape of the earth and making the marching motions with my feet and legs. The children were fascinated by this towering, middle-aged man singing a strange song and making unseemly movements. They gaped at me, their eyes as wide as saucers. The tension in the room dissipated. The teachers, as well as my guide, were beaming and clapping their hands. In short, as a result of my playfulness, I was no longer a cause for wariness. The class was now looking for a song to sing, trying out this and that one by humming a few bars or playing parts on the reed organ. Finally, one said, "I've got it, how about the new song we learned?"

Will it happen when the night is over?
My dearest wish.
Will it be fulfilled when the year is over?
My dearest wish.
If only I can see in my dreams, Great Father General—
Forever, forever, beloved in my heart.

Their eyes were filled with deep, tender emotion as they bent their upper bodies forward, expressing their longing for the Great General. As far as I could tell, they picked the song in the most spontaneous manner, free from all anxiety, and sang it as they usually would.

It made me recall my childhood days when I sang "In the Garden" as a choirboy on Sundays: "And He walks with me, and He talks with me, and He tells me I am His own." Remembering the pride and intimacy I had felt thinking that I was a friend of the Lord, I could understand how the children felt as they sang.

The Great Father General was god in a nation where there was no god. A guide who was used to arguing with visitors from the South once said, "You believe and worship an invisible god as a father. Why can't you believe and follow a living leader as a father?"

GIFTS FROM THE FATHER

The national consciousness of the family-state is formed and held together through routine everyday experiences. The installation of portraits, writings, and paintings of the Leader in everyday living spaces serves as a reminder of the ever-present "Father, the Great Leader" and his ever-benevolent care and affection. Outside the home, people saw, heard, and confirmed "virtue vignettes," which they have read in textbooks, that were physically embodied in various living venues. Every year, the birthdays of the leaders are celebrated with a greater festivity than any other holiday on the calendar; they are occasions on which people can look forward to small delicacies and breaks amid the harsh conditions of everyday living. The "familyism" that binds the people together in the family-state is achieved through such symbolic gestures.

To the children, the General was someone who gave special surprise gifts that they would remember for their entire lives. For example, a teacher at Kim Jong-Sook Nursery proudly told us visitors in a voice full of passion that "the Great Leader had sent an imported carpet as a gift for the playroom, and the children are now dancing on it." At the Pyongyang No. 1 Middle School, the most prestigious school for gifted students from all regions of the nation, we were told that an imported car, a rare sight even on the streets of the capital, was being used for students' driving education. The leader had sent it "to the students as a gift, with the heart of a parent." Each of the thousands of students who participated in the Arirang Mass Games also received a special gift from their Supreme Leader, Kim Jong-Il, a color television set.

We Ate Tangerines!

"We ate tangerines sent by our Great General," boasted a child at a large nursery we visited in Pyongyang. The children had eaten them a few weeks earlier, but the memory of the sweet and sour taste of that marvelous fruit was still lingering on the child's taste buds.

The children met us in a large and sparsely furnished room where it was so cold that our breath turned into white mist. All winter long, the vegetable diet of the children probably consisted of nothing more than a few stalks of cabbage kimchi from the previous fall. I could only imagine what wonder these wan children must have felt at the sight and taste of the colorful citrus fruit from the South that does not grow in the North. The child at the nursery boasted to me that she "ate one whole tangerine."

In the summer of 2009, I met a professor at Jeju National University who had been involved in the campaign to send locally grown tangerines to North Korea. He was delighted to hear that nursery children in Pyongyang had indeed eaten the tangerines. The campaign had left a bitter taste in his mouth; at the time he was organizing it, he was ridiculed by people who said that, his good intentions and genuine efforts notwithstanding, the tangerines would only go to fill the bellies of troops and party cadres in the North. Some believed that his campaign was nothing more than an example of what Koreans called *peojugi* (the provision of excessive relief). He was comforted to learn that the children had enjoyed the fruit after all. He now realized that the North, too, did care about children in its own way, a thought that dissipated the doubts he had harbored for years and made him emotional. He reminisced about the time when the loading of the ship carrying the tangerines had been delayed at the port, how worried he had been that the tangerines would freeze from the cold, and how he had worked to ensure that his plans were implemented. He now felt vindicated for all the trouble he had endured.

Some may still feel uncomfortable about the fact that the children in Pyongyang were not told that the tangerines had been a gift from the people of Jeju Island. Some might still insist that we shouldn't give food relief supplies unless we distribute them ourselves and see with our own eyes that the children actually get to eat them. However, the North Korean authorities have been consistent in saying that they refuse any gift that comes with any such conditions. "Gifts" in North Korea are given by the General only.

Birthday Candy

The most important gifts come on holidays commemorating the birthdays of the Supreme Leaders. On such occasions, all children in the nation receive candy and confectioneries, sometimes even new clothes. For children hungry for sweets, such rare items are most welcome gifts at the end of a long wait and are a special joy to remember. This practice reminded me of my own childhood, when I ran to church on Christmas Day to receive candy. The experience would be similar to those of many children across the world today, waiting for gifts from Santa Claus. In North Korea, the one who gives all such special gifts to children is "Our Father, the General." The children feel his presence tangibly and periodically through such "gifts." Such gifts reaffirm the care and concern of the General, who is said to have special love for the children of North Korea.

Securing "gifts" for children in commemoration of the General's birthday is a task of utmost importance for party workers. At the height of the Great Famine in the late 1990s, I met with North Korean delegates in Beijing to negotiate an expedited shipment of powdered milk to the country. We South Korean delegates said it was a "gift" of genuine sincerity from children in South Korea and that we would like to deliver the supply ourselves directly to children in the North. The North Koreans flatly refused.

While we thought we were humbling ourselves in saying that ours was only a small "gift" and that we would be happy to deliver it ourselves "directly," our words seemed to have bruised their pride. By emphasizing the aid's nature as a "gift," we wanted to convey the fact that our supply was small but sincere, that it was nothing big or in any way ostentatious. However, in the North, the term "gift" is strongly associated with the idea of the "loyal gift"— something that only the Supreme Leader gives out. Loyal gifts are given in the name of the General, on special days, and in special ways, like Christmas gifts in other societies that are bought by parents that are given to children with spectacle and fanfare, and perhaps even signed "From Santa Claus."

Figure 1.3.   The gift from the General: Children receiving bundles of gifts from the Leader. Source: Gi-Man Choi, Taeyanggwa Chongchun *[The Sun and the youths]. (Pyongyang: Geumsong Youth Press, 1999), 122.*

To the North Korean delegates, what we proposed must have amounted to heresy—it was as if we wanted to become Supreme Leaders ourselves! That was not all; gift giving on the birthdays of the Supreme Leaders was the most important event of the year, the brightest moment in what amounted to North Korea's national holiday, the most critical mise-en-scène required for the maintenance of the family-state-cum-theater-state. What we proposed to do, in fact, amounted to staging this most critical act ourselves. I felt embarrassed when I realized this. I remembered unsightly charity events I had witnessed during holiday seasons in the South. At orphanages, the children were lined up in front of a few apple crates for the sake of a photo-op for the donors. We had to soul search and come clean. Were we any different from those donors, who required publicity in exchange for their gifts? We rescinded our request to deliver the milk ourselves.

Once the atmosphere between the two sides became more genial, the North Koreans became more open, asking if we could deliver sugar in addition to the powered milk. They explained that they had to give out candy to children nationwide as gifts marking the General's birthday, but they did not have sufficient resources. We pondered whether or not to acquiesce to this request. In the end, we decided to deliver only the powdered milk, but I could not help feeling a mix of emotions. We were South Korean adults who had set out, ostensibly, to save North Korean children, and all we had was a few tons of powdered milk. Sitting across from us were North Korean adults whose main concern was securing "the General's birthday candy" to distribute to millions of children. Given the enormity and gravity of the food situation in the North, I was struck by how preposterous it was that we were quibbling over the issue of in whose name the "gift" should be distributed.

The powdered milk we sent could have been used to make milk candy. I had to take solace in conjuring up images of the millions of children in the North who would savor the sweet taste of the candy given to them by the General on his birthday.

The Lowered Dining Table

In early 2000, a small group of visitors once went to Chongryugwan a *naengmyeon* (cold noodle) restaurant near the banks of the Botong River in Pyongyang. The weather was bitterly cold. We were told that Pyongyang *naengmyeon* is best eaten in winter. However, the restaurant was not properly heated, and every time anyone spoke, puffs of white steam came out. North Korea was going through its worst period of shortages, not only in terms of food but energy as well. Perhaps to divert attention from the cold, my guide began telling a story about a "lowered dining table," which was located in the restaurant's "Family Room" on the floor below.

> For citizens of Pyongyang who love *naengmyeon*, the Great Leader ordered the construction of the famous Okryugwan on the banks of the Daedong River and Chongryugwan on the banks of the Botong River and personally named the restaurants. One day, he came to Chongryugwan and personally stopped by every room in the restaurant. When he came to the Family Room on the lower floor, he sat down at one of the tables and worried if perhaps the table was too high. The escorting party comrade told him, "It's fine, sir." The Great Leader then instructed, "It's fine for adults, but too high for children. Would the parents be comfortable looking at the children eating in discomfort? Lower the table."[5]

After hearing such a heartwarming story, I suggested that we check out the Family Room right away. The guide, who was ever wary of any spontaneous action, made an exception in this case, willingly leading me to the room downstairs. A family eating their noodles in the cold was taken aback by the sudden appearance of an outsider. They all stood up. The guide explained that a visitor from the South had come to see the lowered table. Upon hearing this, the tense surprise on their faces gave way to proud smiles.

The lowered table story is one famous example of a "vignette of virtue" that every North Korean hears in early childhood. These vignettes are said to be based on true stories that reflect the noble virtue of the Great Leader and his boundless love for the people. The family was now encountering an ignorant outsider who did not know the story. Even the family's grade-schooler looked at me with a charitable smile as I listened, fascinated.

An analogue can be seen in the myth of George Washington and the cherry tree. Whether the anecdote is true or not, its message about their founding father has become engrained in the minds of Americans.

There are countless other "field guidance" vignettes, which relay the Great Leader's guidance on everything from kitchen table height to educational tools in nurseries, kindergartens, and schools, and to hospital and factory facilities. For example, there is a "tilting desk" at the Pyongyang Grand People's Study House, the largest public library in North Korea. The official narrative is that Kim Il-Sung sat at one of the desks and said, "Make a desk that people can adjust according to their seated heights, and with a tabletop that can be tilted for the comfort of reading books."

These are beautiful stories. But I thought it strange that the lowered table and tilted desk should be found at particular venues only. In fact, it would be prohibitively costly to make all tables in restaurants and all desks in libraries adjustable. What is exceptional, rather than commonplace, would be more instructive. Just as mythological heroes leave traces of Herculean feats and miraculous events on mountains, in fields, on the seas, and in forests, the impact of the vignettes comes from their very exceptionality, not from putting heroic ideas into universal practice. The exceptional traces and stories left behind by the Great Leader wherever he went are all variations on the theme of "the love and benevolence, warmth, and touch of thoughtful consideration from Father, the Great Leader."

FATHER TO ORPHANS

I boarded an Air Koryo flight for the first time in early 2000, headed for Pyongyang from Beijing. At the time, there was a widespread sense that the crisis faced by the North Korean regime was deepening due to the famine and the country's international isolation. The Soviet-era Ilyushin aircraft was shoddier than I had expected, from its fuselage down to the seats and safety belts. With modest smiles, the flight attendants handed out the pictorial journal *Chosun* as they guided passengers to their seats.

From the cover photo of Kim Jong-Il's visit to Mangyongdae Revolutionary School in the early hours of New Year's Day, snow fluttering in the air, the photos captivated me. The children were dressed in military uniforms and cheering wildly as Kim hugged some of them. These photos confirmed for me the symbolic meaning of the "guerrilla state" and the "family-state" that I had only heard of. Other photos in the series showed dining tables for children, each loaded with a range of banquet dishes. The abundance of the food for the children, despite the recent famine, meant that the school was privileged to receive special support from the state.

Mangyongdae Revolutionary School

Mangyongdae Revolutionary School opened in October 1947, soon after the liberation of Korea from Japan, as Pyongyang Academy for Bereaved Revolutionary Children. It was a boarding school for elementary and secondary education, built solely for the orphaned children of Korean independence fighters. The school opened at breakneck speed because both Kim Il-Sung and his wife Kim Jong-Sook took special interest in the project.

Kim Il-Sung politically adopted the orphans as his own children, for they were the children of comrades slain during the armed struggle against Japan. He made sure that they were well educated and looked after with special care. This was a signal that the legitimacy of the soon-to-be-established Democratic People's Republic of Korea was to be founded upon the narrative of the armed struggle against Japanese imperialism for the liberation of Korea.

Figure 1.4. Dear General came to Mangyongdae Revolutionary School: Kim Jong-Il visits Mangyongdae Revolutionary School on New Year's Day. Source: Minjokui Oboi [The father of the nation] (Pyongyang: Pyongyang Chulpansa, 2012), 90.

While schools for orphaned children can be found in other socialist countries, Mangyongdae Revolutionary School has been especially pivotal in North Korea's evolution as both a guerrilla state and a family-state.

Later, a few more revolutionary schools for orphans were built outside of Pyongyang "in order to take in children of those revolutionaries who died in battles as far away as Nakdong River in the South fighting American imperialism in the Great Fatherland Liberation War [the Korean War]."[6] Again, these schools were built by the Supreme Leader to raise the orphaned children of revolutionary fighters as his own. In common with the No. 1 School, the students wore military uniforms with red stripes on their pants as a symbol of the blood sacrifice of their parents and their status as the future vanguard of the unfinished revolution in the fatherland. As in training schools for military officers, they lived in school dormitories.

By the late 1960s, the first generation of "revolutionary orphans" had grown up and graduated from these schools. Since then, their children and selected children of party cadres have attended the schools in successive generations. In other words, these are special schools where admission is mainly determined by bloodline; such schools are called "revolutionary breeding grounds" (*hyeongmyeongui weonjongjang*). In this regard, these schools are even more special than Pyongyang No. 1 Middle School, a school for elite students who are selected by merit at the national level. The revolutionary schools located at Mangyongdae and four other locations are where North Korea's military and political cadres, female cadres, and diplomats are trained.

At the first kindergarten we visited in Pyongyang, I heard about an episode that took place at the very special Mangyongdae Revolutionary School. A class of five-year-old children were listening to the following story:

> The young General Kim Jong-Il was five years old when he visited Mangyong-dae Revolutionary School with his Mother Kim Jong-Sook and the Beloved and Respected Generalissimo. . . . Upon seeing the Beloved and Respected Generalissimo, what did the children in the school do but run forward shouting "Father!" and cry in the wide bosom of the Generalissimo? The Young General asked, "Why do these children cry upon seeing my father?" Mother Kim Jong-Suk explained, "These children do not have their fathers, because they were revolutionary fighters who died while fighting courageously against Japanese imperialism. Our Generalissimo is feeding, dressing, and educating these children. So he is the father to all of these children. They are crying because they missed their father and because now they are so happy to see him." "Well, my father should come more often then. That would solve the problem," said the General. "Generalissimo cannot come so often because he has to look after the whole country," said the mother. Then the Young General suggested making lots of pictures of his father and giving them to the children."[7]

This explains why there are framed pictures of Kim Il-Sung and Kim Jong-Il in every North Korean household. In other words, the origin story of the supreme leader who became the "Father" of the nation has its roots in the establishment of the Mangyongdae Revolutionary School.

The children of trusted families in North Korea grow up with privileged support from the state, which could easily make these children the target of jealousy from their peers. However, attacks of this sort are unheard of, as the privileges they receive are justified by propaganda campaigns that emphasize the sacrifices and contributions that their parents, grandparents, and great-grandparents made to the nation. In light of the ideals that thrust the original cast of the revolution into the whirlwind of history, the North Korean revolution today, after the passage of many generations, has a different face.

Yet growing up in such a sheltered and privileged environment poses its own problems for students at the revolutionary schools. Namely, they tend to have an excessive sense of entitlement. They may possess a shocking lack of understanding of the lives of ordinary people, which could make them incapable of providing effective leadership in the face of social problems.

In 1989, Lim Su-Kyung, a South Korean college student, went to Pyongyang without government approval to attend the Thirteenth World Festival of Youth and Students as the representative of Jeondaehyeop, the leading student movement organization at the time. As a young female activist who came directly from the front lines of the ongoing democratization struggle in Seoul, she became an instant star among the young in North Korea. Later, an eyewitness privately testified that the North Korean student leaders who had gone on a hunger strike with her at Panmunjom were not as disciplined as Lim when faced with the harsh conditions and that they had to be fed behind the scenes.[8]

These student leaders looked impressive in their uniforms and were good at marching in response to orders. However, in terms of willpower and leadership, they were no match for the leaders of the student movement fighting at the forefront of the democratization struggle in the South. While they became familiar with revolutionary slogans and military training at school, in real-life situations, "resistance" is an unfamiliar concept to them, and the "protesting spirit" stranger still. A revolutionary struggle *against* power cannot but be fundamentally different from the chanting of revolutionary mottos *in compliance with* power.

In the spring of 2004, I had an opportunity to meet and have a few drinks with a graduate of Mangyongdae Revolutionary School who had defected to South Korea. He said that whereas he had always held important positions in the North, he now lived in low-income housing subsidized by the government and was receiving welfare. He pitied his fallen status and was heartbroken. He wanted to tell his former revolutionary classmates in the North, from the bottom of his heart, "Comrades, defend our-style socialism to death." I wondered what he meant by "socialism." As for the modifier "our-style," he himself seemed well enough aware of its layered meanings. He spoke with irony, but his sense of the loss of his special class privileges was too palpable to laugh off what he had said as entirely a joke. Elite class consciousness does not die easily.

Korean People's Schools in Eastern Europe

"North Korea is different." The Cold War–era Romanian ambassador to North Korea, whom I met in the suburbs of the capital, Bucharest, flatly responded in this way to a question about the possibility of regime collapse in North Korea. The conversation took place in July 2003, a few months after the US military takeover of Baghdad. In the previous year, in his State of the

Union address, George W. Bush had defined North Korea as part of an "axis of evil," along with Iraq and Iran, renewing the pressure on Pyongyang. By July 2003, it was widely believed in international circles that the next regime to fall would be North Korea's. Keeping in mind the tragic end of Nicolae Ceauşescu (1918–1989), the Romanian dictator and a close friend of Kim Il-Sung during their lifetimes, I asked the ambassador about his assessment of the prospects for the Kim Jong-Il regime.

"You can't compare Ceauşescu and Kim Jong-Il. North Korea is really a big family. Not just for the leaders and the elite, but for the vast majority of the people; they are bound together by a common destiny," he told me. A graduate of Kim Il-Sung University, the ambassador described North Korea as a family-state. It surprised me since I had been expecting a sophisticated political analysis from this seasoned diplomat. To support his argument, he told me a story about Kim Il-Sung as "the father of war orphans."[9]

Starting in 1952, when the Korean War was still raging, 1,500 war orphans from North Korea were sent to Romania, where they attended boarding schools in Targoviste and in Siret. Kim Il-Sung sent the orphans on trans-Siberian trains, along with teachers and curricula. Furthermore, he regularly sent an official delegation to deliver gifts to the students and to encourage them in their studies. He wanted them to remember their home country, and he wanted the schools there to function as temporary refugee schools that nurtured the Koreans, who were to return to their home country after the war. Through all the educational programs that took place inside and outside of the classrooms, he wanted to make sure that the students felt his presence as a father figure waiting for them at home.

Georgeta Mircioiu was a teacher at one such school in Romania. She remembered vividly the students who were crying their hearts out when the scholarship delegations arrived from North Korea, so dearly did they miss their home and country. The pain they suffered from losing family members in the war and from living away from home was compensated by their sense of belonging to a huge everlasting family that was their country; they were also overwhelmed with emotion by the love and care that they felt they were receiving from their Father.[10]

Over four thousand war orphans were sent to Romania (1,500), Poland (1,200), Hungary (500), East Germany (600), Czechoslovakia (200), Bulgaria, and other Eastern Bloc countries. The largest number were looked after in China (approximately 20,000). In addition, Mongolia (200) and the Soviet Union (undisclosed numbers) accepted war orphans. In total, it is estimated that over twenty-five thousand war orphans were raised in fraternal socialist countries. The Soviet Union, as the socialist suzerain, allocated one billion rubles to supporting international war orphans.[11]

Figure 1.5. North Korean war orphans in Poland: North Korean war orphans being educated at the North Korean People's School in Eastern European socialist countries. Source: Connected Pictures, Children Went to Poland *(documentary film), 2018.*

The war orphan aid programs that operated under the socialist concept of human rights were based on revolutionary camaraderie, their goal being the delivery of collective relief. This contrasted with charity programs seeking to deliver individual relief under the Western, capitalist concept of human rights. There is no doubt that both approaches are based on compassion. But they are also based on alliance politics. In terms of execution, the socialist relief model took the collective, rather than the individual, as its basic unit of relief, emphasizing social relations, organization, and education.

Armed with a critical consciousness of imperialism and racial discrimination in the Western nations, the socialist countries recognized the importance of the war orphans' cultural identity and ideals of national liberation. Their goal was to raise the war orphans as historically conscious people who would fight to overcome social contradictions.

North Korea did not shy away from taking full advantage of the socialist humanitarianism of the time. Thus, while it was the unilateral beneficiary of wartime aid, it was uninhibited in demanding respect for its autonomy by fellow socialist donor countries. The overseas "dispatch" of war orphans took place in the name of "International Socialist Educational Cooperation." Accordingly, the "student delegates" sent overseas were not limited to war orphans. North Korea selected students who it deemed needed "special" protection and education, including children of "war heroes"—meaning children who had lost at least one parent. The youths who were educated were thus imbued with a sense of patriotic duty, a sense of obligation to return to the fatherland and dedicate their lives to the advancement of the nation. As such, Kim Il-Sung was their political father—not only the symbol of their pride but also their protector.

While listening to stories about the North Korean schools in Romania, I thought about the South Korean orphans sent overseas for adoption. As late as the mid-1960s, it was common to see war orphans in South Korea going door to door carrying tin cans and begging for food. Of course, that is not to say that there were no orphanages in South Korea. In fact, there were many ostensible "charity organizations" operated by religious organizations as well as orphanages run by individuals and poorly subsidized by the state. The orphan children, who were isolated from society and whose welfare depended solely on the conscience and competence of individual facility operators, frequently ran away when they could no longer endure the harsh conditions.

In South Korea, child rearing is considered the sole responsibility of parents; thus, even relatives were reluctant to adopt orphaned kin. The solution was to have them adopted by families in more economically advanced countries. However, by the 1960s, many years after the end of the Korean War, overseas adoption of children from South Korea took place en masse and systematically through international adoption agencies, such as Holt International. Over the years, adoption of children from South Korea became an international industry, where approximately two hundred thousand children have been sent abroad, among them about 75 percent adopted in the United States.

The goal of Western children's relief organizations, such as those that became the backbone of the adoption industry in Korea, is to send underprivileged children from poor countries to middle-class families living in highly developed countries to grant them material abundance and family love. In the context of Cold War competition, the blessings bestowed upon the lucky orphans became evidence that the United States and other Western capitalist countries were "heaven on earth."

Individual stories about international adoption based on the model of personal salvation are introduced in the media mainly in the form of success stories. However, some adoptees suffer from severe identity crises and psychological trauma. In fact, some came back to South Korea as adults with resentment and scars.* The trauma caused by the sudden change in language

---

* While South Korea has become one of the most advanced economies in the world today, it is still the world's biggest "exporter of orphans." Tobias Hübinette, *Comforting an Orphaned Nation:*

and culture, and the identity crisis experienced by members of an ethnic or racial minority, are not the kinds of hurdles that can easily be overcome by personal love alone.

The North Korean war orphans educated abroad in Eastern Bloc countries all returned to North Korea in the 1960s. The main reason for this was the signs of liberal culture change taking place in East European countries; North Korean leaders feared the political influence of such change on their students. When the students returned, they were put through intensive reeducation programs. Some reportedly failed to adapt back to life in North Korea due to severe culture shock. However, having experienced a superior education in the socialist countries, most evolved into a cohort of professionals, taking on leadership roles in various fields from diplomacy and language interpretation to science and technology. Indeed, they became testaments to the special love of "Our Father the Supreme Leader."

According to the former Romanian ambassador, who had ample experience with these students in Pyongyang and Romania, cohorts of people who have had such a special relationship with Kim Il-Sung function as a balance against the collapse of the regime in the face of international isolation and other crises. The elites in North Korea have maintained family ties and a sense of shared destiny over several generations and more than seventy years of division and Cold War tension. The bonds were forged as they overcame historical crises together, becoming even stronger when those crises evolved into long-term situations.

Ethnic Korean Schools in Japan

"Thank you, Generalissimo Kim Il-Sung!"

Until the 1990s, one was bound to come across red-lettered Korean-language billboards bearing this slogan on subway rides through almost any metropolitan city in Japan. These were signs promoting ethnic Korean schools (*jaeil Chosun hakkyo*) in Japan.

Ethnic Korean schools in Japan are not schools for orphans. They are for the Koreans in Japan who became stateless refugees in the niche between Japan and their divided home country. At the time of Japan's defeat in August 1945, about 2.4 million Koreans had gone to Japan either for work or through forced conscription as imperial subjects for wartime labor. After the war, the Japanese government deprived Koreans of Japanese citizenship.[12] The majority repatriated to their ancestral home in the southern half of the

Representations of International Adoption and Adopted Koreans in Korean Popular Culture (Stockholm: Stockholm University, 2005).

Korean Peninsula, leaving 650,000 in Japan by 1946. Like the orphans of the Cold War, they were dispossessed. Kim Il-Sung took the initiative from an early stage in supporting their ethnic education financially and providing a curriculum modeled on North Korean values and priorities, thereby gaining an image as their symbolic father in the homeland.[13]

A large-scale ethnic Korean education system was organized in Japan immediately after World War II by Korean residents. The top priority for this system was the revival of the Korean language and Korean names, the use of which had been strictly prohibited during the period of Japanese rule from 1910 to 1945. It was both a vehicle for cultural liberation and a component of preparations for a return to the homeland. However, in October 1947, the US military occupation forces in Japan ordered the ethnic Korean schools to merge with Japanese schools. Korean minority educators and parents fiercely resisted this move. Their conviction grew even stronger because of the violent suppressions of communists in South Korea. Ethnic Korean schools in Japan continued to operate, showing their resistance by raising the North Korean flag during and after the US occupation which ended in 1952.

In such circumstances, the "Scholarship Fund for Educational Aid" that Kim Il-Sung sent in April 1957 was a lifesaving source of financial assistance for the ethnic Korean schools. The fund, a huge amount by the standards of the time, was used to found schools in many locations across Japan.[14] For many ethnic Koreans, it was the pivotal experience that convinced them that their home state is North Korea, and it can mean a lot to them. To this day, they sing of the overwhelming feelings they felt then.

Never thought in the dream of dreams
That our country will send money.
The huge amount of the Scholarship Fund for Educational Aid is precious.
. . .
The supreme leader sent it with the heart of a father.
Ah—the lofty and great love of the supreme leader
Shall be praised for ten thousand years over the generations.[15]

The funding from North Korea became the catalyst for the mass "repatriation" (*gwihwan*) movement from Japan to North Korea, started in December 1959. Over forty-nine thousand "returnees" embarked in 1960 alone, and 93,340 made the journey over the full span of the project, with the last voyage taking place in July 1984.[16] The fact that the fatherland was no paradise became well known relatively soon. As Tessa Morris-Suzuki puts it, those "returnees" who chose to be repatriated experienced great suffering after their arrival in the North. After undoubtedly being pushed by forces within Japan and lured by misleading propaganda from North Korea, they nevertheless tried to make their own choices within the limited range of possibilities afforded to them.[17] Those who did not see a future of social self-fulfillment in Japan, with its entrenched culture of discrimination toward minorities, felt a sense of duty to leave and seek to build a better nation in North Korea.[18]

The Korean ethnic schools in Japan from kindergarten to college were wildly popular and grew rapidly during the 1960s and 1970s. In 1966, the number of schools reached its height with 142 schools and 34,388 students. Though the numbers of students and schools have declined in recent years, many schools, which were established during this period and offer elementary to university-level education, are still in operation today.[19] Most graduates of these ethnic schools did not repatriate to North Korea, but many still believed that these schools were places where one prepared oneself to return to the unified fatherland and that life in Japan was to be temporary and transitional.

South Korea and Japan concluded the Treaty on Basic Relations in 1965. After that, an increasing number of Koreans in Japan started to take South Korean citizenship, and this affected the enrollment in pro–North Korean ethnic schools (*Chosun hakkyo*). From the early 1970s, the number of students started to decline because of low birth rates and growing criticism of the North Korean curriculum for children living in Japan.

At least until the mid-1980s, many Koreans in Japan had a strong self-identity as part of a larger force working toward the unification of Korea. In my first visit to Japan in 1983, I was surprised to meet some of them who still maintained a strong sense of hope that they would ultimately return to a unified Korea. These were powerful motivators that brought enormous energy to ethnic Korean education programs in Japan.

Students in these schools use Korean names, and lessons are taught in Korean. What is extraordinary about this is that the teachers are third- and fourth-generation Koreans living in Japan teaching fourth- and fifth-generation Koreans in a language that they themselves are not completely familiar with and that neither instructors nor pupils have much opportunity to use outside of the schools. This insistence on using Korean is derived not from the functional value of the language in Japanese society but from a desire to promote ethnic pride and cultural identity as Koreans.

The discriminatory acts against the Korean minority that periodically surface in Japan by no means undermine the Korean schools. On the contrary, such racist incidents only serve as real-life evidence strengthening the rationale for their existence. When the iconic *chima jeogori* (Korean-style skirt and top) uniforms worn by female students of pro–North Korean schools were mocked or torn up in acts of anti–North Korean hatred in the early 2000s, such incidents were immediately incorporated into a play, a dance, and a film in order to raise awareness of ongoing discrimination toward Koreans in Japan. Such crimes are a reminder that discrimination is a reality and not simply part of history; they reconfirm the raison d'être of the schools.

Some parents send their children to such schools in order to spare them from becoming victims of bullying and discrimination at Japanese schools. But, more proactively, in sending their children to these schools, the parents are hoping to minimize generational conflict with their children and maximize family unity, based on the expectation that, by virtue of attending such schools alone, the children will acquire an unwavering sense of ethnic identity.

With the democratization and economic prosperity of South Korea in recent decades, most ethnic Koreans in today's Japan are no longer passionate about North Korea. But the pro–North Korean ethnic schools still exist, albeit with a significantly reduced number of institutions, each having fewer students and teachers. As of 2017, there were 102 ethnic Korean schools and 6,185 students in Japan, less than 20 percent of the number half a century earlier.[20] The majority of them, almost 70 percent, now have South Korean citizenship. However, their curricula still include some materials from Pyongyang, and their North Korean–style performing arts are still active, although their repertoire has become less revolutionary and more traditional.[21]

High school graduating classes often still go on school trips to North Korea. What makes these trips most meaningful are the surprise gifts from the Dear General. Kim Jong-Il surprised visiting students who were hiking on Mount Myohyang by delivering gifts to them via helicopter even during the difficult times in the late 1990s; the students were deeply moved. Even today, the "Leader" or "General" is still the "Father" who symbolizes the homeland at such ethnic Korean schools.

For decades, North Korea supported ethnic Korean education programs in Japan in the name of the Father. The relationship between these schools in Japan and the Supreme Leader in North Korea is built on strong historical ties that are not unlike the emotional relationship built between parent and child over the span of a lifetime.

SOCIAL ENGINEERING

"It's scorching in here!" the guide said in a loud voice as we walked into the "triplets" room on the upper floor of the Pyongsong Orphanage. Unlike the room on the lower floor where the air was ice cold, the triplets room had a hint of warmth. Two sets of triplets were crawling on the floor. Each set of triplets was identical. Unlike the toddlers on the lower floor, who were wearing yellow clothes, these children had on red onesies with epaulet-like shoulder buttons. Within the same orphanage, triplets were kept in a special space and received special treatment.

I picked up one of the babies in my arm and asked the staff, "Are these children also orphaned?"

"No. They have parents, but we raise them here as part of a special arrangement until they are five," one worker responded.

I gathered that the parents were allowed to come and see the children now and then. However, I did not immediately grasp the attractions of an arrangement in which parents had to come to an orphanage in order to be with their children.

Not too long afterward, back in South Korea, I saw a TV documentary about a low-income couple who had triplets. Tasked with the care of the three infants, the couple was unable to work, eventually filing for bankruptcy. Even in affluent South Korea, it is difficult for a nuclear family to look after three infants at once. Unfortunately, there is no special support for parents in such rare cases of multiple childbirth in South Korea. In the case of the triplets I saw in North Korea, they would have faced the same difficulties as other children in the famine-ravaged country at the time had it not been for the state's support.

Blessed Triplets

Triplets in North Korea also have special symbolic significance. I was told that triplets are "national treasures" and thus receive special love and care from the General. In the past, triplets often likely died during birth or became disabled. Healthy triplets were thus proof of the advanced nature of the socialist scientific medicine in North Korea. In a book about the special place occupied by triplets in North Korea, one author wrote, "Dear Leader Comrade [Kim Jong-Il] readily mobilizes not only trains and automobiles but also emergency airplanes for triplets; he would not hesitate to spare millions of dollars."[22] In short, triplets receive special attention because they symbolize the socialist medical welfare system highlighting its superiority to that in capitalist systems.

Triplets are also considered "a good omen for the nation," and as such, they represent the future. Thus, the General "gives them even silver knives for boys and gold rings for girls as a gift of love that would be handed down for generations."[23] Pyongyang Maternity Hospital, the cutting-edge hospital for expecting mothers, has a separate "triplets ward" that provides a comprehensive service for families with triplets, from birth to child rearing. It was said that on the day that the one hundredth set of triplets was born at the

Figure 1.6. Triplets are the treasures of the nation: (top) triplets in an orphanage, (bottom) triplets in Young Pioneer uniforms named Chong-Il, Pok-Il, and Tan-Il, combined meaning "Chongpoktan (total bombs)." Top: Eric Lafforgue. Bottom, source: Chosun, June 2001.

hospital, Kim Jong-Il ordered the newspapers that were ready to go to press to redo their typesetting in order to trumpet the news on their front page. He also personally met and embraced the triplets.

What does such special interest and expectation in relation to triplets signify? In the early days, the policy seems to have been simply a social response to a rare phenomenon. However, more recently, it seems to have become more important as a form of social investment. What does the regime expect from this investment? A book titled *Blessed Triplets* (*Bokbadeun Ses-sangdungideul*), distributed widely by the regime, explains:

> The triplets who receive so much love from above feel that the bosom of the Dear Leader is the bosom of their mother as they grow up from year to year, and they entrust their fate completely to him; they do their best to be loyal and pious so as to give him great joy and satisfaction.[24]

The fact that the target of loyalty and piety here is not the Great Leader (i.e., Kim Il-Sung) but the Dear Leader, or the General (i.e., Kim Jong-Il), tells us that the triplet policy was Kim Jong-Il's project. Triplets are given names as a set, each including a character related to loyalty or piety. They grow up as a set, become soldiers, musicians, or rural propaganda leaders as a set, and "lead the file of loyalty."

A Brave New World

By intervening not only in the birth and rearing of triplets but also in their education and careers, Kim Jong-Il showcased them as a model for future generations. Kim Jong-Il's policy on triplets smacks of the social engineering experiments and expectations of efficiency derived from human cloning that Aldous Huxley refers to in *Brave New World*. In this novel, based on the power of biological and educational engineering, every member of society voluntarily accepts their social status and performs their given tasks in society without conflict.

Yuval Harari warned that if revolutionary new technologies, such as bioengineering and artificial intelligence, are combined with the "ideological values" of a dictatorship, this amplifies the possibility of a totalitarian dystopia because "it is often assumed that the new technologies and science of the 21st century would weaken the (false) belief systems, but instead [they] make them stronger." That is how the combination of "old myths and new technologies" amplifies both the opportunities for and the disintegration of future society.[25]

Currently there is a big gap between North and South Korea in levels of scientific and technological development. However, where a nation's scarce resources are concentrated and what fields become advanced in a nation are matters of social priorities and political will. A good example is the North Korean development of nuclear arms and ICBMs. Harari points out that, unlike in South Korea and other liberal societies where different social groups have conflicting interests, the political regime in North Korea has absolute power. He notes that North Korea could easily introduce driverless vehicles nationwide, apply the results of genetic experiments, and build and operate a centralized surveillance system by utilizing available smart-phone technologies.[26] Its choice, however, lay in investing heavily in atomic weapons. Today, North Korea is isolated, neither it nor the world has much stake in the other, and, in any case, it does not readily comply with the demands of the outside world. Given these circumstances, North Korea has the highest potential for realizing the Huxleyan dystopia of postmodern totalitarianism.

THE YOUNG GENERAL

North Korea's three intergenerational power successions were achieved through state-organized spectacles.[27] In order to place Kim Jong-Un—then twenty-seven years old and a political neophyte—in the most powerful position in the nation, an all-out propaganda campaign was waged for several years after Kim Jong-Il suffered a stroke in August 2008.* The country was in crisis, and the power succession had to be completed as soon as possible. The propaganda campaign had two key messages: Kim Jong-Un is the legitimate heir to his father, and he represents change.

On September 27, 2010, Kim Jong-Un was photographed in front of the Geumsusan Memorial Palace with the members of the Central Committee of the Workers' Party to commemorate being formally awarded the title of "General." The release of this photograph was the first occasion on which information about the "Young General Kim" became public in North Korea.

Almost two years prior to the public unveiling of Kim Jong-Un's photograph, spectacular fireworks lit up the night sky on February 16 (Kim Jong-Il's birthday), April 15 (Kim Il-Sung's birthday), and May 1 (International Workers' Day) of 2009. The public was later informed that Young General Kim had directly "created and guided" the spectacular shows at a time when only his approaching footsteps could be heard, figuratively speaking.[28] The international community was aghast as estimates of the cost of the unprecedentedly spectacular fireworks ranged to approximately $5 million.[29]

---

* In a theater state, national symbols and rituals signify power itself. Accordingly, all political processes are shaped and signified culturally. Clifford Geertz, *Negara: The Theatre State in Nineteenth-Century Bali* (Princeton, NJ: Princeton University Press, 1980).

However, North Korean authorities needed this fanfare in order to introduce the new leader of their theater state to the world.

The fact that Kim Jong-Un "personally directed" the show was a hint that he would play a similar role to his father, who produced and directed the enormous Arirang Mass Games. It also hinted that the Young General's performance as leader would be more spectacular and provocative than that of his father, even though the scale of the event that he staged was smaller than the games his father had directed. In fact, Kim Jong-Un soon switched his medium from festive firework shows to repeated long-range artillery training exercises and missile launches. Calling him "Rocket Man," US president Donald Trump both sneered at and issued a warning to the young leader.

"So Alike!"

When Kim Jong-Un at last formally appeared on stage, the world was at first taken aback by his strange attire and looks. He wore an archaic *inminbok* (Mao suit) and boasted a slicked-back hairstyle unbecoming of his age. He was overweight and had a strange manner of walking. In short, the image that he projected was not one of a young leader of a contemporary nation. However, it must be remembered that his weight is part of a carefully cultivated image, one of a third-generation leader who has inherited charismatic authority, and not the result of a voracious appetite or a regretful lack of exercise.*

North Koreans immediately recognized his looks, gestures, and manner of speech. They evoked those of their original charismatic leader, Kim Il-Sung. Kim Jong-Un's looks gave them an idea of what to expect going forward in terms of the country's politics. This sentiment is reflected in a children's poem, "So Alike."

Master Kim Jong-Un
You empower us a hundred and a thousand times.
So alike you are to
Father General.[30]

Kim Jong-Un's succession was completed in 2012, following the death of Kim Jong-Il. In that year, more cultural events and artworks were produced to celebrate the one hundredth anniversary of the birth of Kim Il-Sung than to commemorate the death of Kim Jong-Il. This was in part an attempt to erase

---

* According to Fujimoto, a Japanese chef for the Leader, Kim Jong-Il frequently told his son, "Make sure you eat plenty and maintain dignity." Hong-Min Cho, "Kim Jong-Unui 'Wurin Wae Meugeul Geuk Upna' Geuggeonghae Nolla" [(Fujimoto was surprised to hear that) Kim Jong-un was worried, "Why don't we have food?"], *Kyunghyang Shinmun*, October 10, 2010, https://www.khan.co.kr/politics/north-korea/article/201010102220305.

Figure 1.7. So alike! Kim Il-Sung (1948) and Kim Jong-Un (2013). Left and right, source: Chosun Central News

the tragic memory of the famine that had begun in 1994, the year that Kim Il-Sung died. Kim Jong-Un copied the looks and mannerisms of his grandfather more than those of his father, cultivating a mystical image of himself as his grandfather reincarnate.

He wanted people to remember Kim Il-Sung—the leader who had not only led the liberation of the nation from Japanese colonialism but succeeded in achieving rapid economic growth, guiding the nation as it rose from the rubble of the Korean War in what British economist Joan Robinson called the "Korean Miracle," hailing Kim Il-Sung as a "messiah rather than a dictator" in her 1965 report.[31] In summoning that memory, Kim Jong-Un wanted to sow hope for economic revival.

Kim Jong-Un appeared on the stage of this revolutionary drama as its protagonist. He transformed his role into that of the leading man in a contemporary drama involving dynamic social change. While appropriating the political symbols and mannerisms of his forebears as his own, he also retooled them to meet the demands of his time. His role demanded that he deliver a new act with an old script. That is to say, the propaganda hardware was still the same. Like his father before him, he toured various military and industrial sites in order to deliver "field guidance" while also producing massive artistic and cultural spectacles.

However, the substance had to change in order to meet modern (or material) desires. Accordingly, Kim Jong-Un was on the ground, for example directing and "guiding" the construction of a ski resort and theme park that became the symbol of change in his era. He introduced pop music concerts and idol stars, Western-style restaurants and department stores, and high-rise apartment buildings and neon signs that transformed the urban landscape.

He simultaneously transmitted messages of repetition and change, endeavoring to illustrate novelty in the context of the familiar. To kindle nostalgia among the middle aged and elderly, who had experienced the economic stability of the 1960s and 1970s, he ordered the reproduction of Kim Il-Sung–era artworks, such as the song, "Nothing to Envy." To encourage members of the younger population to take pride in their country and give them a sense of the change that was coming, the answer was sensational arts performances, such as those by the Moranbong Band, and a fancy theme park. For children and youth, he held large-scale Youth League events at which he frequently appeared in person. In doing so, he wanted future generations to remember him as a leader who was young, approachable, and friendly.[32]

In a country such as North Korea, in which the political process is opaque to the outside world, only the main actors are in the spotlight. One could therefore easily conclude that there were simply no other actors, that life and politics moved in perfect top-down order as the Supreme Leader formulated plans and made decisions, either alone or in concert with select members of the elite. However, many of the twenty-four million people in this theater state participate actively in the production as writers, actors, extras, staff members, and spectators. They in fact have a great degree of influence on the content, structure, and presentation of the drama.

By the end of the 1990s, in the wake of the catastrophic famine, *jangmadang* (private field markets) had become an integral part of everyday life. Concurrently, due to the increasing number of defectors, smugglers, and workers officially sent overseas, the cross-border flow of information, goods, and people had also increased, making it increasingly untenable for the ruling elite to rely on self-contained, socialist-style propaganda in order to secure the consent of the people.

The introduction of hybrid capitalist elements in entertainment and consumption, as well as in popular performance events, was the North Korean state's response to bottom-up pressure and the demands of the changing times. If for no other reason than to ensure the survival of the regime, the ruling power could no longer delay the liberalization of the country. It could only hope that such change would take place in an orderly manner that permitted the preservation of the entrenched hierarchy. The dramatic inter-Korean summits in 2018, as well as the ensuing US–North Korea summits in Singapore and Hanoi, reflected North Korea's genuine desire for change in this context.

From "Rocket Man" to "Good Friend"

In her study of Japan during World War II, anthropologist Ruth Benedict observed that symbols of power can be effective when a nation undergoes dramatic change. North Korea is now seeking such dramatic change. Considering Japan's experience, there are a number of possible scenarios for North Korea. In the first scenario, the protagonist of the theater state stops the play and changes the script. In World War II, the Japanese emperor, who had been worshipped as a living deity, personally announced Japan's surrender in his first public statement and radio broadcast, thereby allowing all Japanese soldiers, from the South Pacific islands to Manchuria, to disarm at once. The emperor then also announced that he was not a deity but a human being, symbolically supporting postwar regime change and securing his position on the throne until his death in 1989.

In another scenario, new directors can pursue reform using existing symbolic power figures. For example, the Meiji Restoration (1868) that laid the groundwork for the establishment of modern Japan was brought about by reform-minded, low-ranking samurai who utilized the power of the emperor as a traditional political symbol. History shows that, in either case, the culturally trained actors, staff, and spectators of the theater state can be equally passionate in immersing themselves in the changing trajectory of the play.[33]

As a theater state, North Korea can also minimize sacrifices and proceed to a new act. The role of the protagonist, the central figure of the theater state, is crucial—not only for maintaining the regime but also for generating the possibility of change. Although Kim Jong-Un is young and his political experience limited, he is still the new producer and the leading actor; he is not someone "unworthy of mention," as one South Korean paper put it.[34] He is no longer an individual but is emblematic of a system.

In fact, the international press exhibits a relentless obsession with Kim Jong-Un's age, looks, and gestures, building a caricature that is variously strange, boorish, or ridiculous. At the same time, he is constantly demonized as ruthless, cruel, and crazy. Since his debut, external spectators have come to know the lead actor of this closed theater state via such images.

After Kim Jong-Un's recent appearance on the world stage, a different kind of cognitive error began spreading. President Trump gave Kim Jong-Un a thumbs-up evaluation, calling him "a smart negotiator" and "a good friend." The South Korean press also began softening its stance toward the North Korean leader after an inter-Korean summit in 2018. However, Kim Jong-Un's seemingly casual and spontaneous comments and behavior in informal settings, not to mention the contents of his official speeches and exchanges, are all part of a carefully constructed reality show. The image he projects is precisely the impression that he wants to convey.

It must also be remembered that theater is not a one-way performance. The actor is constantly aware of, and responsive to, his audience. The two are interdependent. When the new star of the North Korean theater state stepped onto the global political stage, the stage went live. This means that the outside world now has the power to influence his performance. What kind of performance does the international community want to see? What role do we want him to play? What lines do we want him to say, and what kind of dramas do we want him to show us?

Just as internationally popular South Korean dramas constantly modify their scripts, rearrange their casts, and change their endings according to the responses of viewers, North Korea, too, has been engaged in the production of a dynamically changing power drama as if it were responding to the reactions of the outside world. The day may yet come when the world sees Kim Jong-Un as a young, fit, sartorially elegant, and astute if unconventional politician.

THE THEATER STATE

When the event known as the Arirang Mass Performance and Games was first held in 2002, much of the country was still hungry, the scars of the famine still far from being healed. Just months earlier, President George W. Bush had designated North Korea as part of an "axis of evil," along with Iraq and Iran. The threat of the resumption of the US-led war with North Korea loomed large. Even veteran North Korea watchers had a hard time understanding the regime's intentions in mobilizing people and resources on such a massive scale for the spectacle. Many interpreted it as "a response to the World Cup games" in South Korea, or as "a means of earning foreign currency." Soon, commentators noted that the regime had failed to bring in foreign tourists to view the performance. Others even went so far as to say that the festival was "the last convulsion of the 'brain-dead state' of North Korea."[35] These are examples of typically self-serving analysis by outsiders who do not understand the workings of the theater state.

The Arirang Mass Games

The Arirang Mass Games is the largest mass arts festival ever organized by North Korea. For the 2002 performance alone, one hundred thousand performers and twenty thousand "image card holders" were mobilized, and four million visitors came to see the performance. Between 2005 and 2013, millions of people attended the event, which became the "performance of the nation" (*gukmin gongyeon*), both in name and substance.* On October 9,

---

* The year 2002 marked the ninetieth anniversary of the birth of Kim Il-Sung, the sixtieth birthday of Kim Jong-Il, and the seventieth anniversary of the founding of the Korean People's Army. The Arirang Mass Games opened on April 15 in honor of the Day of the Sun (Kim Il-Sung's birthday). Within the first two months of the event's opening, the show was performed fifty-four times. Yeong-Seon Jeon, "Bukanui Daejipdanchejo Yesulgongyeon 'Arirang'ui Jeongchisahoejeok, Munhwayesuljeok Uimi" [The politico-social and literary-artistic significance of the North Korean mass performance

2010, the eve of the sixty-fifth anniversary of the founding of the Workers' Party, Kim Jong-Un appeared in the VIP section of the festival stadium with his father, Kim Jong-Il. It was the first time that the younger Kim had appeared in public. The regime had chosen the site of this massive national ritual to declare, at home and abroad, the continuity of the power center.

Darkness was fast descending that chilly evening in October 2005 as I entered the Reungrado May Day Stadium to attend the Arirang Mass Games. Although I knew that the stadium was built to accommodate 150,000 people, I was struck by its actual size once inside. The arena was already packed, and when the entourage from South Korea and foreigners from other countries entered their designated sections, a huge number of people waved and applauded in welcome. I could feel the incandescent curiosity of the North Koreans seated in neighboring sections. It seemed that we, the foreigners in the stadium, were a major spectacle for them.

The stadium was brimming with lights, voices, and excitement. Even before the start of the performance, lights shone brightly and rainbow-colored beams danced about, perhaps part of the final checks before the start of the show. These illuminations contrasted starkly with the darkness of the Pyongyang night outside beyond the stadium, devoid of the glow of neon signs and streetlights. The North Koreans at the event must have felt the contrast even more than I did.

The performance started with a portrayal, in a plaintive color scheme, of the harsh lives of the people oppressed under Japanese imperialism. The stadium was draped in inky darkness, and a melodramatic song played as dancers moved about the stage portraying a desperate situation. Suddenly, bright lights illuminated the card section of the stands, where the card holders had turned their cards over to create a massive image of a snow-covered Mount Baekdu and its crater lake. The large picture then began to change, inch by inch, as a red sun rose over the mountain. Murmurs of "the General, the General!" could be heard from the crowd. Now the sun reached its apex, its rays bouncing off the golden dresses and fans held by the thousands of dancers blanketing the stadium floor, its light rapidly washing over the stadium from end to end. The crowd was enthralled. "Great Leader, Great Leader!" They leaped to their feet, hands clapping wildly, as if the morning light had pierced their bodies and entered their hearts. In North Korean iconography, the red sun symbolizes the founder of the nation, Kim Il-Sung. It was as if the crowd was welcoming him personally, basking in the warmth of his morning sun.

'Arirang'], *Jungso Yeongu* [Sino-Soviet affairs] 26, no. 2 (2002). The performances were held at a similar pace and scale until 2013, with the exception of 2006, when they were canceled in the face of large-scale flooding throughout the country.

Figure 1.8. "Smile Broadly!" A performance by children at the Arirang Mass Game. Takashi Ito

The Arirang Mass Games are a reenactment of a drama already familiar to the crowd but presented with great spectacle in a manner affording an immediate sensory experience; it is a form of call-and-response. In other words, the performers on the ground, the students in the image card section, and the members of the audience in the stands are all playing roles in this shared drama. The performance is engrossing, and the response of the crowd equals it in sheer passion; these elements coalesce to create a festival of enthralling performance and enthralled participation.

What is the goal of investing so heavily in such a grand ritual at a time when state finances have all but collapsed? With the money and resources spent on the production of the massive performance, one might think, perhaps the regime could have instead bought more food or more weapons. But the games are a characteristic response of a theater state to economic and political crisis.

Theater states typically exert more effort to move the hearts of their people than to expand their territories or bolster their forces. In such states, the political system and the bureaucracy often prioritize the preparation and execution of national rituals over the pursuit of the nation's economic or even military interests. In this context, the Arirang Mass Games function as a confirmation of national grandeur and pride.

The more the state is belittled, the more need there is to display its gravitas, both at home and abroad. The Arirang Games are the summation of culturally familiar creative and artistic efforts. In other words, the performance reaffirms the political legitimacy of the anti-imperialist struggle symbolized by Kim Il-Sung; it demonstrates the power of Kim Jong-Il's *songun* (military-first) politics, forged to protect the autonomy of the nation; and it projects an image of the future utopia of a unified Korea in which it will forever be the center of the world.[36]

The essence of the message is that while Kim Il-Sung is dead, his son and grandson have successively inherited the role of the "exemplary center" in order to safeguard and even more perfectly reproduce the state system that he founded. Mobilizing such national symbols and rituals, the regime pulled off two charismatic power successions that would be inconceivable in a modern nation-state, despite the general crisis brought on by widespread famine.[37]

The Immobile Center Finally Moves

In the extravagant performances of the theater state, the central cast members—the Leader or the General—rarely make appearances. When they do on special occasions, they remain in their VIP seats, their faces expressionless and their hands clapping mechanically. In trying to describe the role of a king in this regard, cultural anthropologist Clifford Geertz evokes T. S. Eliot, characterizing the ruler as "the still point of the turning world."[38]

In the rituals of the theater state of Negara, the "half-divine" king was "immobile, tranced, or dead at the dramatic center."[39] In other words, he was "the still point of the turning world," and, as such, "his job was to project an enormous calm at the center of the enormous activity by becoming palpably immobile."[40]

The frequent absences of Kim Jong-Il from grand national events, and the passivity he showed when he did appear, corresponded precisely with what Geertz describes as the king in a typical theater state. Kim Jong-Un's public debut was also marked by a conspicuous display of expressionlessness and measured ceremonial movement; he, too, was the quintessential "still point of the turning world" playing out its symbolic function.

In the grand finale of the Arirang Mass Games, a group of dancers circles around a giant globe, suggesting that Korea is the center of the earth as well as the center of the cosmic order. The leader is the immobile central axis that makes the orderly movement of the globe possible. It is not his ability or activity but his *being* itself that is symbolically important.[*]

---

[*] As a symbol and an icon, the leader of the theater state serves as the purpose and object of national rituals. Roland Barthes introduced the concept of the "hollow center" in order to express a

However, as the new producer-cum-leading actor of the theater state, Kim Jong-Un began speaking for himself as he consolidated his own power base. In September 2018, during the inter-Korean summit in Pyongyang, the entourage from the South was invited to attend a performance featuring highlights from the Arirang Mass Games. At the Reungrado May Day Stadium, Kim Jong-Un spoke personally to the people of Pyongyang, introducing President Moon Jae-In before his historic speech there. This revealed that the so-called hermit kingdom was changing. At the same time, it was a dramatic proclamation of its intention to continue to change.

The Geumsusan Memorial Palace versus the Ho Chi Minh Mausoleum

In February 2019, after the breakdown of talks with Trump in Hanoi, Kim Jong-Un made one last official stop in Vietnam before returning home, visiting the Ho Chi Minh Mausoleum. One can only imagine the emotions that the young leader must have felt as he confronted the fact that his dream had just been dashed. He had been full of hope of ending long-standing hostile relations with the United States and opening "a new era" for North Korea.

Only a few days earlier, he was on his train ride from Pyongyang to Hanoi, a symbolic sixty-five-hour journey following in the footsteps of his grandfather more than half a century earlier. During the past half century, the positions of North Korea and Vietnam have dramatically reversed. Kim Il-Sung's North Korea was a country that ended a war with the United States with an armistice, recorded as a "victory" in North Korean history books. Moreover, the country had achieved a "Korean miracle" and was regarded by some as a leading success story of the socialist bloc in the Cold War. On the world stage of nonalignment diplomacy in 1954, Kim Il-Sung stood shoulder-to-shoulder with Sukarno of Indonesia, Tito of Yugoslavia, and Zhou Enlai of the People's Republic of China. On his second visit to Vietnam in 1964, Kim Il-Sung offered encouragement to Ho Chi Minh, a hero who was leading another postcolonial nation in a war with the United States, and promised aid to the downtrodden country.

Today, second only to China, Vietnam has emerged as a success story of "market socialism." Kim Jong-Un, on the other hand, is now in the position of having to seek help and support, as shown in his "wish" for Vietnam to "share its experience of nation building and economic development."[41] In past decades, North Korea succeeded in developing nuclear arms and ICBMs that

---

similar notion in his discussion of Japanese culture. Roland Barthes, *Empire of Signs* (New York: Hill and Wang, 1982).

pose a threat to the United States. However, this success has worsened the country's international isolation, wrought havoc on its economy, and clouded the fate of the regime and the nation itself in uncertainty.

When the talks in Hanoi broke down, Kim Jong-Un was left empty-handed, his hopes of a dramatic breakthrough, a departure from years of costly military buildup, crushed. During his exit, as Trump tantalizingly left open the possibility of continuing talks, Kim found himself in a position where he could neither cast a chill over the talk nor return to the past. As he stood at the grave of his grandfather's comrade, Ho Chi Minh, what was going through his mind?

I had opportunities to visit the mausoleums in both countries, which allowed me to think about differences in each nation's national character-istics and leadership styles. Let me first share what I saw, heard, and felt during my visit to the final resting place of Kim Il-Sung, which took place in October 2005.

When Kim Il-Sung died, Kim Jong-Il renovated his father's official resi-dence and transformed it into a tomb, calling it the Geumsusan Memorial Pal-ace, in order that the people may keenly feel the eternal life of Kim Il-Sung. Kim Jong-Il reportedly spent $300 million on the remodeling project, which took place during the disastrous famine, saying that nothing must be spared in the task of preserving for generations the eternal resting place of his father, whom he deems the Sun for all progressive peoples of the world.[42]

The palace itself is massive, not merely ostentatious. Standing in its vast plaza, I spontaneously exclaimed, "Taj Mahal!" It overwhelmed me not so much with its aesthetic beauty but with its scale, the massive building having been entirely transformed into a mausoleum.

At precisely seven o'clock in the morning, our bus stopped at the east gate of the Palace and we were asked to disembark. As at an airport security checkpoint, everything in each visitor's possession was put through a scanner, and all visitors were required to pass through a metal detector. Not so much as a stray pen was allowed through. It seemed to me that the thoroughness of this inspection process had a significance beyond security purposes.

After the security check, we boarded our bus again to head to the side entrance of the mausoleum. Two soldiers, each holding a bayonet, were on guard on either side of the gate, and one with a particularly boyish face was dozing off while standing up. Inside the gate, we were ordered to stand side by side in a line and tidy ourselves up just outside the mausoleum. We pushed through a heavy door and entered the ceiling-to-floor marble lobby. Again, soldiers with bayonets stood guard, a pair at the bottom and another pair at the top of the spiral stairway leading to the second floor. Soaring marble columns and a giant chandelier, unlit, decorated the expansive second-floor hall. Supersized paintings hung on every wall, portraying common people stricken with grief at losing their Great Leader, and Kim Jong-Il comforting them.

The next room was the central hall in which Kim Il-Sung's body was preserved. To enter, one had to pass through a small chamber between two layers of curtains. Pushing through the first red curtain, I entered a small, dark room and was startled upon being suddenly showered with some sort of mist from above. I smelled perfume. It reminded me of how visitors are sprinkled with holy water at the entrance to Catholic churches, a religious purification gesture. Was I contaminated?

Passing through a second red curtain, I finally entered a large room that was dimly lit with red bulbs. I saw the body of Kim Il-Sung, which was encased in a glass sarcophagus atop a stand at the center of the room. People standing in a long line bowed respectfully at his feet. Upon closer inspection, I noticed that the North Koreans were bowing a full ninety degrees, while the foreigners were only bowing their heads. Starting at the dead leader's feet, they moved in a clockwise direction, bowing four times in total, once on each side of the crystalline coffin, before exiting.

Dressed in a black suit and covered in a red flag up to the chest, the corpse's face looked puffy, perhaps because of the layer of makeup it wore. So this is what he looks like in death, I thought, the one who was—and still is—the symbol of the nation and the object of the most ardent worship. The sight did not stir a sense of awe in me but one of futility. Watching the people bowing with resolute expressions on their faces and moving solemnly through the hushed space brought to mind the highly standardized mise-en-scène of a historical drama.

As a person visiting North Korea for the purpose of delivering food relief for famine victims, I found it hard to believe that the renovation project had been simply an expression of Kim Jong-Il's filial piety. It seemed to me that through such idolization, he himself had wished to become "the Sun of great love in true likeness of the Great Leader." In fact, Kim Jong-Il now lies side by side with his father.

In June 2010, a few years after my visit to the Geumsusan Memorial Palace, I paid a visit to the Ho Chi Minh Mausoleum in Hanoi while on a trip to Vietnam. At eight o'clock in the morning, there was already a long line of visitors, and I was already drenched in sweat. Perhaps because it was a Sunday, most of the visitors were families with children, and there was also a group of red-scarfed Youth League students and their teacher. People of all walks of life stood waiting in a line a few hundred meters long, shaded by a cloth canopy. Peddlers came and went, some selling flowers to those waiting. Families talked loudly, as if they were enjoying a fun excursion, and children ran about without a care. Everyone waited in the sweltering heat for their turn to go in.

The Ho Chi Minh Mausoleum opens at seven in the morning and closes a half hour before midnight. I was told that it was visited by an average of approximately sixty thousand people each day and that the line was already so long by nine in the morning that anyone arriving later might not be able to enter. A staff member took my camera and handed me a numbered ticket. There was no other security check process, per se. Watching the soldiers standing guard in their long-sleeved white uniforms made me feel even hotter. Perhaps they felt proud to serve as honor guards, for their faces were solemn.

In comparison to the Presidential Palace of Vietnam, which was originally constructed in an ornate style to house the French governor-general of Indochina, the Ho Chi Minh Mausoleum is a relatively simple structure. Even up close, the red granite mausoleum is not too imposing. Upon entering the building, one immediately feels the cool breeze of the air conditioning. As the visitors went up the stairs to the second floor, the crowd gradually divided into two orderly lines. Following one line, I entered the interment chamber through an open door. Inside, the room was dark, with only the glass box holding the revolutionary leader brightly lit in the middle of the room. A white-haired Ho Chi Minh in light beige work clothes lay there, his face clearly made up. At the four corners of the base beneath the glass box stood four honor guards, each holding a bayonet.

Visitors were guided to exit the chamber in two lines along the pathway that encircled the casket. Parallel to the pathway for adults was a separate, raised pathway for children that enabled them to see "Uncle Ho" (Bac Ho) without their line of sight being blocked by taller adults. I was struck by the conspicuous absence of any form of religious gesture by the visitors. Everyone simply walked along the route as if in any other ordinary space. It seemed appropriate to pay respect in this way to a socialist revolutionary hero.

I have often wondered what Kim Jong-Un felt upon his visit to the Ho Chi Minh Mausoleum. Paying respect at this simple mausoleum, did he not feel that the Geumsusan Memorial Palace was too extravagant? Or, on the contrary, did it reinforce his belief in creating the basis for the highest respect for the North Korean leader? Did he reflect on the mechanism of familial power succession through the symbols that his father had put in place? Did he realize that the road to a "normal state" like Vietnam would inevitably involve a voluntary process of dismantling such multiple emblems? After returning from Vietnam, Kim Jong-Un sent an unusual message in the form of a letter to the Convention of the Local Party Propaganda Workers in North Korea not to deify him. "Should the revolutionary activities and character of the leader be mystified in the name of emphasizing his greatness, truth will be veiled," the letter read. "The leader and the people are not far from each other as beings."[43]

NOTES

1. Oxford Poverty and Human Development Initiative (OPHI), "Bhutan's Gross National Happiness Index," https://ophi.org.uk/policy/bhutan-gnh-index.

2. Joan Robinson, "Korean Miracle," *Monthly Review* 16, no. 9 (1965): 541–49.

3. The Mangyongdae Children's Palace in Pyongyang is a public facility where selected elite schoolchildren engage in extracurricular activities, such as learning music, foreign languages, computing skills, and sports. It was established on May 2, 1989, and is the largest of the locales in North Korea dedicated to children's cultural activities.

4. Kim Il-Sung's notions of the liberation and unification of Korea (*haebang choguk* and *tongil choguk*, respectively) borrow many symbolic images from millenarianism, which envisaged the overthrow of the order that perpetuated social inequality and advancement toward a utopia on earth. Millenarian movements arose in a number of colonial and semicolonial societies plundered by Western imperial powers in the period from the late nineteenth to the early twentieth century.

5. "Najajin Papsang" [The lowered meal table], *Chongnyon Munhak* [Youth literature] (Pyongyang: Central Committee of the Federation of Chosun Writers, printed by Munhak Yesul Jonghap Chulpansa) December 2003, 26.

6. Gyoyukdoseo Chulpansa, ed., *Haebanghu 10 [Sip] Nyeonganui Gonghwaguk Inmin Gyoyukui Baljeon* [The improvement in people's education in the DPRK in the ten-year period after liberation] (Pyongyang: Gyoyukdoseo Chulpansa, 1995).

7. Transcript of a personal recording of the kindergarten class, March 6, 2000.

8. Personal testimony of a North Korean defector who was involved in arranging Lim Su-Kyong's schedule in North Korea during her visit there at the time.

9. Personal testimony of the former Romanian ambassador to the DPRK (interviewed July 30, 2003, Bucharest, Romania).

10. Hyeon-Suk Kwon, *Rumaniaui Yeonin* [Lovers in Romania] (Seoul: Minumsa, 2001); Kim Duk-Young, "(Suyogihoek) Mireuchoyu, Naui Nampyeoneun Jojeonghoimnida" [Wednesday feature series: Mircioiu, my husband is Jo Jeong-Ho], (South Korea: KBS-1 TV, June 23, 2004).

11. According to Charles Armstrong, the North Korean war orphan support project was "the only case of the socialist countries joining hands together to carry out a joint project that has accomplished harmony." Given that the Cold War was in its inchoate stage internationally, a competitive response to the humanitarian aid programs led by the United States and the Western countries was an important international solidarity project for the socialist countries. As news of North Korean people "fighting valiantly and enduring the indiscriminate bombing by the US imperialists" spread widely in socialist countries, floods of demands to save North Korean war orphans facing danger came voluntarily from the bottom up. Charles K. Armstrong, "'Fraternal

Socialism': The International Reconstruction of North Korea, 1953–62," *Cold War History* 5, no. 2 (2006): 161–87.

12. American occupiers adopted and reiterated Japanese discriminatory views, thus contributing to the designation of this unwanted minority group as the "Korean problem" in Japan. Matthew R. Augustine, "The Limits of Decolonization: American Occupiers and the 'Korean Problem' in Japan, 1945–1948," *International Journal of Korean History* 22, no. 1 (2017): 43–51.

13. Sonia Ryang, "The North Korean Homeland of Koreans in Japan," in *Koreans in Japan: Critical Voices from the Margin,* ed. Sonia Ryang (London: Routledge, 2000).

14. To this day, the entrances of every North Korea–supported ethnic Korean school in Japan has display boards with information such as the following: "The Number of Times Aid Funds Have Been Received from the Fatherland: 165 times. Total Amount: 48,443,730,390 yen (as of April 2019)." The amount is updated every year.

15. Lyrics of the song "Chogugui Sarangun Ttasarowara" (The love of the fatherland is warm).

16. Tessa Morris-Suzuki, "Exodus to North Korea Revisited: Japan, North Korea, and ICRC in the 'Repatriation' of Ethnic Koreans from Japan," *Asia-Pacific Journal: Japan Focus* 9, no. 22 (2011), https://apjjf.org/2011/9/22/Tessa-Morris-Suzuki/3541/article.html; Sonia Ryang also deals with this controversial issue in detail in "Japan, North Korea, and the Biopolitics of Repatriation," *Asia-Pacific Journal: Japan Focus* 21, no. 6 (2023), https://apjjf.org/2023/6/Ryang.html.

17. Tessa Morris-Suzuki critically analyzes the roles of the Japanese state and the International Committee of the Red Cross (ICRC) in planning and promoting the mass-scale repatriation to North Korea; *Exodus to North Korea: Shadows from Japan's Cold War* (Lanham, MD: Rowman and Littlefield, 2007).

18. The vast majority (over 90 percent) of returnees did not come from North Korea, as most Koreans in Japan originated in South Korea, including Jeju Island.

19. Ki-Chan Song, "Jongcheseongui Jongchieseo Jongcheseongui Kwanriro" [From identity politics to identity management: The ethnic education of the *Chosun hakkyo* and the identities of Zainichi-Koreans], *Korean Cultural Anthropology* 51, no. 3 (2018): 207–78.

20. Ki-Chan Song, "From Identity Politics to Identity Management," 229.

21. Sonia Ryang, "The Rise and Fall of Chongryun—from Chōsenjin to Zainichi and Beyond," *Asia-Pacific Journal: Japan Focus* 14, no. 15 (2016), https://apjjf.org/2016/15/Ryang.html.

22. Sang-Gyun Shin, *Bokbadeun Sessangdungideul* [Blessed are the triplets] (Pyongyang: Geumsong Chongnyon Chulpansa, 1993), 3, 100.

23. Sang-Gyun Shin, *Bokbadeun Sessangdungideul,* 31.

24. Sang-Gyun Shin, *Bokbadeun Sessangdungideul,* 101.

25. Yuval Harari, *Homo Deus: Miraeui Yeoksa* [Homo deus: A brief history of tomorrow], trans. Myeong-Ju Kim (Paju: Gimm-Young Publishers, 2017), 212–16.

26. Yuval Harari, *Homo Deus,* 6–11.

27. Heonik Kwon and Byung-Ho Chung, *North Korea: Beyond Charismatic Politics* (Lanham, MD: Rowman and Littlefield, 2012), 183–92.

28. DailyNK, "Jongyeonghanun Kim Jong-Un Daejang Dongjiui Widaeseong Gyoyang Jaryo" [Educational material for learning (about) the greatness of Honorable General Comrade Kim Jong-Un], *Daily NK*, October 6, 2009.

29. So-Won Oh, *Hadaka No Kitachosen* [Naked North Korea] (Tokyo: Shinchoshinsho, 2013).

30. Commemorative poem. Rodong Sinmun, "Widaehan Kim Jong Il Dongjiui Ryongjonenun" [To the memory of the Great Comrade, Kim Jong-Il], *Rodong Sinmun*, December 30, 2011.

31. Robinson, "Korean Miracle," 541–49.

32. Yeong-Seon Jeon, "Kim Jong-Un Sidaeui Munhwajeongchi, Jeongchimunhwa" [Cultural politics, political culture in the Kim Jong-Un era], in *Kim Jong Un Sidaeui Munhwa* [Culture in the Kim Jong-Un era], ed. Yeong-Seon Jeon (Seoul: Haneul Chulpansa, 2015).

33. Byung-Ho Chung, "North Korea: Beyond Charismatic Politics," *Asia-Pacific Journal: Japan Focus* 16, no. 13 (2018), https://apjjf.org/2018/13/chung.

34. Young-Jong Lee, "Kim Jong-Un Jeonsaegye debwuinal," *JoongAng Ilbo*, October 11, 2010.

35. Yeon-Gwang Kim, "Good-Bye! Kim Il-Sung," *Weolgan Chosun* [Chosun monthly], December 2005.

36. Sung-Mo Kim, Sung-Il Tak, and Chul-Man Kim, *Chosunui Jipdanchejo* [Mass Games of Korea] (Pyongyang: Oegungmun Chulpansa, 2002).

37. Heonik Kwon and Byung-Ho Chung, *North Korea*, 187–89.

38. Clifford Geertz, *Negara: The Theatre State in Nineteenth-Century Bali* (Princeton, NJ: Princeton University Press, 1980), 130.

39. Geertz, *Negara*, 102.

40. Geertz, *Negara*, 131–32.

41. Young-Kyu Min, "Kim Jong-Un 'Beteunam Gyeongjebaljeone Gipeun Insang, Gyeongheom Gongyu Huimang'" [Kim Jong-Un 'impressed by Vietnam's economic development, hopes to share experience'], *Yonhap News*, March 2, 2019, https://www.yna.co.kr/view/AKR20190302037200084.

42. Heonik Kwon and Byung-Ho Chung, *North Korea*, 29–33.

43. Letter sent on March 6, 2019, on the occasion of the Second Local Propaganda Workers' Congress of the Workers' Party of Korea.

Chapter Two

The Arduous March

THE SCARS OF FAMINE

The famine in North Korea became known to the outside world in the wake of the floods and droughts of 1995 and 1996. Given that it was impossible to set foot in North Korea at the time, I met with North Korean refugees crossing the Chinese border in order to assess the media reports on the North Korean famine. It was painful meeting survivors of the famine to confirm the scars that the prolonged disaster left on their bodies and minds, and to hear of their suffering. A famine was indeed in progress. It was worsening, slowly and silently, right next to us, across the DMZ. The disaster was taking the lives of enormous numbers of people and leaving indelible scars on many more.[1]

The famine was exacerbated by the collapse of the international socialist trading system following the breakdown of the socialist economic bloc. Until the late 1980s, North Korea exported industrial goods to its "socialist brothers" and imported food and energy from them according to a system of barter exchange. The decisive blow that set off the famine was the fact that after 1990, with the collapse of the Soviet Union and COMECON (Council for Mutual Economic Assistance) for the socialist states, such friendly trade disappeared while a US embargo continued to lock North Korea out of much of the world trading system. Without the capacity for international credit settlement or foreign exchange reserves, North Korea could not buy the food and energy it had traditionally imported through the socialist trading system. In addition, the isolation that resulted from political and military pressure from the outside world further aggravated the famine.

Wide, Deep, and Silent Famine

The North Korean famine was notable for its wide, deep, and silent aspects.[2] "Wide famine" refers to a phenomenon in which a majority of a nation's population is approaching a critical level of malnutrition as a result of strict state control of food supplies. There is no effective relief method other than to gradually improve overall nutrition by providing large-scale food aid to the entire population over an extended period.

"Deep famine" refers to famine in which the damage deepens exponentially and prolongs the crisis. Typically, such famine occurs when natural disasters compound a food crisis among people already critically malnourished due to structural problems in the food supply system. In the case of children in particular, the damage spreads fast and the wounds are profound, making timely intervention with relief activities difficult.

"Silent famine" refers to famine that spreads unbeknownst to the outside world due to the isolation of the affected population. For political reasons, famine-affected countries often do not provide accurate or complete information to the outside world concerning the scale of the famine, nor the extent of relief activities or responses, thereby aggravating the situation. Thus, in the case of North Korea, many of its East Asian neighbors, located in one of the world's most economically prosperous regions, were not fully aware of the depth of the famine and consequently could not provide the necessary help until more than one million people had already died of hunger. Relief was also limited by the political isolation of North Korea.

Responses in South Korea under the Politics of Division

The famine deepened in 1995. South Korea at the time was abuzz with speculation that North and South Korea would unify as suddenly as the two German states had only a few years earlier. South Koreans were also enjoying material abundance for the first time in the nation's history. It was a few years before the International Monetary Fund (IMF) bailout crisis.[3] Thick, fragrant clouds of smoke from grilling meat filled the air in cities and towns throughout the South. According to South Korean statistics from this period, the value of food wasted in the country each year exceeded US$8 billion. It was also during this period that news of the food shortages in North Korea began circulating widely, along with news of flooding there. When I saw images of children sick and hungry from the famine, I decided to do something to alleviate the problem. My goal was simple: I would collect relief supplies and send them to the suffering children.

The division of the peninsula into North and South, however, made even a straightforward humanitarian initiative difficult. The South Korean

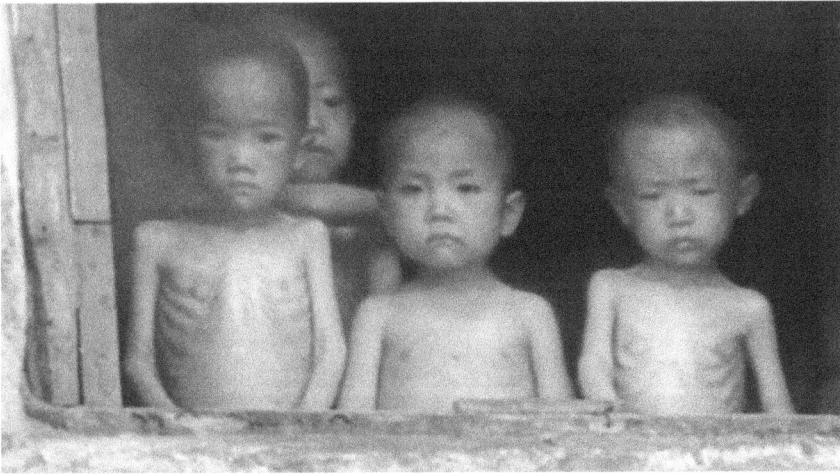

Figure 2.1. North Korean children dying of hunger: famine-stricken children gazing at the camera. World History Archive

government, then led by President Kim Young-Sam, banned relief fund-raising for North Korea by grassroots organizations in order to increase its own bargaining power with North Korea. This made it difficult to send food relief to starving children in the North.

According to the Korean Red Cross, the total relief it sent to North Korea in 1995 for flood relief was one hundred thousand packages of ramen noodles and a few thousand blankets. At first, I felt that the Red Cross package was incomparably larger than anything grassroots organizations could have collected and that government support for the relief efforts was making a huge difference. But I soon learned that flood victims in the border city of Sinuiju alone numbered more than two hundred thousand. What the Red Cross had sent would not have been enough to provide even a single full meal for half of the victims there, let alone those in other areas. Yet news about the package in South Korea focused on concerns that this aid would be diverted for military use.[4] This type of framing opened my eyes to how decades of war, division, and hostile confrontation had left South Korea with a deep-rooted sense of distrust of the North.

To learn more about the damage wrought by the famine, I obtained and began reviewing the "Request for Emergency Food Assistance to North Korea" prepared by five UN agencies that had already started relief efforts in North Korea. The UN report gave me an idea of how dire the situation was, but it wasn't until years later that authoritative figures became available. Empirical studies on the famine include a report by Good Friends, an international nongovernmental organization (NGO) based in South Korea, which surveyed North Korean refugees in the Chinese border areas over a period of many years, and a mortality survey by the Johns Hopkins University Public Health Research Institute.[5] While limits exist in generalizing the results of these reports to the North Korean population at large, the reports make clear that at least one million people died from the famine. It was a major historical catastrophe.

The only official mention of the deaths by the North Korean authorities was an announcement in 1999 that 220,000 famine deaths had occurred between 1995 and 1998.[6] Due to the nature of the North Korean system, where information does not flow freely, it is doubtful that those in power had accurate information on the overall situation.[*] In a closed society, information is not only controlled but also subject to internal distortion. But even if we were to accept that "only 220,000 people starved to death," as per the official announcement, was this not a terrible enough disaster? The outside world was completely oblivious to a truly staggering loss of life.

However, during the period when the famine was entering its most devastating phase, the Kim Young-Sam administration prohibited all civic organizations, including the Red Cross, from sending aid to North Korea and even prevented the delivery of relief supplies that had already been collected in the wake of an incident involving a North Korean spy submarine infiltrating South Korea in the fall of 1996. With the passing of each day, I felt the harsh ramifications of the politics of division on the Korean Peninsula.

Considering the economic prowess of South Korea in the period between 1995 and 1998, when the North Korean famine was at its height, the country's response was incredibly passive. This was in part due to an expectation that the North Korean regime would soon collapse due to the famine. The logic was that no matter how terrible the ongoing famine was, any relief efforts would only prolong the tragedy so long as the regime that had caused the famine remained in power. Therefore, the right thing to do was to wait for the regime to collapse (or to actively bring it down), thereby saving the nation in one fell swoop. In retrospect, such logic was due to ignorance of the effects of famine. No matter how severe it may be, a famine alone will not bring down a regime, because hungry people have neither the strength nor the composure to resist power. This is a fact that research on famine around the world has confirmed.[7]

In socialist countries in particular, massive losses caused by famine do not necessarily bring down the regime itself. This is because both the movement

---

* Hwang Jang-Yup, the highest-ranking North Korean defector, asserted that there were approximately 2.5 million casualties by 1997. Jang-Yup Hwang, "Bukhanui Jinsilgwa Heowi" [The truth and falsehood of North Korea], Institute for Unification Policy, 1998. Even now, opinions on the exact scale of the damage caused by the famine differ widely among sources in different positions.

of people and the exchange of information are strictly controlled. It is said that in the case of the famine during the Great Leap Forward in China, for which the scale of the damage only became known in recent years, thirty million or more people died. However, this did not destroy the political system.[8] When we understand the characteristics of a socialist famine, we can see that reading the North Korean famine as well as the number of defections during this period as signs of imminent regime collapse was simply wishful thinking influenced by Cold War consciousness.[9]

As for North Korea, despite the mass death and damage, the regime was unshaken, and the contradictory images coming out of the country were confusing for onlookers. We saw pictures of emaciated children, only to be met with kindergarten children dressed in pretty clothes singing and dancing. There were images of homeless children in open-air markets eating crumbs from the street, which contrasted sharply with scenes of lively mass games featuring tens of thousands of apparently healthy children. Which of these showed the true picture of North Korea? Uncertainty swirled in relation to whether a famine had actually taken place at all, whether it had once ravaged the country but had been overcome, and whether it was still ongoing but only in limited areas. Responses were called into question. Were immediate relief efforts still necessary, or would it be better to pursue other types of response, such as long-term development cooperation? It was difficult to assess the reality of the famine.

In a socialist system, the damage caused by famine is not, as is often imagined, sustained equally by everyone. In the exigencies of famine or war, when the distribution system cannot function properly, all food supplies controlled by the state (e.g., those involving domestic agricultural produce, international aid packages, and imported food) are allocated according to social status. In other words, they are first supplied to military personnel, bureaucrats, and residents of strategically important cities. This is a policy that has as its primary goal the protection of people considered most important to the state.[10] In the case of North Korea, which has long been in a constant state of quasi-war, a food crisis results in resources being concentrated in the center, Pyongyang, which serves as a showcase city for outsiders as well as for North Koreans themselves. Thus, the gap in survival conditions between center and periphery inevitably widens. By the same token, during emergencies, even within a city or a region, limited food supplies are distributed even more strictly based on the sociopolitical hierarchy of each individual.*

---

* International aid agencies had difficulties carrying out activities related to famine relief in North Korea due to transparency issues. In other words, agencies doubted the transparency of the regime in its distribution of relief packages. In addition, the more critical the crisis situation, the less likely it was that the regime would allow outside intervention in prioritizing food distribution. The result was

Figure 2.2. Train ride by famine refugees: traveling in search of food on a windowless train packed to the rooftop. Source: JTS, 1999.

In 1994, the year Kim Il-Sung died, the cessation of public food distribution began first in North and South Hamgyeong Provinces, which are located far from the Military Demarcation Line, the boundary between North and South Korea. This decision was based on national security considerations as North Korea's leadership was consumed by security obsessions. However, the shock of closing down the public distribution system in one region caused paralysis in the food-rationing system nationwide—with the exception of Pyongyang—as other regions prioritized securing their own food. Thus began a state of social panic, the first sign of the onset of famine.[11]

The breakdown of the food-rationing system, the underpinning of the North's socialist economy, led to general paralysis in the social system, including medical care, welfare, and education. Conscious of the gaze of the outside world, Pyongyang was kept running at the minimum level of normalcy. The state's social control functions nevertheless weakened as people began moving in order to survive. When it became impossible for authorities to stop the migration, famine refugees began crossing the border into China to obtain food. This was the start of the "North Korean refugee problem." However, even these utterly desperate North Koreans were considered illegal immigrants in China. As such, they were exposed to potential deportation, as

that the outside world, including South Korea, found it difficult to grasp the severity of the famine in the North and the effectiveness of relief efforts.

well as the possibility of becoming victims of human rights violations, such as forced marriage, human trafficking, and labor exploitation.

North Korean Refugees: Wanderers of the Post–Cold War

Along with experts in various fields, including cultural anthropologists, physical anthropologists, psychologists, nutritionists, doctors, teachers, and relief activists, who had been working together to provide famine relief, I organized joint field research that began in the summer of 1999. Through the vivid testimonies of the North Korean refugees we met, we gradually comprehended the scope of the damage inflicted by the famine. As expected, the situation was difficult to grasp fully using literature and statistics alone.

A sixteen-year-old boy we met in Yanji, the capital city of the Yanbian Korean Autonomous Prefecture in China, was a mere 132 centimeters (4'4") tall. He slept under a bridge over a small stream and was suffering from a nasty cough due to tuberculosis. Speaking to us as he scratched the mosquito bites that covered his body, he said that life wasn't so bad because at least it was summer. His face was that of a child, but he spoke gently with an expression that belied his age, saying, "I have to return to my family, who are starving across the river." A few days later, I heard that the boy had crossed the Tumen River with the money he had scrounged up so far. He had gulped down the money in a small plastic bag to hide it from the search of North Korean border guards.

We also met an eighteen-year-old young man who was worried because his voice had still not dropped, and a seventeen-year-old girl on the cusp of womanhood who had the face and body of a prepubescent girl. Long-term malnutrition had resulted in such discrepancies between natural and biological ages. The problems of growth and development, which we had speculated about through fragmentary data and statistics, materialized in concrete form in the bodies of the young people that we met. It was heartbreaking. Studies show that when nutrition is administered in an intensive and stable manner to adolescents who have suffered malnutrition, they can make up for their stunted growth at a rapid pace. For the young people that we met in the border areas during that time, there was scant chance that their reality would change dramatically any time soon, if ever. Each of them was in a desperate situation, but we were unable to help them in any meaningful way with our limited resources.

The children themselves were also sensitive to their growth and development issues. A child once asked me to buy him a gift, a "medicine" to make him grow tall. Upon hearing this, the child next to him chastised him, saying that he shouldn't be asking someone he had just met to buy him such an expensive drug. Even at a young age, these North Korean refugee children already had the toughness and maturity of adults earning a living.

The youths that we met in Yanji in the Korean Autonomous Region of China raised money for their families who were still in North Korea. They traveled everywhere on foot, no matter how long the trip. Some children secretly hopped on trains to and from Shenyang, Dalian, and Beijing. Although they were young and small, they had persistence and vitality that allowed them not only to starve for days at a time but also to escape after being caught by Chinese police or North Korean soldiers. Despite their bleak circumstances, the children had dreams. One of them said, in quite an adult-like manner, "My dream is to live and not die." Another told me she wanted to become a celebrity singer. A sixteen-year-old girl with an ashen face said she wanted "to read a poetry book." I had asked her what I could buy for her when she was hiding in the house of an ethnic Korean in China.[12]

The reality of the famine that I learned about through these children was harrowing. Most of them had lost family members to starvation and disease. Grandfathers and grandmothers had been the first to go. I heard over and over again about grandparents who had died while forgoing food themselves so that their grandchildren could eat first. Food rationing had already become obsolete in most areas prior to the 1995 floods. Because of energy shortages, factories were incapacitated, and workers in industrial areas such as Ham-heung suffered greatly as a result.

The children we met said that when the public distribution system all but collapsed, their fathers had become helpless. Using words and phrases that were typical, they said that their "depraved"—that is, despairing—fathers clung all the more to alcohol and cigarettes and became sick, while their mothers tried to earn money on the black market or left on extended trips to faraway places in search of food. Many children told us that one or both of their parents had died or left, never to return. The phenomenon of families broken by famine was more widespread than I imagined. When the situation became critical, the older children said, they had left home in order to remove the burden of one extra mouth to feed in the household. That is how they became *kkotchebi*, the wandering child beggars likened to fluttering swallows.

Of course, not all children became *kkotchebi*. According to children I spoke to, in one border city in North Korea, most schools remained open even during the height of the famine, but many students were absent. Even the teachers were busy looking for food, so the school kept running in name only. Many children fled North Korea only to return later and even reenter school without drawing much attention to themselves. In other words, mass absenteeism was chronic.

In any given classroom, about a quarter of the students came from "a family of means," meaning a family with a relative who was a party cadre or in a foreign country. These children came to school with lunch boxes and prepared studiously for exams. Another quarter came to school with nothing for lunch and went hungry all day. Yet another quarter came to school and stayed only for the important morning lessons on such topics as the childhood of their great leader, General Kim Il-Sung. The remaining quarter, including those who had died from the famine, did not come to school at all.

"Cowards! Leave, If You Will!"

A group of people on the North Korean bank of the Yalu River were standing in a row, facing China on the other side, waving their arms like marching soldiers and belting out a military song, the words to which went, "Cowards! Leave, if you will! We protect our fatherland." They sang with such gusto that the lyrics rang out clearly all the way to the Chinese side of the river. I witnessed this scene in August 1999 near Changbai in China. I was there observing an area in Hyesan, a city located on the North Korean side of the river, as the glow of a summer evening faded into night. Hearing the song, my heart sank, for I was reminded of some of the North Korean refugees I had met in China in their hiding places near the border. Some of them told me, "They said I'll get an apartment in South Korea if I go, but I do not want to betray my country." In their extremely desperate situation, what was the "fatherland" to them, and what did it mean to betray it?

For North Koreans at the time, crossing the border was not simply a bid for survival. It was also an act of resistance as extreme as suicide.* For over half a century, North Korea had socialized its people as members of a partisan (guerrilla) state. Leaving the nation's community was considered a cowardly act of betrayal and treason. If found out, punishment would not stop with the individual perpetrator. Family members and relatives would also face severe consequences. For that reason, North Korean refugees lived with the constant fear of being caught and repatriated. Their concern was not only about their personal fate after repatriation but also about the pain and punishment their families would face on account of their actions.

Such fear was often combined with extreme guilt. As soon as refugees were able to rest in safe places and eat well, many struggled with a pervasive sense of guilt for the families they had left behind in North Korea. The

---

* In North Korea, suicide was in fact interpreted as resistance to the regime. It is said that many families took their lives together under the extreme conditions of the famine.

thought that their defections were cowardly acts of betrayal stayed with them for years. Not knowing when they would be arrested and repatriated to North Korea by Chinese police authorities, chronic fear pervaded their lives.

Fear weakened them, making them helpless, even when suffering unthinkable human rights violations. A young mother from Chongjin, North Korea, left her child with her sister when she ventured to China to obtain food. No sooner had she made it across the border than she was caught and sold as a bride to a Chinese bachelor with few marriage prospects in a remote village. The entire village remained on guard so that the new bride, bought for a hefty sum, could not escape. Within months, she was pregnant. Once pregnant, she was hesitant to cross the Tumen River back to North Korea. Soon, she gave birth. All the while, she was going mad with the thought that her child in Chongjin must have died of starvation. She wept as she told her story, saying that she could not go back now with her baby in her arms, adding that, either way, one of the children would die. Worse still, even under these circumstances, every time an unfamiliar vehicle drove into the village, she feared that Chinese police were coming to apprehend her, so she would jump into a cornfield with the child and stay there all night to avoid arrest.

It was rare to come across any young girls among the North Korean refugees wandering the streets of Yanbian. When I asked why this was, a boy said, matter-of-factly, "Girls just disappear as soon as they cross the border."

We would learn that no matter how small the child, a girl could be sold quickly and at a high price. An extremely unbalanced male-female ratio among young adults across the region became a demographic background of the forced marriages imposed on the female border crossers.[13] We met a sixteen-year-old girl who had crossed the border at the age of thirteen and was immediately caught and sold to a man who was almost forty. Within a year, she had given birth and was now the mother of a two-year-old child. We also came to know several other girls who had become mothers in similar fashion. There were also many women who had been trafficked not just once but multiple times. After being sold off as brides, they had made daring escapes, only to be caught and sold again and again in an unending cycle.[*]

A middle-aged man we spoke to told us he had escaped North Korea with his wife and daughter and was hiding in the mountains. One day, he returned from a logging expedition to find both his wife and daughter missing. He learned they had been sold off, and there was no way to find them. He said he would go back to North Korea, even if it meant going to jail. If his wife

---

[*] The everyday trafficking of North Korean refugee women is a serious human rights violation that leaves a particularly deep, multilayered wound in the victims. The problem is that many people in remote areas of China saw it as a way for desperate women to survive. At times, women themselves, cornered in dire situations, have also accepted it as their only means of survival.

and daughter were also caught and repatriated, at least the family would meet again, he lamented.

At the end of each of our field study trips to China, during which we learned of such horrendous situations, we would arrive back in Seoul in a mere two-hour flight. I spent the next few weeks feeling devastated. Life in Seoul felt unreal. I was tormented by feelings of guilt for abandoning those I had met to their suffering.

What we had heard and seen was truly the stuff of historical fiction. One half of the Korean nation, separated from the other half for more than half a century, was living under extreme hardship. Those who argued that national borders no longer held any meaning in the postmodern era angered me. In South Korea, the trend seemed to be to cut off North Koreans, as lizards cut off their tails, and saunter ever so unencumbered into the postmodern world. Having seen with my own eyes the reality faced by North Koreans, I could not allow myself to so callously cut them off. My heart ached at the realization that the history of the Korean nation's suffering was not over.

GLORIFICATION OF CATASTROPHE

It was around dusk, and the heat of the midday summer was receding. In the North Korean village across the Tumen River, no cooking smoke rose from the chimneys. Despite being a fairly large town, there was no movement. It was as if all life had come to a standstill.

"It seems that they are in a state of exhaustion due to the prolonged famine," said an activist from a South Korean aid organization who was monitoring the situation across the river from the Chinese side, speaking in a low voice. It was the summer of 1999.

There are countless eyewitness testimonies concerning the North Korean famine, dating from the time of its earliest stages to the present. They include hellish tales of stealing, of the consumption of human flesh, and of public executions, as well as heroic tales involving individuals making unimaginable sacrifices for their families and serving their communities under extremely challenging conditions. It felt impossible that a single disaster could be spoken of in such differing terms. Such inconsistencies made some question the veracity of the stories altogether. According to an anthropological study comparing various famines worldwide, famine has three stages of development: vigilance, resistance, and exhaustion. Let us take a closer look at the development of the Great Famine in North Korea with these three stages in mind.[14]

In the early "vigilance" phase of famine, anxiety from hunger brings people together. While it varies from region to region and from situation to situation, communal altruism is highest in the early stages, when the famine is gradually taking hold. This altruism disappears when the deprivation becomes more acute. In North Korea, the early days of the famine witnessed many acts involving people helping others and sharing resources, even when conditions became more severe as rations were cut off.[15] As more and more people moved around the country desperately searching for food, the social control mechanisms that regulated long-distance travel collapsed. Vagrants hopped onto the roofs of trains, sleeping in train stations and other public places. Due to the dangers involved in traveling in this manner, the unsanitary lodgings, and disease and hunger, many died in transit. A boy testified that when he had been living as a *kkotchebi*, sleeping in a train station, the police had given him a small piece of corn bread daily as payment for removing the dead bodies of the homeless.*

Most regions except Pyongyang entered the "resistance" stage around 1996–1997. Due to the spiraling energy deficit, productivity declined, and social relations eroded, leaving only the bonds of family in the struggle for survival. People began consuming things that had never before been considered food, and competition for supplies of such non-foodstuffs became fierce. Where there was food, there was competition and fighting. Theft was rampant, and fields and warehouses had to be guarded. As the famine prolonged, even public goods were destroyed, with factories ransacked for machinery and parts and wires stripped from power lines.

From 1997 to 1998, "exhaustion" began to set in widely across the country. Even family units collapsed, leaving individuals to fend for themselves. Hungry children left their homes and formed gangs of *kkotchebi* who begged and stole. At times, hungry children were more ruthless than adults.**

When a famine intensifies, the possibility of organized riots or revolution plummets because everyone is busy struggling for individual survival. Not only that, but the extreme experience of deprivation and social conflict leads to a desire for a stable social order. It has been observed that people can become even more obedient to a ruling power if it controls food resources and maintains its authority in times of need. A community in the exhaustion stage is characterized by its passivity, regardless of its size. The bizarre tranquility of the village I witnessed across the Tumen River was a sign that the famine there had entered the exhaustion stage.

---

* Other North Korean refugees have testified to the countless deaths they witnessed while they were moving about, including those they witnessed while riding trains (interviewed in August 1999).

** A television documentary showed a case of violent robbery by a group of *kkotchebi* (wandering beggars), children running amok in a *jangmadang* (private field market). KBS, "97 Jigeum Bukhan Museun Iri Ireonago Inneunga" [97 what's happening now in North Korea], (South Korea: KBS-1 TV, 1997).

March with a Smile though the Roads Are Rough!

"March with a Smile though the Roads Are Rough!" The signboard stood in the middle of a barren hill behind the village across the Tumen. Its huge red letters lent an uncanniness to the eerily quiet village. March what roads? People were dying of starvation left and right. On the Chinese side of the river, which was only as wide as a large stream, the verdant fields were thick with soybeans and corn. North Koreans on the other side could only gaze at the fields as they starved to death, the slogan exhorting them to smile all the while. The slogan rang hollow, even tragic. I couldn't help but wonder what people suffering in extreme pain from the famine thought when they saw such signs installed all over their country.[16]

The famine, in which at least one million people died of starvation and sickness, is commonly referred to as the "Arduous March." Historically, the term evokes a specific march made by partisan guerrillas in Manchuria, led by Kim Il-Sung, pursued by Japanese troops from the end of 1938 until the following spring. Trapped under enemy siege, their march lasted about one hundred days, the partisans battling off cold and hunger in the most severe ordeal experienced by the troops. North Korean history commemorates the escape as the Arduous March and records the period as a glorious time comparable to that of the Long March of the Chinese Revolution.

The North Korean novel *The Arduous March* depicts the deep camaraderie among the hungry partisans, who share a handful of roasted grain in the cold, and the love of the leader, who gives up his one ear of corn for the troops. Finally, having escaped the enemy, the partisans cheer as the sun rises over Mount Baekdu, declaring: "It was truly a moment we could never forget. For this joy, our revolutionary squad would walk the path of battle, the path of revolution, the path of freedom and liberation with a smile, even if we had to go through the same long ordeal as we did last winter again, ten times or a hundred times."[17]

The regime tried to instill the optimistic conviction that difficulties could be overcome so long as there was trust in the leader and camaraderie among the people. However, it is a bitter contradiction to equate a hundred-day escape operation involving trained combatants with a five-year calamity in which tens of millions of civilians were trapped. The problem was not simply a matter of rhetoric, because the damage caused by such a cognitive error was enormous. Bizarre measures were taken. For example, the survival principles used by the legendary partisan heroes were applied at face value to civilians, including the elderly and children. In other words, perhaps in an attempt to emulate the battle logic of the partisans, Kim Jong-Il declared the advent of his *songun* (military-first) politics, making the brutal decision to prioritize the military over the civilian population in the fight against hunger. But, for the

Figure 2.3. *March with a smile though the roads are rough!* (Top) anti-Japanese guerrilla fighters are glorified for having overcome the Arduous March (1938–1939) with a smile; (bottom) the painting Chagangdo Saramdeul *(The people of Chagang Province)* glorifies the suffering of the Great Famine (1995–1999) in the same manner. Top, source: Sang-Soon Kim, Juche Yesului Bitnaneun Hwapok [Splendid paintings of the Juche art] *(Pyongyang: Pyongyang Yesul Chonghap Chulpansa, 2001), 10.* Bottom, source: Hyo-Ryun Kim, Taeyangui Pomsokesu Kotpyunan Jaenyunui Hwawon [The garden of talents blossoming in the bosom of the Sun] *(Pyongyang: Munye Chulpansa, 2018), 5.*

actual partisans, civilians were the key to their survival. When attacked by the enemy, the partisans immediately left the villages, heading into the mountains supposedly to reduce civilian casualties. This type of obvious contradiction was overlooked.[18]

The period of famine glorified internally as the Arduous March will be recorded in world history as a catastrophe of historic proportions, the "Great North Korean Famine." During the famine, the character of the nation and its people changed radically. While the regime maintained its appearance, the way of life changed in substance. North Korea as a nation before and after the famine were profoundly different, and the two realities now coexist in today's North Korea. I will discuss this in the following chapter, "Changing Undercurrents."

Growing Exercise and Growing Medicine

As I walked along the hallway of a kindergarten in Pyongyang, I heard the loud voice of a teacher coming from one of the classrooms. On the blackboard, the words "Growing Exercise" were written in large letters. Next to them were large pictures depicting various kinds of exercise, such as chinups, ladder climbing, and basketball. The teacher twisted her face like an actress and spoke clearly in an exaggerated tone.

"Hey, Ogi! I'm taller, right?"

"No, you're shorter."

"What? *I'm* shorter?"

"That's right. Yongsu does growing exercises every day, and he is taller."

The class all repeated after the teacher, sentence by sentence, in a loud chorus.

"Our young comrades must do lots of growing exercises and resolve to grow tall. We must all stand with tall legs and give joy to the great leader, General Kim Jong-Il. Can you do that?" The teacher asked her class.

The children replied all at once with a short, loud "Yes!"

It was frustrating to witness such a scene. The children were small because there was not enough food, yet they were being taught that they must exercise harder and resolve to grow tall.

Spiritualization, which demands that subjects overcome material limits using mental power, is hardly unique to North Korea. It is a widely practiced educational philosophy in modern East Asian countries, which share the Confucian cultural tradition. Meiji-era Japan, in particular, emphasized genuine exertion and mental power above all else through its newly instituted public education system.

Figure 2.4. *Growing exercise: children are taught to overcome growth problems due to malnutrition with "growing exercises" such as basketball, jump rope, and chin-ups, among others. AP Photo, Maye-E Wang*

It goes without saying that one cannot will oneself to be taller through exercise alone. When a homeless North Korean youth in Yanji, China, asked me to buy him "growing medicine," I understood that he was conscious of his small stature and that if a magic growing pill existed, as in a fairy tale, he would take it in a heartbeat to make himself grow taller. Alas, doctors and scientists I met in Pyongyang the following year also talked about the task of developing such a pill.

Becoming aware of the phenomenon of "growing exercises" and the search for "growing medicine," I felt that there was an expectation of magic through pseudoscience by the state regime in North Korea. I use the term "magic" here because the efforts to devise exercises and develop drugs to make children grow tall, when they are undernourished, are comparable to the dreams of alchemists in the Middle Ages who tried to squeeze gold out of basic metals. These are fantasies of creating something from nothing. Of course, the scientists did not seem entirely on board with the aspirations of the regime, which had ordered such a task. As such, it seemed to me that the regime was shifting its responsibility to health professionals and children with its emphasis on spiritualism and bootstrapping while it was busy promoting medieval magical aspirations.

"Like a Cascade of Eggs!"

In the face of the famine, the power elites in North Korea placed more emphasis on political propaganda than commonsense economics. Rather than taking basic measures to ameliorate the food shortages, scarce resources were concentrated on attempts to solve problems "in a single breath!"

The latter period of the famine witnessed the launch of a large-scale project involving the reorganization of arable land. Fields that had been cultivated by families for generations were plowed and replaced by new farmland with straight rows in order to "create a new history of mechanical farming." In a country with nothing but manpower, this enormous project was carried out via mass mobilization, the goal being to facilitate future machine farming. International food experts were stunned that this full-scale farmland reorganization project was being undertaken in the middle of a famine. While it is true that reorganization could ultimately result in a little extra land to farm on, in this case, to date, the result has been reduced production for a considerable period of time.

In January 2000, Kim Jong-Il gazed out at a "sizable and neatly readjusted" field in North Pyongan Province. "Now, even if former landlords tried to find their land with documents in hand, they would not be able to find it. This has become land befitting a socialist state," he said with satisfaction.[19] I often heard in Pyongyang that economics was nothing compared to politics. I realized that this was an example of that approach.

Science and technology have been prioritized not only by Kim Jong-Il but also by his successor, Kim Jong-Un. North Korea's military industry developed nuclear weapons and missiles to flaunt their might to the world. The agricultural and fisheries sector also tried to produce food through the use of innovative science and technology. The leaders' "field guidance" tours focused on advanced agricultural and fishery facilities rather than on ordinary food production sites.

Kim Jong-Il eventually overcame the worst of the famine through an inter-Korean summit. Shortly after the historic North-South summit in June 2000, he toured a chicken factory in Pyongyang. When he saw eggs passing by on a conveyor belt, he exclaimed, "It looks like a cascade of eggs pouring down!" However, there was no mention of how much capital, technology, and energy it would take to build and operate a mechanized poultry farm, how much chicken feed would be needed, or how the ingredients used for the chicken feed could be used to feed the people. As economic cooperation between the two Koreas began in earnest, the North Korean authorities repeatedly demanded support for capital-intensive, technologically advanced machinery and production facilities for the agricultural and fisheries sector, such as industrial greenhouses, livestock factory facilities, and fish farms.

Their demands dovetailed with South Korea's desire to show off its advanced mechanized farming methods.

A few years later, in the fall of 2006, I was in a car passing through open country outside Pyongyang. I observed that the crops in the rice paddies and farming fields were thin and sparse, the natural result of poor soil and a scarcity of fertilizer. Seeing the miserable cabbages and radishes growing in the dry fields, I was particularly concerned about the long winter ahead, during which North Koreans would have to get their share of vitamins through kimchi.

Around the same time, Fidel Castro of Cuba was promoting eco-friendly organic farming in Havana and at various other locations in an attempt to overcome the local food crisis, which had also begun with the collapse of the international socialist economic system. Alternative agriculture in Cuba has been labeled an agricultural revolution. In July 2004, I visited Cuba and went to see the urban organic farms. Everywhere I went, the farms were simple but lively. By establishing a system that supports organic farming socially, Cuba achieved remarkable results in overcoming its food crisis. To help North Korea, which has neither fertilizers nor pesticides, South Korean organic farming groups proposed to support sustainable and eco-friendly farming methods. However, officials in both the North and the South were not interested. Both wanted high-cost, high-energy "scientific and technological" farming methods that would supposedly bring them breakthrough yields in food production but in fact ignored the stagnation in subsistence agriculture.

CHILDREN'S SUFFERING

In early May 1996, five UN agencies warned that one in five North Korean children under the age of five were at risk of suffering growth irregularities. The UN made an urgent request for nutritional compound foods and vitamins as well as electrolyte solutions for children worth one billion won (approximately US$1 million) per month. However, the international community, including South Korea, did not respond positively to this or other requests. One year later, in May 1997, one out of every two infants in North Korea had already become underdeveloped, meaning that in addition to high-nutrient foods, full-fledged treatment drugs were also needed.[20]

The most meaningful statistical survey results related to the North Korean famine came out after the United Nations Children's Fund (UNICEF), the World Food Programme (WFP), and the European Union (EU), working jointly with the North Korean authorities for famine relief, conducted a random-sample survey of the nutritional status and growth of children six months to seven years old between August and September 1998.[21] The results showed that 60 percent of all children were underdeveloped due to chronic malnutrition, 30 percent of those aged twelve to twenty-four months were malnourished due to lack of baby food, and 18 percent of infants under twelve months old were malnourished due to maternal malnutrition. In such circumstances, high morbidity and mortality were inevitable.

Meanwhile, the study provided additional, unintended insights. Comparing the national average height of children in the North and the South in 1998, there was already a difference of twelve centimeters (4.7 inches) for seven-year-old children. Considering the growth and development pattern of South Korean children and comparing it with that of North Korean children, this gap would widen to up to twenty centimeters (7.9 inches) by the time these children reached puberty unless a breakthrough was made in the supply of nutrition. These were average demographic differences. In real life, such differences can be much greater in terms of how they are perceived. As an anthropologist who studied issues involving discrimination against minorities, this was a shocking revelation.[22]

Anthropologically speaking, small stature is not a problem in itself, as it may be a sign of successful adaptation to scarce resources in the environment. However, when meetings and exchanges take place between North and South Koreans, such visible differences in height can lead to complex problems involving stigma and discrimination. In today's South Korean culture, in particular, marked by an obsession with height and appearance, North Koreans with small stature are likely to suffer discrimination. Like any other form of social stigma, such discrimination can be a repressive factor for those affected. The socioeconomic differences between children in the South and the North are already great. What kind of difficulties will they face in the future?

Famine can not only cause complex developmental problems on the physical level but also in areas such as behavior, emotion, and sociability. Children who were malnourished and suffered from associated illnesses during their formative years are more likely to have lifelong disabilities and suffer from chronic diseases. The suffering does not stop with the individuals. The cost of the burden to families and to society at large is enormous.

Children Are the Kings of the Nation

"In our country, the children are the kings of the nation."

"We spare nothing for the children."

Large letters bearing these quotations from Kim Il-Sung hung on the walls of an orphanage in Pyongsong, the capital of South Pyongan Province. The mottos were hardly convincing to those of us there to deliver famine relief supplies. The white lime plaster was peeling off the walls of the dilapidated hallways, and the room where we met the children was cold. There were 120 orphans there.

Our hosts explained that they had so many orphans "because this is the only facility in South Pyongan Province," which meant that it was supposed to be large and high in quality. "The Great Leader is the founder, and with the care and attention of the Great General, we are doing well, despite the difficult times," we were told. This was certainly true for those children who had made it to this facility. I knew, because a few months prior to our visit to Pyongsong, Doctors Without Borders had withdrawn from this city citing transparency issues, leaving behind the six hundred homeless, starving children they had been looking after. Considering the options those children faced, most of whom would probably have become *kkotchebi* by that time, the children in the orphanage were undoubtedly privileged. They were under the care of the state, after all.

However, even here, many children were suffering from severe malnutrition. Even at a casual glance, I could see that their skin was breaking out and their abdomens protruding; there were ringworms on their faces and bald spots on their heads—all classic signs of malnutrition. Even the guides from Pyongyang who had brought us here were having a hard time maintaining their steely, expressionless demeanors. The children all had candy in their mouths, perhaps to induce smiles during our visit. However, the expressions on most of the children's faces were blank. A few were too emaciated to even stand.

When we arrived at the orphanage, the staff bore stiff expressions, and I broke the ice by saying that I worked at a day-care center in the South. At last they let down their guard, one of them responding cheerfully, "But you're a man. How could you have run a nursery?" At that, we all sat down on the floor and talked shop about raising children. In the meantime, I held some children in my arms, stroking the heads of some, pressing down on the protruding bellies of others, and patting the buttocks of yet others.

"She's so young to have no diaper. When do you start toilet training for the children?" I asked, noticing the lack of a diaper on one child.

"We start at eight months."

"So early? In the South it's much later."

"We do it according to the Childcare Education Law of our country."[23]

The teachers were clearly quite proud of their system. But experienced staff from any child-care facility know what it takes to toilet train infants at such an early age. Intensive training must take place long before the diapers are actually taken off. At this point, I was reminded of the World War II–era studies on comparative toilet training practices in the United States and Japan. Anthropologists carried out the studies in order to compare national characteristics.*

"That's amazing," I replied. "Can I see the diapers?"

"Oh, what for? They're all the same."

"I want our nursery staff in the South to have full and proper knowledge."

Begrudgingly, the worker showed me a diaper. Her face flushed as she handed it to me. The double-folded patch of ashen cloth she had produced was scarcely larger than a handkerchief. The cloth was wrapped in rectangular plastic pieces recycled from fertilizer bags sent by the Canadian Foodgrains Bank in order to prevent soiling. The diaper must have been used heavily, for the threadbare cloth had several burn marks. It seemed that, lacking soap and detergent, the staff boiled the diaper cloth in lye for disinfection. It was obviously sheer devotion on the part of the staff that had made such makeshift solutions possible in the absence of proper supplies. I could not help feeling resentment, again, at Doctors Without Borders for having withdrawn from the city, leaving the helpless to fend for themselves.

Two years later, an administrator from Doctors Without Borders came to see me in Seoul where I was running a school for North Korean refugee children. Bringing an interpreter, the visiting official said that they had launched a psychological counseling project for youth who had defected from North Korea and that the budget for the project was in the hundreds of thousands of dollars. They had come seeking my advice.

International relief activities for famine victims in North Korea had suffered major setbacks in the aftermath of the withdrawal of the famous Nobel Peace Prize–winning NGO, all the more because the organization had made a huge fuss by issuing a statement condemning the North Korean government's lack of transparency. Having left the orphans in dire need of help in Pyongsong to sink or swim on their own, they now wanted to help North Korean youth in South Korea who were already receiving funds from the South Korean government and were covered by universal health insurance. I asked them where the money was coming from to pay for youth counseling with interpreters in Seoul, where costs of living and labor were high. I suggested they should go to the Chinese and Mongolian borders, and to Vietnam, and help the North Korean refugees in life-or-death situations there instead. They said that in socialist countries such as those, it was impossible

---

* During World War II, British anthropologist Geoffrey Gorer and American anthropologists studied Japanese and German national characteristics. In the study, they were interested in correlating rigid sanitation training from early childhood with the later development of authoritarian behavioral characteristics in adulthood. The study was highly criticized for being too simplistic. However, it had a major influence on the postwar liberal child-rearing paradigm.

to carry out relief activities their way, which is why they had come to South Korea.

I had had enough of them. "Their way" amounted to carrying out relief activities by handling the governments and bureaucrats of certain poor countries as if the latter were their own colonial underlings. Did they think "their way" would work like magic in North Korea, China, and Vietnam? As for the proposed project, could you really call South Korea an underdeveloped country in terms of health care? Is that what they had claimed in their fundraising campaign for the project? Though my English was rusty from disuse, I chased them away, yelling at the top of my lungs in my nonnative tongue.

I lost my temper thinking about the fertilizer-bag diapers in Pyongsong. But, in retrospect, I was angry at both the North Korean regime and Doctors Without Borders simultaneously, angry at the former for claiming that children were "the kings of the nation" while making their lives so miserable, and angry at the latter for approaching their humanitarian aid work with such self-centered principles while ignoring the famine conditions at the time in North Korea.

A few years later, I met Professor Han-Shik Park at the University of Georgia, who had also visited the orphanage in Pyongsong. He said that the malnourished children there had reminded him of his own childhood experience. Immediately after the liberation of Korea from Japan, at the end of World War II, his family had left Manchuria to return to Korea and had been caught and interned in a refugee camp where everyone went hungry. He said that he was still the shortest of his siblings because his growth had been stunted at the refugee camp. Visiting the orphanage decades later, he was so angry when he saw the malnourished children there that he pounded the chest of the North Korean bureaucrat who had accompanied him there, crying, "What have these children done wrong? Why can't you, all of you, do any better?" As he cried his heart out, he told me, the bureaucrat and the guide knelt down beside him, and they cried together. In the face of such an utterly tragic reality, genuine sorrow and anger can provide real consolation.[24]

Soy Milk Trucks Are the King's Trucks

"The soy milk truck is here," said the vice principal of Pyongyang First Middle School as he glanced out the window at the commotion outside. It was now "Intermission Gym and Soy Milk Distribution Time." The students moved outside in an orderly fashion in their class groups. They exercised as they waited their turn for the soy milk. Those who had finished their glasses of the drink shook their bodies left and right and sang in loud voices before marching off back to class. Perhaps energized by the soy milk, many students broke away from the marching line and hopped about freely. Now and then one of their peers, presumably a Youth League leader, would try to rein in the stragglers, but the line soon broke again. The vice principal said, "They should all be marching in a straight line. Look, look, look at them going alone—they are all liberals!" He tut-tutted.

Being the certified liberal that I am, I was taken aback hearing the term "liberal" being used to criticize a selfish person. While he was chastising the stray students with his words, the smile in his eyes betrayed his tender feelings for them. Seeing this, I mimicked his voice, saying in the direction of the students, "Nice jump, nice. . . . Hey! No more liberalism now! Get your act together!" The two North and South Korean adults looked at each other and shared a hearty laugh.

In North Korea, a soy milk truck is also called a "king's truck" for a reason. When the soy milk truck is on the road, all other vehicles must yield to it. It is a national priority to deliver the freshest possible soy milk to children, who are "the kings of the nation." Our guide told us that the Great General had given instructions to guarantee the provision of soy milk, even when the Great Famine was at its height. Thus, between 10:35 and 10:55 each morning, students at all schools across the country receive a cup of soy milk. This is what I was witnessing at Pyongyang First Middle School. I wonder, though, to what extent the trucks actually made the daily rounds, and if indeed all schools and all areas received daily visits.

Looking at the children lined up for soy milk at the edge of the school grounds, I was reminded of a similar scene from the 1960s when I was an elementary school student in Seoul. I remembered waiting in line in front of a somber-looking structure behind the main school building to receive corn bread and powdered milk mixed with warm water. The entrance to the building was marked with the USAID (United States Agency for International Development) logo, which featured an American flag and an image of a handshake. I remember clearly to this day the words "From the American People" written below the flag. America was the richest nation in the world, and we children were grateful to the Americans who fed us every day when we were hungry.

Later, when I was in the United States as a graduate student, I came across publicity materials from the period produced by the US Department of Agriculture and USAID about why they were sending wheat flour, corn, and powdered milk to Japan and Korea in the postwar period. They explained that rice was the main staple of East Asians and that if they could change people's tastes by providing aid during the difficult postwar period, these people would become dependent on US wheat, corn, and dairy produce. The documents explained to Americans that changing the tastes of Korean and Japanese children was an investment for future US farmers. Thus, with the surplus grain from American farms, aid to Korea continued well into the 1970s, some twenty years after the Korean War armistice. In the meantime, Korean and Japanese governments encouraged flour-based food in their national diets. Farmers in Korea, who could not make a living through rice farming alone due to the low grain prices regulated by the government, left their farms and joined the urban labor force en masse.

The Great General sent warm soy milk using "the king's trucks" to hungry children every day. I cannot help thinking that it is heartfelt gratitude for the compassion the children received every day that is echoed in the phrase "Beloved Father! Great General!" belted out by both adults and children in North Korea at the top of their voices.

"Our Soy Milk Is Not Like Your Soy Milk"

When we decided to help the children in North Korea, we had to find a way to deliver the supplies in a semiperishable state so that the North Korean regime could not convert them for military use. This was partly in response to the demands of the South Korean government as well as public opinion at the time. However, we also wanted to make sure that the relief supplies reached the most vulnerable population: children and mothers with newborn babies. The objective here was to send food that couldn't be stockpiled for military purposes and to have it distributed and consumed immediately.

However, we soon saw with our own eyes that these concerns were mostly based on groundless Cold War obsessions. We did not know any better beforehand, primarily because we knew little of the reality in North Korea, but also because little knowledge or resources related to international relief work were available in South Korea. We learned gradually that international aid programs were conducted from the culturally biased perspectives of donor countries, meaning mostly advanced Western nations. In addition, we learned that relief programs and aid delivery worked essentially in the same manner as colonialism, with priority given to the industrial interests of donor countries, not the interests of the recipients.

When we sat down with North Korean officials for the first time to deliver our relief supplies, the first thing we learned was that the internationally recognized food relief that we had brought—high-energy biscuits and powdered milk—were not considered food but mere snacks by our counterparts. We explained that they were for children, but to no avail. During the Korean War, the chocolate and cheese that US troops had given out were high in calories, but they still could not fill the stomachs of hungry people. In the same manner, no matter how popular South Korean Choco Pies were among North Koreans, we could hardly insist that they provided nutritional value.

The idea of providing soy milk from South Korea came together into a real plan after we spotted the government soy milk trucks. At the time, we were trying to find a form of food relief that would work well with local logistics as well as suit students' palates. The plan did not materialize right away, for we were still caught up in the task of finding a nutritional snack similar to high-energy biscuits. It was doctors in North Korea who finally steered us away from following in the footsteps of international relief organizations. Unlike bureaucrats, who are trained as professional negotiators, these doctors had real expertise in famine relief, and they let us know, sincerely and desperately, what would help most.

However, like the bureaucrats we had spoken to, the doctors also began by explaining how hard they were working to keep the socialist preventive medicine and nutrition management system in operation, despite the harsh reality that supplies were insufficient. They would then mention, as if in passing, that there were certain urgent needs. Of course, it was difficult to adjust our perspective according to the on-site conditions and realize that we had to essentially start over from scratch. But we learned over time that true relief is provided when those offering it understand on-site truths and adjust their plans accordingly.

The North Korean doctors pointed out that they were unable to produce formula milk for babies born to mothers who did not have enough breast milk due to malnutrition. What they needed was a single ingredient called lecithin, an emulsifier. A standstill in the production of formula milk in the country meant the imminent death of thousands of newborn babies. The doctors never made an explicit request, but once we understood the problem, it was obvious that formula milk was more urgently needed than the biscuits we had brought. We knew about the lack of food. What we did not realize was that due to a lack of raw materials and energy, the country was unable to manufacture types of medicine and processed food that had been produced in the past, and that this situation had led to a problem more serious than we were aware of. There was always the lingering possibility that some unforeseen political issue might erupt that would put a swift end to the flow of international food relief. We were not confident that we would be able to provide an uninterrupted supply of necessary ingredients from outside. We had to make a decision, and fast. We decided to provide basic facilities and ingredients for manufacturing formula milk locally.

The base of the formula for newborns would be the soy milk already familiar to North Koreans. In addition, we decided to set up manufacturing facilities in order to increase the supply. For technical advice, I contacted a leading

Figure 2.5. A soy milk factory: Okedongmu Children (South Korean NGO for famine relief) supported the building of a soy milk factory. Byung-Ho Chung

soy milk manufacturer in South Korea, but talks for cooperation broke down immediately. They mentioned using raw materials imported from Europe for the vacuum packaging and explained that the minimum production volume for package processing would start in the millions. There was no point in talking with them further after that. While they were willing to reduce the unit price for such a good cause, they were not interested in giving advice on independent, on-site manufacturing. For our relief plan to work, we had to think outside the box and began searching for options other than the soy milk found in South Korea. We found an alternative at a Chinese soy milk manufacturing facility. The preservation period was short, but for one-fifth of what we would have had to pay in South Korea, we could produce fortified soy milk for children packaged in simple plastic containers. When we took the trial product to the South Korean company, they laughed, calling it "soy water." However, nutritionists who analyzed our product said that because it did not have as much sugar as the soy milk sold commercially in South Korea, it was actually better for children's health. Following all these twists and turns, a South Korean NGO eventually succeeded in establishing soy milk production facilities in Pyongyang. Our facility produced two tons of soy milk per day, providing formula milk and soy milk for 3,500 newborns and infants up to age three. We also processed formula milk in powder form, sending it to maternity hospitals in various regions. Later, we were also able to produce 250 tons of powdered soy milk per year for two thousand infants living in remote mountainous areas.[25]

The next obstacle to overcome was the tradition of donor identification, whereby relief supplies had to be identified as such in print. However, considering the political system and social organization in North Korea, the most efficient method of distributing the soy milk was via the "king's trucks." North Korea already had a complete production and supply system. If mutual trust could be achieved, the most rational course would be for us to set up additional production lines in order to increase output at the existing facilities and fortify the milk with added nutrition.

Still, some continued to argue that the drinks had to be identified in print as having come from South Korea, because otherwise the children would think it had come from their Supreme Leader, which would benefit the enemy regime. It was difficult for us to ignore this argument. The older generation of South Korean politicians, who could recall receiving relief supplies bearing the USAID emblem with its American flag during the Korean War, argued that anything going to North Korea had to be clearly marked: "Republic of Korea." For this very reason, the North Korean authorities were sensitive about any trademarks or letters printed on relief packages. However, we came to learn in the field that soy milk delivered via the "king's trucks" in the name of the Great General had less chance of being siphoned off, and that use of the "king's trucks" ensured that the supplies would be delivered to their intended recipients, the children. The stronger one felt about the urgent dietary crisis faced by the children, the more one preferred the certainty of successful delivery using the most efficient means available. If only we could better feed the hungry children; that was the true transparency. Do not let your left hand know what your right hand is doing.

We came to learn that what is etched in the hearts through real understanding is more important than any letters etched on packages. One day, a North Korean researcher we were working with in Pyongyang grabbed my hand quietly in a darkened hallway, his eyes fixed on the faraway distance. He held it tightly, ever so quietly saying, "Thank you, thank you." I was overcome by emotion and uttered, as if talking to myself, "I'm sorry we cannot do more."

He gripped my hand even more tightly and said, also as if talking to himself, "It's the heart, the heart that we are grateful for." His words brought me close to tears. I did not want to put him on the spot with my sentimentalism. I had to turn my head and look up.

FAMINE RELIEF ACTIVITIES AND OBSTACLES

The sickening pictures of malnourished North Korean children taken by outsiders at orphanages and hospitals in the early years of the famine were occasionally used in fund-raising campaigns for relief supplies, but more frequently in anti-regime campaigns emphasizing the North Korean state's failures and denouncing its human rights violations. Whereas the North Korean authorities allowed such photos to be taken in the early days in the hope of receiving much-needed relief supplies, they later censored the international media as well as visitors in order to prevent the circulation of such images. However, the photographs were already widely available and are still used extensively today in anti–North Korea political rallies in the South.

From the mid-twentieth century onward, countless children have died of malnutrition due to war and natural disasters in countries such as Biafra (1967–1970), Ethiopia (1983–1985), Somalia (1992), and elsewhere in Africa. The tragic pictures of suffering children remain unforgettable images of Africa to the present day. But how many children has the international community saved after circulating so many awful pictures? How many North Korean children have we indeed saved by gazing at their scrawny bodies in these photographs?

A South Korean NGO that I was involved with from its inception in 1996 started a relief campaign for children in North Korea. We named the campaign "Hello, Friends!" We wanted children in the North and South to be able to imagine themselves as friends. In so doing, we wanted to emphasize friendship, not pity. We were desperate for donations but did not want to sow a sense of alienation and superiority in South Korean children by parading tragic pictures of their North Korean peers in front of them. We wanted children in the South to think of their peers in the North as their classmates and asked them to draw pictures of themselves to send to their faraway friends. We suggested that we send gifts along with their self-portraits, as their peers in the North were going through some really hard times. The campaign was a huge success. However, blocked by the wall of division and adult politics, we still have not fully delivered the innocent affection and care displayed by so many of the children who participated in this campaign some twenty years ago.[26]

Facing the disastrous reality in the North and the limitations in our resources, we had to prioritize our relief efforts. Meetings with nutritionists and doctors suggested that nutritious and easy-to-store items, such as high-energy biscuits, enriched soy milk, and baby formula, were good options. We also consulted with North Korean officials and experts to assess the most pressing needs of children in the country. Then came negotiations with the

North Korean officials, obtaining permission from the South Korean government, and finally production and shipping. None of these processes went smoothly. We had to deal with—and sometimes even fight—bureaucrats and red tape in both countries. Such bureaucratic barriers were no lower when we worked with international organizations such as the UN. I would like to share a few episodes for the record and as guidelines for future efforts.

Anthelmintic or Nutrition Enhancer

When the famine became protracted, North Koreans took to the mountains and fields in a desperate search for food. By reviving folk knowledge concerning traditional famine foods, nutrients were obtained from the roots of herbs and the bark of trees. People also found creative ways to eat a variety of things that had not been customarily eaten in the past. These experimental survival strategies were accompanied by significant risks and side effects. Vomiting, diarrhea, and parasitic infection were common problems. When immunity was compromised due to malnutrition, even such minor conditions could become fatal.

"Dragonflies, grasshoppers, snails, frogs, toads, snakes, rats"—North Korean youths who had left the country by crossing the Tumen River listed the names of the various insects and wild animals they had eaten in North Korea. They also had extensive knowledge of edible fruits, flowers, and herbs. To me, many things they listed were familiar, but some were new. I had no difficulty understanding their stories because, as a child in the 1960s, I too had ventured into the mountains and down to the rivers in order to catch and eat grasshoppers, frogs, crayfish, and shellfish with my friends. However, experts caution that eating wild creatures runs an inevitable risk of parasite infection.

I was curious about how North Korea dealt with intestinal worms. None of the young refugees I met in China said they had ever taken an anthelmintic, a drug that expels worms from the system. When I asked refugees who had been doctors in North Korea, they said that before the famine, anthelmintics had been administered, but distribution had been halted due to a severe side effect involving weakly stimulated roundworms piercing the intestines. We informed parasite experts in South Korea about this situation and sought advice. They said that the anthelmintic used in South Korea today was a vast improvement over those used in the past, meaning that patients could now get rid of almost all of the parasites by taking just one pill a year. They also suffered very few side effects, and manufacturing costs were also very low. Hearing this made me realize that if only we could figure out how to supply this drug to North Koreans, it would be a very effective relief strategy. It would stop the parasites from taking 12 to 15 percent of the already scarce nutrients from those infected and prevent deadly diseases caused by parasitic infections.

With an air of confidence, I explained to the North Korean representatives our plan to supply the anthelmintic. Without so much as a moment of consideration, they refused.

"There is no such squalid problem in our republic. We have excellent public hygiene, and our preventive medicine is advanced. We do not have that problem. Don't even speak of such a thing."

I couldn't understand this reaction. I explained the plan again at informal meetings and looked into the matter further. The truth was that the North Korean representatives could not accept something they thought might embarrass the regime. They could be sharply reprimanded for doing so. What a reason for a refusal! I was blown away. Bureaucrats are infamous across the world for the extreme lengths to which they will go for the sake of self-preservation, but in this case it was difficult to come up with a solution given the limited contact channels and mutual distrust.

However, supplying the antiparasite drug was too important to give up on, and we mulled over ways to convince our counterparts to accept our proposal. Then it struck us: what if we called the drug a "nutrition enhancer"? We came up with a new proposal. We introduced a "new" drug that enhanced nutrition by 12 to 15 percent if taken once a year, and samples of the drug were repackaged accordingly. Of course the ingredients were properly listed along with details of the medicinal efficacy of the anthelmintic.

"We can accept a drug like this!" The North Korean representatives we met the following year smiled broadly, delighted by the proposal.

North Korean doctors who saw the label with the ingredients immediately understood what it was. "Ah, mebendazole! This is a strong medicine. We can make it ourselves, but since we are short on supplies, we can accept it if you supply it." The doctor said this to save face, but his expression showed that he was genuinely grateful. He nodded, saying, as if talking to himself, "If one tablet a year is so effective in getting rid of worms, that really would be remarkable."

With the sponsorship of a South Korean pharmaceutical company that understood our goal of providing relief supplies without any fuss, thirty-seven million "nutrition enhancers" and twenty million doses of antibiotics were supplied to North Korea over a three-year period, from 2000 to 2003. In February 2004, the North Korean Ministry of Public Health confirmed that the drugs had been distributed in all nine provinces and three cities as planned.[27]

The project of supplying the deworming "nutrition enhancers" was not widely known at the time because we organizers refrained from publicizing it. Authorities in the North also did not want to recognize it openly, perhaps because they still considered it embarrassing. However, having learned from field contacts how serious the problem was for victims of the famine, this was the most rewarding relief activity for me personally. A North Korean refugee youth whom I taught at Hanadul School gave an eyewitness account that someone had been selling a "nutrition enhancer" at a market in a mountainous region of North Hamgyeong Province. Whatever the channel, and whatever the method, the antiparasitic drug was quietly and extensively distributed among North Koreans.

Sea Vegetables from the Southern Seas

We were in Pyongyang meeting with doctors and discussing nutrition and development problems among children during the famine. A young North Korean researcher chimed in rather suddenly, perhaps sensing the sincerity of the South Korean visitors: "There is an issue of iodine deficiency among children and mothers in mountainous regions." We recognized the seriousness of the problem immediately.

Iodine deficiency in infancy causes hormone problems in the thyroid gland, which leads to poor mental and physical development. A lack of iodine during pregnancy increases the risk of miscarriage or premature birth and causes brain damage to the fetus and breast-fed infants, in turn causing hearing impairment and growth retardation. Once such problems set in, brain growth and physical development damage cannot be reversed, even if appropriate nutrients and treatment are administered later. Korean folk wisdom led new mothers to consume sea mustard soup in order to prevent such problems from occurring.

Experts from the South convened an urgent meeting in Pyongyang, seeking to address the problem of iodine deficiency among children in mountainous areas first. However, the junior researcher who had raised the issue was nowhere to be seen at our next meeting. "Gone on training," the North Korean officials told us.

In fact, the researcher hadn't disclosed anything new. Already in 2002, a joint investigation by the European Union, UNICEF, and North Korean authorities had confirmed and even announced that 19 percent of children in mountainous areas suffered from severe iodine deficiency. However, this announcement was buried under various other famine-related news items. After returning to Seoul, we notified the relevant government agencies as well as various other offices of the iodine deficiency problem and sought

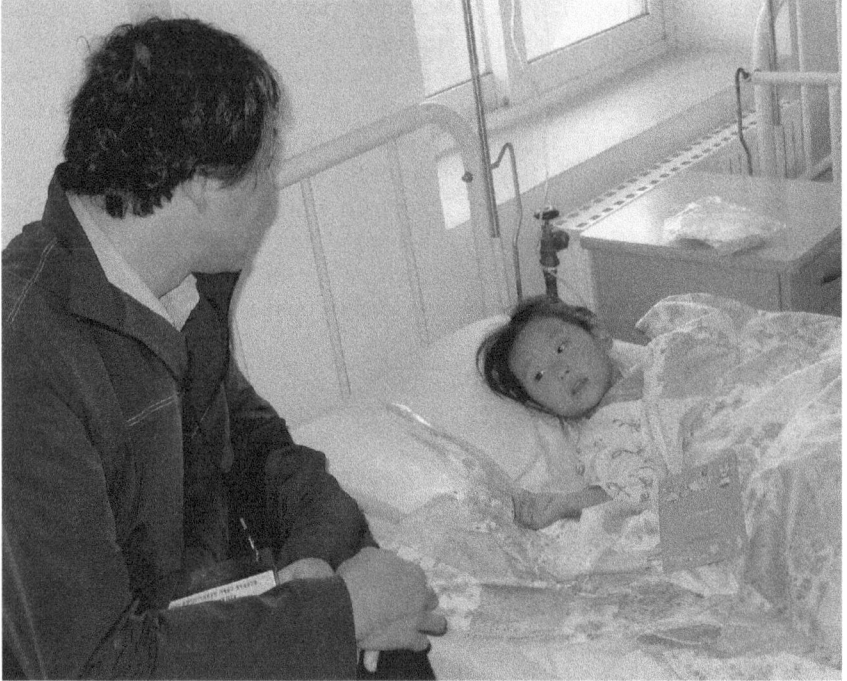

Figure 2.6. Children's clinic specializing diarrhea: Pyongyang Okedongmu Children's Hospital. Byung-Ho Chung

support, but the issue was never addressed when relief packages were prepared for the North. In the meantime, the South got a new conservative administration. As inter-Korean relations cooled, the problem was forgotten altogether.

Ten years later, in early 2012, a teacher at a school for North Korean refugee youths sighed, "Some of the children arriving these days have very severe learning disabilities. Could it be the effects of iodine deficiency in infancy that you mentioned years ago?" She said that the refugee children she had been teaching so far had no problem learning. Even if they were stunted physically, their cognitive skills were fine. However, starting two or three years prior, she had begun to see children with cognitive impairments. They did not understand her, no matter how much she explained. "If one kilometer is one thousand meters, how many meters is two kilometers?" An eighteen-year-old young man, born in 1994, could not solve this problem, just staring blankly. The teacher said that it was frustrating because these youths were so different from the former *kkotchebi* youths, who lacked learning experience but were still clever. The youths with cognitive impairment were usually short, tired easily, and were generally very weak.

My heart sank when I realized that the generation I had worried about had finally arrived. The life path that these children faced was a daunting one, and I worried how they would fare. The lack of essential micronutrients, such as iron, zinc, and iodine, is a problem that can be solved by eating a small amount of sea salt or marine plants common in Korean cooking. After ten years of being unable to tackle the problem, children who suffered these deficiencies were now appearing before us as young adults aged fifteen to twenty. Desperate, I wrote a newspaper column calling for emergency assistance to send seaweed from the seas off the southern coast of Korea to children in mountainous areas of North Korea.

> Iodine is an essential micronutrient, so even a very small deficiency can cause fatal disorders. The intake amount to satisfy nutritional requirements is also very small. The solution is simple. Marine plants are abundant on our southern and western coasts. Dried marine plants are easy to collect and inexpensive to transport and store for a long time. They have no military significance, either. Let us send sea mustard from the southern coast and dried laver and salt from the western coast to the mountainous regions of Hamgyeong and Pyongan Provinces in the North. In the end, we must help each other and live in this land together. Let us raise healthy children together. Let us raise children who grow up healthy with the benefits of nature and love of the people from the South.[28]

My humble wish was not fulfilled.

The North Korean regime deserves the strongest possible criticism for failing to provide its children with essential nutrients while continuing to conduct nuclear weapons tests. But we must ask ourselves, what have we done for these same children? What have we—adults in the South as well as people around the world, for that matter—really done for them? Both North and South Korean government authorities were well aware of the issue. They barked that when the big problems were solved, the little problems would be solved automatically. Twenty years have passed, and the malnourished children have either died or grown up with disabilities they need not have acquired. Politics in both the North and the South have always put face-saving first, whether in relation to giving or receiving. Bureaucrats and NGOs in the South have also prioritized big projects, big buildings, and big events in order to flaunt its influence.

Politics and bureaucracy in South Korea presented their own hurdles for North Korean relief efforts. The conservative Lee Myung-Bak administration (2007–2012) always insisted in the media that it would not block "humanitarian aid" to North Korea. However, when local NGOs prepared supplies and sought permission, government officials invariably requested that new, supplementary documents be prepared. In the worst case, we had to apply for permission more than forty times for the same package. Eventually they would ask for impossible data or unconditionally withhold our supplies, citing political conditions involving inter-Korean relations. Baby formula ingredients, laxatives, and saline solution materials for North Korean infants and toddlers that were tied up in customs warehouses at the port of Incheon had to be thrown out when they reached their use-by dates. Precious items embodying the concern and care of countless South Koreans were tied up or discarded in such profligate ways. In the meantime, many North Korean children withered away and perished. The grave problems the children are facing are the fault of all those adults in North and South Korea and around the world who have not worked harder and with more urgency. It is my fault, and yours too.

Iodized Salt and International Organizations

When inter-Korean relations were at a standstill, the only open conduit was the UN. The WFP and UNICEF both had resident secretariats in Pyongyang and claimed that they had a food aid distribution system established throughout North Korea. The then UN secretary-general Ban Ki-Moon had previously served as the South Korean minister of foreign affairs and trade during the Roh Moo-Hyun administration (2002–2007), when inter-Korean relations were active. Hanwha Group decided to provide five thousand tons of Australian sea salt containing ample iodine. If the UN agency provided the supply channel, we could supply five kilograms of sea salt each to one million households. It was also reassuring that the company that had supported the supply of anthelmintics without press publicity was on our side again. The company quietly understood the need for emergency relief.

The problem was the WFP officials. Surprisingly, they said they wouldn't take the salt. With the help of the UN secretary-general's office, we held several consultations, but in the end we were unable to deliver the salt we had secured. During working-level discussions, the person in charge would be gone for a month on vacation. In another case, the staff member in charge seemed not to want to take on the job during his term in office. We had to start the discussion all over again when his successor came in. They kept repeating that we should give cash rather than salt. It is true that North Korean bureaucrats, too, prefer cash over anything else. The final answer from the WFP was that it couldn't accept our supply package because it was "too big." Too big?! I felt I had finally met head-on the infamous UN bureaucracy that I had previously only heard rumors about. Diplomatic meetings were more important than the on-the-ground reality. Meetings were held repeatedly, ad nauseam, but nothing was accomplished.

I contacted UNICEF to see if there was any way to unblock the dead end we had reached with the WFP. The UNICEF representative in Pyongyang was aware of the problem. She informed us that, according to a survey, the number of children affected by iodine deficiency under the age of five had increased from 19 percent in 2002 to 26 percent in 2009. She also informed us that because the shortage of sea salt and algae had not been resolved, iodized salt factories had been established at three locations, but they were unable to fulfill their quotas because of shortages of certain raw materials and a nationwide electricity crunch. In a great hurry, we put together a plan to supply facilities and raw materials to get the facilities running and consulted the relevant ministries in South Korea. This time it was the South Korean officials who blocked our progress, refusing to provide us with the necessary government permit. We became acutely aware of the inhuman characteristics and limitations of the bureaucratic system established by nation-states and international organizations in today's world.

Two years later, in 2014, I met a young woman in Seoul who said she was from the UNICEF office in Pyongyang. She boasted that she had raised the issue of the iodine deficiency among children in mountainous regions with the group of young leaders who had taken power with Kim Jong-Un, informing them of the need to provide iodized salt. She seemed completely unaware of the prior activities and discussions related to this issue. Still, I was able to confirm that the documents I had prepared and sent here and there in desperation had seen the light of day, at unexpected times and in unexpected ways. I had to take solace in that.

In the meantime, did the elite officials in Pyongyang, aware of the iodine salt issue, solve the problem for the little children in remote mountainous regions while they went ahead developing nuclear missiles and constructing high-rise buildings? In South Korea, the policy priorities of leaders in the era of development dictatorship were the same as those of the North Korean leaders. Until the 1970s and 1980s, social welfare, especially for the vulnerable, was always pushed to the bottom of the list of priorities. Until the early 1990s, the difference in height between urban and rural students, for example, was plain to see.

A North Korean refugee youth who had crossed the Tumen River in 2016 came to visit me on campus one day. Pointing to a group of female students passing by with his chin, he asked me, "What did they eat that they are so tall?" He had been born in a remote mountainous village in North Hamgyeong Province in 1997 during the Arduous March.

Frozen Tangerines and Sick Cows

In 2000, the tangerine harvest was exceptionally bountiful on Jeju Island in the South, and farmers faced the possibility of a drastic fall in prices. The government decided to purchase the surplus crop and send it to North Korea rather than buying it and burying it. After many twists and turns, the fruit ended up being sent. However, what came back in return from the North were not words of thanks but complaints that too many tangerines had arrived frozen. The North's response had been similar two years earlier when Chairman Chung Ju-Yung (1915–2001) of the Hyundai Group donated one thousand cows. The North complained that too many of the cows had bits of plastic in their guts, that they were no good for working, and that they had died shortly after their arrival. Such complaints from the North prompted some in the South to say that we should never again send gifts to our Northern neighbors. Each time, rather than thanking South Korea for the genuine generosity of its gifts, North Korea complained about them. I explained the cultural meaning of this to South Korean bureaucrats from the perspective of cultural anthropology.

In South African Bushman culture, there is no tradition of giving thanks or offering praise for any gifts received. This demonstrates the cultural principles of an egalitarian society. For example, when a hunter catches a large animal and distributes the meat to everyone in the village, they enjoy the meat in a communal meal and complain that the meat is too tough. It is said that the harsh words are meant to cool the excited heart of the successful hunter. One Western anthropologist, Richard B. Lee, who stayed in a Bushman village bought a fat cow to thank the villagers for their hospitality. Everyone had a feast, but they scolded him publicly for giving them such a scrawny cow.[29] Such is the gift culture of an egalitarian society, where actions are taken to dampen any sense of superiority that the gift giver might feel.

I had an opportunity to personally witness North Korean youths' critical attitudes toward the gift givers. Mrs. Mutsuko Miki, the wife of the late Japanese prime minister Takeo Miki, visited Seoul in the fall of 2003 and met refugee youth from North Korea. In the wake of the 1995 floods in North Korea, she had organized an NGO and sent bananas and eggs to the country. She asked them if they had ever received any. A boy asked her how many she had sent; she told him one hundred thousand eggs and ten thousand bunches of bananas. The boy immediately shot back, "Well, with that much, did you think there was ever a chance for them to make it to us?" He understood immediately that the amount sent would not even have been enough to provide one snack for the people of his hometown.

Gratitude is not something one expresses immediately or on the spot when gifts are given and received. It is reciprocated in kind or with an even more generous gift after the passage of an appropriate period of time. When visited by a group of relatives, the Bushmen of the Kalahari Desert share water to the last drop, no matter how dire the drought they may be experiencing. Such cultural practices are the key to their survival in the harsh desert environment. In response to Chung Ju-Yung's cows, the North Korean authorities gave Hyundai exclusive permission to develop tourism on Mount Kumgang to the people of Jeju Island who sent the tangerines, they gave special permission to fly them directly to Pyongyang on chartered planes. In other words, the North Koreans did indeed reciprocate the goodwill of the South Koreans in both cases, only not immediately and not in the manner that was culturally expected by the donors.

A Cold Night by the Tumen River

A former student of mine from the refugee youth school, who has been in Seoul for around a decade, once wrote on Facebook, "Nothing beats long johns. It's the best gift of filial piety." An arctic cold front had been gripping the country for days. The sentiment expressed in his post was not something that a South Korean youth, growing up in a well-heated apartment, could have come up with. He must have been thinking of the family he had left behind in North Korea, about gifts for his parents that, wish as he might, he could not give them.[30]

I had experienced similar freezing conditions once near the Tumen River, in China, at the border with North Korea on a winter's day just a few days prior to the turn of the millennium. There, a coughing child in shabby clothes snooped about the entrance to a store I was in, and I had him come in. He was from Hamheung and eighteen years old, although he still looked boyish. He was soon to enlist in the military, he told me. He said he could not leave his sick father behind to join the army, and that was why he had crossed the river a week earlier. He had come to ask his aunt living in the United States for help. The aunt, who had gone to the South in the Hungnam Evacuation during the Korean War, apparently ran a dry-cleaning shop in New Jersey. With the help of a broker, an ethnic Korean in China, the boy had been able to make a few calls, urgently asking for money, but was rejected. When there was no prospect of money, he was kicked out of the broker's house. After wandering the streets for three days, he had caught a cold.

"Is this what you call a family?" With anger rising in his face, he sighed like someone three times his age, uttering each word with difficulty. He knew that the United States and South Korea were rich countries, contrary to the message conveyed by state propaganda. But when he spoke that day, he seemed more resentful of the well-off relative who had refused to help him in an emergency than with the regime that had deceived him. He said he just couldn't understand such a "family" and told me more about his family troubles.

In the summer of the previous year, three of the teen's aunts living in the United States had come to Yanji and had a reunion with their brother, the young man's father. They had promised that they would come back soon to see him again, and also to visit Mount Baekdu. The boy's father, being ill, asked the aunts to send him the money instead to help with the family's living expenses. From then on, the boy's aunts did not even answer the phone. Since crossing the river, he had come to learn about the high living standards in China and the even higher living standards in South Korea. Yet he told me he planned to return home because of his family and his sick father.

I bought him a bowl of hot soup and saw that the bottoms of his socks had large holes. I took off a layer of socks I was wearing and gave them to him. At night, when he stepped onto the bank of the Tumen River, where the wind was fierce, the thin jacket he was wearing on his thin body looked far from sufficient. I took off the sweater I was wearing, hesitating for a moment because it had been given to me by my deceased father as his last Christmas gift.

I wondered about the fate of the boy with the cold who crossed the frozen Tumen River that night. If he survived, he would have returned home to his parents and enlisted in the People's Army. Considering the sound of his cough, I should have given him my thick down jacket that night. I still feel the same pang of regret whenever I think about that night.

Whenever the weather gets cold, I think about the North Koreans, for whom the weather would be even colder. I am reminded of an arduous procession of people I once saw digging up and hauling off tree roots because there was no firewood. As I mentioned earlier, poor nutrition can turn even a minor cold into a fatal illness. For them, a cold is no mere nuisance but a matter of life or death. Politics must be separated from humanitarian aid. The Red Cross movement began with the care of wounded enemy soldiers on the battlefields. That is what humanitarianism is. There is no give-and-take. It is unconditional, and it must be so.

I hope that when we think of extending a helping hand to "our neighbors," this group will include those North Koreans whose lives can be saved by a pair of long johns. Since meeting them, I worry about the rice fields in North Korea whenever droughts drag on, because they do not have much groundwater there. When torrential rains drench the land, I worry about flooding and about the terraced hillside fields, for there are no trees in the mountains there. They are our neighbors, living in the land immediately next to us. "Is this what a nation is?" I am reminded of the face of the scrawny boy on the banks of the Tumen.

NOTES

1. Byung-Ho Chung, "Bundanui Teumsaeeseo: Talbuk Nanminui Sarmgwa Ing-won" [In the interstices of North-South division: The lives and human rights of North Korean refugees], *Dangdaebipyeong* [Contemporary criticism] 16 (2001): 236–55.

2. Byung-Ho Chung, "North Korean Famine and Relief Activities of the South Korean NGOs," in *Food Problems in North Korea: Current Situation and Possibil-ity*, ed. Gill-Chin Lim and Namsoo Chang (Seoul: Oruem Publishing House, 2003), 239–56.

3. The IMF crisis was caused by South Korea's severe foreign exchange short-age when it was on the brink of default in December 1997. South Korea was bailed out by the IMF and other international financial supports. The crisis was officially ended in August 2001 when the South Korean government declared the prepayment of IMF credit.

4. Hazel Smith, *Hungry for Peace: International Security, Humanitarian Assis-tance, and Social Change in North Korea* (Washington, DC: United States Institute of Peace Press, 2005), 87–88; Ralph C. Hassig and Kong-Dan Oh, *The Hidden People of North Korea: Everyday Life in the Hermit Kingdom* (Lanham, MD: Rowman and Littlefield, 2009), 108–9.

5. Uriminjok Sorodopgi Bulkyo Undong Bonbu (Korean Buddhist sharing move-ment), *Bukhansigryangnanui Siltae (Jaryojip)* [Reality of the North Korean food shortage] (Seoul: Joeunbotdul, 1998); testimonies are available in Joeunbotdul (Good friends), ed., *Bukhansaramdeuli Malhaneun Bukhan Iyagi* [Tales of North Korea told by North Koreans] (Seoul: Jongto, 2000); W. Courtland Robinson, Myung Ken Lee, Kenneth Hill, and Gilbert Burnham, "Famine, Mortality, and Migration: A Study of North Korean Migration in China," in *Forced Migration and Mortality*, ed. Holly E. Reed and Charles B. Keely, 69–85 (Washington, DC: National Academy Press, 2001), https://www.ncbi.nlm.nih.gov/books/NBK223341. Andrew S. Natsios, *The Great North Korean Famine: Famine, Politics, and Foreign Policy* (Washington, DC: United States Institute of Peace Press, 2001).

6. Marcus Noland, Sherman Robinson, and Tao Wang, "Famine in North Korea: Causes and Cures," *Economic Development and Cultural Change* 49, no. 4 (2001): 741.

7. Byung-Ho Chung, "Bukhan Gigeunui Illyuhakjeong Yeongu" [An anthropo-logical study of the North Korean famine], *Tongilmunjeyeongu* [Korean journal of unification affairs] 16, no. 1 (2004): 109–40.

8. Jasper Becker, *Hungry Ghosts: Mao's Secret Famine* (New York: Henry Holt, 1998).

9. Byung-Ho Chung, "North Korean Famine," 111–12.

10. Sue Lautze, *The Famine in North Korea: Humanitarian Responses in Commu-nist Nations* (Medford, MA: Feinstein International Famine Center, Tufts University, 1997).

11. Byung-Ho Chung, "North Korean Famine," 109–40.

12. Byung-Ho Chung, "Living Dangerously in Two Worlds: The Risks and Tac-tics of North Korean Refugee Children in China," *Korea Journal* 43, no. 3 (2003): 191–211.

13. Byung-Ho Chung, "Living Dangerously," 198.

14. Byung-Ho Chung, "North Korean Famine," 129–33.

15. Joeunbotdul, *Bukhansaramdeuli Malhaneun Bukhan Iyagi.*

16. Seung-Hwan Song and Yeong-Su Weon, *(Wiinirhwae Pikkin) Useumui Segye* [The world of smiles (as observed in anecdotes of the Great Man)] (Pyongyang: Pyongyang Chulpansa, 2003), 76–77.

17. Yungi Seok, *Konaneui Haenggun* [The Arduous March] (Pyongyang: Munye Chulpansa, 1991), 713.

18. Heonik Kwon and Byung-Ho Chung, *North Korea: Beyond Charismatic Politics* (Lanham, MD: Rowman and Littlefield, 2012), 174–78.

19. Seung-Hwan Song and Yeong-Su Weon, *(Wiinirhwae Pikkin) Useumui Segye*, 134–35.

20. Byung-Ho Chung, "Bukhan Gigeunui," 109–40.

21. EU, UNICEF, and WFP, "Nutritional Survey of the DPRK," November 1998.

22. Byung-Ho Chung, "Bukhan Eorini Giawa Hanguk Illyuhagui Gwaje" [Children, the North Korean famine, and the task of Korean anthropology], *Korean Cultural Anthropology* 32, no. 2 (1999): 155–75.

23. The *eorini boyuk gyoyang beop* (Childcare Education Law) was enacted and promulgated in June 1976. Enforcement ordinances followed in 1993. The content of the law and ordinances relate to the rearing and education of preschool children at day-care centers, kindergartens, orphanages, and other child-care facilities. https://www.semanticscholar.org/paper/Current-Situation-and-Policies-of-Early-Childhood-Lee-Kwack/0cf21c8e6452497f473d622cd70937207b37727c?p2df (accessed May 31, 2020).

24. Han-Shik Park and Guk-Jin Kang, *Seoneul Neomeo Saenggak Hada: Namgwa Bugeul Galanonneun 12 [Yeoldu] Gaji Pyeongyeone Gwanhayeo* [Thinking beyond the lines: Regarding twelve prejudices dividing North and South Korea] (Seoul: Buki Publisher, 2018).

25. Gi-Beom Lee, *Namgwa Buk Aideuregen Cheoljomangi Eopda: Lee Gi-Beom Gyosuui Maheunahopbeon Bangbuggi* [The children of the North and South do not have a barbed wire fence between them: A travelogue of Prof. Lee Gi-Beom's forty-nine visits to North Korea] (Paju: Bori Publisher, 2018), 86–94.

26. Byung-Ho Chung, "North Korean Famine," 239–56.

27. Gi-Beom Lee, *Namgwa Buk*, 118.

28. Byung-Ho Chung, "Hamgyeongdo Aideurege Namhaeui Miyeogeul" [Sea mustard to the children of Hamgyeong Province], *Hankyoreh*, February 21, 2012, https://www.hani.co.kr/arti/opinion/column/519927.html.

29. Richard Borshay Lee, "Eating Christmas in the Kalahari," *Natural History*, December 1969.

30. Byung-Ho Chung, "Naebongmanhan Hyojaga Eopda" [Nothing beats long johns for filial piety], *Hankyoreh*, January 27, 2011, https://www.hani.co.kr/arti/opinion/column/460956.html.

Chapter Three

Changing Undercurrents

AN INFORMAL ECONOMY ON THE BORDER

In the summer of 1999, I went to Dandong, a Chinese town on the river that forms the eastern boundary between China and North Korea and is known to the Chinese as the Yalu and to the Koreans as the Amnok. My objective was to procure and send food for famine relief. At that time, Dandong was enjoying a booming economy, fanned by the food crisis in North Korea. This visit offered me a window into the complex reality of the North Korean famine that I could only have guessed at from abroad. What I saw, heard, and felt at that time became keys to understanding not only the informal economy and the dynamics of everyday life, but also the ways in which they unfolded in a manner so antithetical to the official rhetoric.

When the public distribution system collapsed during the famine, the informal economy lying dormant beneath it began to stir. To survive, people turned to previously unimaginable activities. While officials in Pyongyang formally held to the position that "politics is more important than the economy," even the lives of these officials themselves became heavily dependent on the underground economy.

In a situation of absolute deficiency, almost all of the consumer goods, raw materials, and parts that could not be procured internally had to be imported. However, due to its lack of foreign currency and the international economic sanctions it faced, the North could hardly import anything. People depended on clandestine trade for everyday necessities. Smuggling was no longer viewed as a serious crime. Rather, it had its own justification, summoning the historical memory of the "supply struggles" carried out by anticolonial partisans who had broken through enemy blockades and secured food for survival. Suddenly, the ruling power not only informally tolerated smuggling but actively took advantage of it.

North Korea's informal economy first appeared in the form of the *jang-madang*, a type of small, open-air market. However, behind the shabby appearances of such sites, a new supply chain began to form that was invisible, broad, and deep. The informal nature of the *jangmadang* makes it difficult to determine the economic scale of their activities, as there are no numbers captured in statistics, and nothing can be either confirmed or denied officially. However, despite the protracted imposition of international blockades and sanctions, high-rise buildings have continued to go up in Pyongyang and elsewhere in recent years, and large volumes of consumer and luxury goods are known to have circulated within the North's borders. One can only guess at the scale of the informal economy from these observable phenomena.

Warehouses in Dandong, China

Dandong is now the most important gateway connecting North Korea with the outside world. After the heavy floods of 1995, most of the relief supplies destined for North Korea passed through Dandong. But these supplies were not simply passing through the city—a considerable number of purchases were made there as well. Before entering North Korea, supplies were also warehoused there and were loaded onto trucks and trains there. In effect, the famine in North Korea fattened Dandong, China.

As representatives of a private South Korean relief organization, we arrived in Dandong intending to buy flour, as sending relief supplies directly from South Korea to the North was not feasible at the time. Our goal was to send at least a few truckloads of flour across the border.

At 9 a.m. on July 27, 1999, I boarded a tour ship under the iron bridge in Dandong, the vessel bringing us so close to the North Korean riverbank that I could almost touch it. I was told that there was no territorial border bisecting the river. Rather, it was an intermediate zone, the waters jointly managed by the two countries. Just out of my reach was Sinuiju, the capital of North Pyongan Province. Concrete piers and buildings, shuttered factories, rusted boats, and dilapidated rides at the riverside amusement park all showed signs of damage from the floods several years earlier and had never been repaired. In the scorching midsummer heat, North Koreans sat along the riverbank, gazing vacantly at us, passengers on a fancy tour ship.

Dandong was thriving. Sparkling skyscrapers with state-of-the-art glass exteriors lined the riverside, while the concrete frameworks for still more buildings could be seen jutting upward between them. At night, the sleepless city was illuminated by bright lights and colorful neon signs that contrasted dramatically with the blackness that blanketed Sinuiju. Not so long ago, Sinuiju had been the up-and-coming modern city and Dandong a simple border town. Now the fates of the two cities had been radically reversed.

I arrived in Dandong hoping to find a more dependable way to deliver supplies to North Korea, because the capricious nature of inter-Korean relations and international politics had often stymied our efforts. Our first stop was a place willing to sell us rice and flour. It was a shabby warehouse, piled high with rice bags clearly marked "Caritas." They said that they were only reusing leftover bags from the international Catholic charity organization. After showing me their goods, they asked if I was interested in buying. How much of what they told me, if anything, was I to believe?

One wall of a large granary was stacked high with large televisions, rice cookers, and even small dishwashers, all of which felt out of place. I was told that they were bound for North Korea. These were among their most popular types of merchandise, the owner said, and sales were good. I had a hard time imagining who would buy such items in North Korea where, famine aside, electricity comes and goes. Where did the money come from? Seeing that I was confused, the owner answered me with a question of his own: "When there are those willing to sell their homes for a few scraps of tofu, why shouldn't there be others taking advantage to line their own pockets?" That is to say, people on both sides of the river were cashing in on the dire circumstances.

Why should I send relief supplies to such a corrupt place? I was tempted to call it quits right then. But I had to come to terms with the reality that North Korea was home to humans who were just as fallible there as they would be anywhere else. It helped to remember that the same had happened in South Korea, too. I had heard stories from the Korean War about refugees in Busan forced to barter family heirlooms in return for shelter. After the war, at every port and warehouse that foreign aid came through, large quantities of supplies were siphoned off. Corruption was rampant. Nevertheless, the international community continued to send South Korea relief supplies, which helped the poor ride out the hard times.

North Korean refugees I met near the border around that time told me that whenever foreign aid arrived in North Korea—or was rumored to have arrived—grain prices at the *jangmadang* dropped. The news of incoming relief triggered the release onto the market of a trickle of food that had been hoarded out of fear of future lean times. If that was the case, it did not matter whether we sent food through official routes or informal ones. Either way, the delivery of relief into the country would help those in need. Still, the few truckloads of food, all that we could deliver at the time, seemed meager in the face of the large and complex nature of the famine.

"We Can Find a Way Together"

In 2010, when a South Korean navy patrol boat, the *Cheonan*, sank near the inter-Korean maritime border, the South Korean government, then led by President Lee Myung-Bak, banned inter-Korean trade and imposed sanctions against North Korea. Doing so only invigorated the trilateral trade in Dandong linking North Korea, China, and South Korea. Kang Ju-Won, an anthropologist working in the Dandong area, reports that the informal economy was bustling during this period despite international sanctions against the North.[1] Ships loaded with clearly marked Hyundai containers from South Korea traveled across the river to and from Dandong and Sinuiju in broad daylight.

In winter 2014, I visited Dandong again. By then, it had completely transformed into a modern metropolis. Everywhere I went, the flags of South Korea, China, and North Korea were displayed side by side on the signboards of restaurants and shops. The city had become a center for trade involving people from all three countries. In the meantime, across the river in Sinuiju, a high-rise was going up, while the dilapidated factories and amusement park rides had been repainted and were back in operation. The Park Geun-Hye administration in South Korea (2013–2017) overlooked such changes in North Korea. Its belief that the Kim Jong-Un regime was unstable and its collapse imminent fanned the flames of the "reunification bonanza."

The Dandong customs service is located not far from the Friendship Bridge that leads into North Korea. Trailer trucks that had been waiting for clearance since daybreak filled the parking lot. Inside the customs building, North Korean government trade workers, ethnic Koreans in China, and entrepreneurs from South Korea bustled through with briefcases full of documents. Bored truck drivers chain-smoked while waiting for the OK to proceed.

Both sides of the large boulevard leading up to the entrance to customs were lined with massive commercial buildings. I had gone there thinking I would find individual stores selling consumer goods at wholesale prices for *jangmadang* operators in North Korea. Instead, what I discovered was a veritable mall of trading companies. You name it, they sold it: automobiles, heavy equipment, engines, chemicals, construction materials, generators, electronic goods, flour, soybean oil, and more. Everything sold there went to North Korea. "Exhibition halls" displayed sample products for wholesale deals. I heard that one such store had made $50 million in sales the previous year.

What caught my eye was solar panels for electricity and solar collectors for warm water. One store also sold solar power generators. In North Korea, power outages are common, making these must-have items for homes and businesses alike. A signboard explained that a small solar panel and current transformer could be used to charge TVs, lighting fixtures, laptops, and

Figure 3.1. Dandong Customs and Import and Export Mall: trading companies and wholesale and retail stores lined up on both sides of the street in Dandong, China, near the Sino-Korean Friendship Bridge (Ueuigyo) connected to Sinuiju, North Korea. Ju Won Kang

mobile phones and that a single large solar panel could power an electric fan, electric blanket, refrigerator, washing machine, and electric rice cooker. The solar panels were all made in China. I was relieved to hear that they were steady sellers; access to hot water alone during the long North Korean winter could help prevent all sorts of diseases.

Signs explained that purchases could be packaged in a way that would pass inspection by North Korean authorities and that pickup at Sinuiju Station or Pyongyang Station could be arranged. The confidence conveyed in such claims was the result of the formal and informal trade that had been taking place in Dandong over the previous fifteen years. I also came across the following ad in Korean in the Dandong city phone book: "Having trouble with North Korean trade? We can find a way. We can connect blocked roads, and where there is no path, we can open one together."

I came across a gateway with a sign written in Korean and Chinese: "North and South Korean Folk Street." True to its name, North and South Korean stores there respectively sold items that were popular among people from the other country. The North Korean stores sold the wild ginseng, deer antlers, *chaga* mushrooms, and blueberry liquor popular among South Koreans, while the South Korean ones alongside them sold the cosmetics, ramen noodles, and banana milk popular among North Koreans.

Eventually I wandered into a large kitchenware store. As I browsed, nothing about it struck me as special until the shop's South Korean proprietor made his pitch, making it easy to conclude that the variety and volume of goods shipped to North Korea far exceeded what one would have imagined. He claimed that his store supplied almost all of the noodle-making machines used in the large *naengmyeon* (cold noodle) restaurants in North Korea, including the famous Okryugwan in Pyongyang. Not only that, he also supposedly supplied the tables with inset barbecue grills for new restaurants springing up in Pyongyang and other major cities. So much secondhand kitchen equipment from defunct restaurants in South Korea went into North Korea through Dandong, he said, that it was impossible to estimate the trade volume.

Another South Korean entrepreneur, the operator of a lingerie shop, also boasted of doing business on an extraordinary scale. Not long ago, he said, he had bought ten thousand items of women's underwear at a fire sale in Seoul for a dollar a piece, sending them to Sinuiju in a freight container. He told me about a well-mannered middle-aged party cadre who was one of his regulars. Every time he dropped in, this man would purchase armfuls of sexy nighties, to the point where it became apparent that they weren't all for him—or his wife. Finally, one day, the store owner jokingly asked him if he was a ladies' man. The Mao suit–wearing North Korean replied that the lingerie had initially been traded secretly within a closed circle made up of wives of higher-ups, but it had become the latest must-have item, touching off a wider surge in demand. He then asked for the wholesale price.

At a hotel in Dandong's so-called Koreatown, I came across North Korean government trade officials in China on business as well as "foreign currency workers," mostly laborers working at foreign factories or construction sites, now on their way back to North Korea. They usually had huge bags with them, filled with whatever sold well at the *jangmadang* back home, I was told. By 2014, there were already thousands of North Koreans residing in Dandong, working either for the North's government or in the private sector. In addition, twenty thousand North Korean workers were reportedly employed by nearby factories, some producing garments and electronics, others involved in the processing of marine products.

In the 1970s and 1980s, South Koreans who had gone to work in the Middle East as construction workers returned home, bringing with them popular consumer products, such as Japanese rice cookers, television sets, cameras, and camcorders. At the airport, they handed these over to brokers for a profit. Now, similar scenes were taking place whenever a train bound for Pyongyang crossed the Amnok into North Korea and pulled into Sinuiju Station. Again, at Pyongsong Station, one stop before the domestic border inspection facilities for Pyongyang, numerous middlemen brokers passed those goods on to the *jangmadang*.

While these consumer goods go through a relatively "official" entry process, many other items are more difficult to bring in because they are either prohibited due to international sanctions or banned by the North Korean authorities. Thus the high demand for "gift" items fit for greasing palms. Many streets near the border in Dandong are lined with shops selling high-end cigarettes and liquor, South Korean instant food and cosmetics, rare tropical fruits, and other goods perfect for such purposes.

Luxury goods and consumables are essential ingredients for creating and maintaining special relationships, rather than fodder for sale or direct consumption. It is said that *jangmadang* and other markets primarily owe their existence to—and derive their function from—such informal "gift politics." In other words, they are necessary for the mobilization of materials, not only in order to supply publicly traded goods but also to curry favor with those in power regulating the flow of goods.

Every day around 5 p.m., the international train from Pyongyang to Beijing arrives at Dandong Station. A variety of people disembark, ranging from executive-looking middle-aged men in the North's signature *inminbok* (Mao suit) to young men and women in sharp Western suits. Those who have been waiting greet them warmly, most speaking with a Pyongyang accent. I recall seeing a North Korean woman, perhaps a trade worker living in Dandong, waiting in the lobby, dressed in a stylish trench coat. When a young man stepped out of the exit, she slipped her arm into his. Together, they walked to a parked car, chatting affectionately. In the square outside, the drizzle cast an aura off the brightly lit golden statue of Mao Zedong, while the South Korean actor Kim Soo-Hyun smiled down at the crowds from a billboard.

"We Need to Teach Them the Taste of Money!"

Most of South Korea's "industrialization generation" are the children of the Korean War who spent their early adulthoods in an era of what may be described as postwar recovery and developmental dictatorship. Many of them became masters at survival, experts at expediency, well versed in the skills needed to cope with hardship. They traveled the world with a relentless can-do spirit, aggressively building one of the world's strongest import-export economies.

"You know, there are probably no people in the world who could understand these types of dealings with North Koreans better than us," a South Korean businessman who had spent many years working with North Koreans told me. Up until and throughout the 1980s in South Korea, it didn't matter what your business was, you had to involve the politicians, the bureaucrats, the police, and sometimes even the KCIA (the Korean Central Intelligence Agency of the Park Chung-Hee regime), he said. You wanted a truckload of goods to go through? You had to pay a "toll" at each checkpoint. Even at local government offices, if you wanted a document to be processed on time, you had to pay an express fee. If you were caught by the police for a traffic violation, some cash was all it took to solve the matter.

"When did all of that disappear?!" he lamented. "After democratization! Young South Korean kids these days probably can't stomach this kind of business."

In 2007, during a period of active inter-Korean exchanges, I visited a primary school in Pyongyang with South Korean businessmen who were interested in inter-Korean projects. The children welcomed us with a performance, after which we took pictures together. A small kerfuffle arose when a hotel mogul from South Korea furtively slipped a $100 bill into the hand of a fourth grader. The girl stood there, frozen, her face belying her confusion. Noticing that something was amiss, our guide took the money out of the child's hand and coolly returned it to the businessman. The quick sense of a seasoned guide defused what could have turned into an explosive situation. Then the businessman said out loud, as if for all of the South Koreans in the group to hear, "We need to teach them the taste of money!"

MARKETS AND TRADE

With domestic resources depleted, securing supplies from the outside world was critical. Fortunately, China was just beginning to enjoy material abundance, a fact that proved key to the survival of many North Koreans. People who had crossed the border illegally into China for food and daily necessities went back to North Korea, some selling the goods they had brought back from China. Some of them gathered goods in North Korea that could be sold in China before crossing the border again to do business.

Smuggling and Bribery

People who had the money to buy food and daily necessities from China to trade in North Korea usually raised capital through family members or relatives living abroad. Sometimes they used foreign connections, collecting sought-after items from North Korea and selling them for sizable profits outside. People who have built up seed money and mastered profiteering are known as *donju*, this term literally meaning "money holders." Among the early *donju*, several are known to have made big money by smuggling antiques. A refugee youth once told me a story about his own experience of a close encounter with such a *donju* that involved robbing old tombs.

The work had to be done quietly in the dead of night. The job of going into the burial chambers was reserved for boys with nerve who were small enough to slide through the small grave openings.

"It's totally dark, and suddenly I see blurry lights like a will-o'-the-wisp. I learned later that they were caused by phosphorus from the corpse. Anyway, I had to keep calm and grope in the dark. Eventually, I felt jars and vessels at my fingertips." The young man shuddered as he told me the story. At the same time, he became boastful as my eyes widened. He went on, saying that he had heard rumors that those who sold these antiques in China had become major *donju*. They paid boys like him a few pieces of bread for each job.

The trading counterpart in China, the *daebang*, sells North Korean items coming across the border, in return procuring packages of food supplies as well as daily necessities and sending them back to North Korea. In most cases, a *daebang* is either a *chosunjok* (an ethnic Korean who is a Chinese national), a *jogyo* (a North Korean national with permanent residence in China), or a *hwagyo* (a Chinese national with permanent resident status in North Korea). However, high-value items, such as antiques, are eventually passed on to a South Korean *daebang*. Some *donju* who have become versed in smuggling try to maximize profits by entering into direct contact with South Korean brokers. Doing so, however, is dangerous, because if they become connected with South Korean intelligence agencies or Christian mission organizations, or if they are suspected of having such connections, this could lead to political catastrophe.

"Steal If You Have To!"

During the famine, people working in mines and factories even stripped copper wire and stole machine parts for sale in China. Given that people were dying of hunger, they felt that they had no other choice to survive. Theft, robbery, and swindling—illegal acts that would have been unimaginable during times of strict social order—became ubiquitous. From hungry children to soldiers, they simply took, without a twinge of guilt, not only food but whatever they saw as having some utility. Whatever it took to survive was acceptable. Once, when a child beggar was caught stealing from a *jangmadang*, the police were called in. An officer hit the boy hard on the back, then whispered to him: "Steal if you have to! Eat and survive!" He then let the boy go. Lawless survival strategies became universal.

Party and military cadres, bureaucrats, and police officers also used their authority or position to engage in illegal activities or have others engage in them on their behalf. For example, if forced by a supervisor to make an offering of flowers for the commemoration of Kim Il-Sung, people fulfilled such requests by mobilizing whatever "informal" resources they could to ensure their political survival.

In the face of such confusion and disorder, the regime carried out public executions by firing squad in similar fashion to summary executions during wartime in order to make examples out of those caught. However, despite the adoption of such extreme measures for maintaining order, which created a pervasive sense of fear, informal trade became commonplace in the area along the border between North Korea and China.

"North Korea Seems More Capitalistic"

A woman who had defected to Seoul in 2015 when she was nineteen told me about the secret trading operation she had carried out using her home in Hyesan, near the Amnok River, as an operational base. Her father worked with the border guards to ferry chickens and goats to the Chinese side every night. In return, he received grain, which sold well at the market. From the age of seventeen, she herself traversed the Amnok, selling grain she had brought back at markets in Hyesan. When she was conscripted into the military, her father bribed a doctor to falsify her medical records, allowing her to dodge the draft and continue helping with his smuggling business.* The Tuman and Amnok Rivers dividing North Korea and China, the lengths of both rivers extending over 1,300 kilometers, are a hotbed for such smuggling.

"Now that I am in South Korea, I think North Korea is the more capitalist country of the two. Money can solve any problem there," the woman told me. Born in 1996 during the famine, she had grown up in an era of deprivation. Now, she observed that many South Koreans seemed soft as a result of their welfare state, while others lacked flexibility. As someone who was already a veteran of smuggling and bartering by her early twenties, she was a hardened survivor.

All types of illegal activities—bootlegging, trafficking, smuggling, blackmailing, theft, bribery, embezzlement, and more—permeated North Korean society and were justified in the name of survival. Anyone caught engaging in such activities could be punished. From people who kept small stalls at *jangmadang* to major *donju*, and from the local officials who supervised them

---

* In order to fill vacancies in the military caused by the famine, lower fertility rates, and avoidance of military service, the state increased pressure on females to enlist.

to the high-level party officers who backed them up, just about everyone was in the business of risk.

Survival required creating and managing interpersonal relationships, which might include ties with members of the power elite, middlemen, and those who took care of the dirty work as well as those who could cause trouble for a shopkeeper, such as market supervisors, local police, border agents, and even one's colleagues and neighbors, whose jealousy or suspicions could mean danger. Many lived in a constant state of anxiety.[2]

In a system closed to the outside world like North Korea's, high-end consumer goods enjoy elevated value. Thus, giving and receiving goods brought in clandestinely from abroad creates special bonds. Such symbolic exchanges carry great utility value. This is a phenomenon not unique to North Korean society. It has been shown that in socialist systems where the official economic model is based on a planned economy, the informal economy and the resulting "bribery economy" are prominent features of the social structure. In order to live in a "command society" operated by central planning and bureaucratic regulations, informal human relations and material exchanges are necessary. Studies on socialist systems such as those of the Soviet Union, Poland, and Hungary emphasize the importance of the "informal economy," the "second economy," the "underground economy," and the "shadow economy."[3]

In 2002, after the worst of the famine was over, North Korea formalized markets through what it called "Economic Management Improvement Measures." With this policy in place, a "general market" was created. Companies were now permitted to engage in market activities, allowing them to operate restaurants and service businesses. However, the authorities still tried to regulate the flow of market goods and incorporate the emergent *jangmadang* markets into the official system. Nevertheless, no system of regulations could check informal economic activities, nor could the new market system reverse the patterns of the formal economy that had grown dependent on the underground economy. Immediately, illegal street vendors known as "grasshopper stalls" appeared in close proximity to general markets.

When the market was formalized, the production and management of factories and enterprises formed an organic relationship with the market. As the market became the locus of economic activities, ranging from the supply of and demand for raw materials to the maintenance of production facilities, the introduction of new technologies and machinery, and the selling of products, the boundaries between the formal and informal sectors became even more blurred.

Among the early *donju*, those who had ties with *daebang* in China and in South Korea and were able to establish ties with the right people in North Korea obtained official trade licenses. Among them, those who had the wherewithal borrowed the names of corporations or trading companies belonging to state institutions, trading officially and reaping profits while bribing informally.

When *donju* joined the market through collusion, their capital increased rapidly, prompting a currency reform in 2009 aimed at checking their power. This extreme measure ruined many of the small original *donju*. However, it also provided an opportunity for the emergence of a new class of *donju* who, again, colluded with power to invest in large-scale projects. The nouveau riche *donju* made investments that were unprecedented in scale, pouring money into major development projects such as high-rise apartments and shopping malls. They raised investment funds through connections and mobilized labor by borrowing the names of state authorities. In other words, a class of *donju* deserving of the name began to emerge.[4]

Some argue that the emergence of these new *donju* as well as rising consumption in North Korea are signs of inchoate capitalism, or a portent of the collapse of the North Korean system. However, *donju* do not own the means of production, nor do they have direct control over labor. As such, they cannot be capitalists. Instead, they exploit the existing power system for their own profit, seeking personal safety and higher social status. The *donju* are newly incorporated into the existing economic and class system by means of marriage and identity laundering. In this type of social change, the members of social classes may change, but the structure does not.[*]

Professor Ito Abito, a Japanese anthropologist who studied the everyday lives of North Koreans, concluded that "exchanges between people of different political rank are carried out in a chain of succession, from the lowest levels of society to the uppermost echelon, and it has become the basic mechanism by which North Korean society is sustained." That is to say, the system needed people who could carry out the work of nonsocialist commerce as well as transactions that party cadres could not perform themselves. In this manner, a complementary interdependence was formed for the survival and benefit of both parties. Accordingly, the expansion of the informal sphere did not pose a threat to the power system. On the contrary, the informal sector has formed a unitary body with the formal sector and become indispensable for maintaining the dysfunctional formal sector. Ultimately, the "durable socialist system in North Korea neither denies nor excludes the nonsocialist informal domain. In fact, the system is being established in such a way that it is becoming incorporated into a single entity."[5]

---

[*] In anthropology, such a phenomenon is called "Sanskritization," and refers to a phenomenon in which the lower castes seek to rise by internalizing upper-caste norms. It is found in class societies with strict hierarchical structures. In Korea, historically, a similar phenomenon was the buying and selling of *yangban* status toward the end of the Chosun dynasty.

The Market as Women's Space

When, in 1994, rations ceased to be distributed in all regions except Pyong-yang and supplies became scarce, most official economic activities came to a screeching halt, including the operation of state enterprises and factories. With the exception of those in the capital, people and businesses were told to "self-rehabilitate." A mad dash for food and necessities ensued. This proved a challenge for those who had been complacent in having their lives controlled by organizations. Clinging to their official status, ideology, and social norms, such people lacked resilience. By contrast, those of lesser social status, nota-bly women, adeptly plugged into the informal economic sector and began feeding their families by employing whatever market-oriented survival strate-gies they could devise.

Jangmadang markets evolved from their initial form as informal farmers' markets, proliferating and expanding rapidly nationwide during the famine. In the early years of socialist state building, even such markets were regarded as vestiges of capitalism. They now proliferated from farmers' markets that were officially permitted as supplements to the planned economy, and the range of products available expanded. Initially, the state strictly regulated the number of venues (one or two sites per county), the frequency (once every ten days), and the goods that were permitted to be traded (agricultural and fishery-sector products only). However, from the 1980s, unsanctioned markets began springing up in increasing numbers in alleys and even private homes, and the range of products grew.

At that time, those involved in these informal markets were often criticized for failing to overcome capitalist ways. The markets were therefore consid-ered places for older women or people whose already low *songbun* (family background) left them with little to lose.

Jangmadang and other markets were and are overwhelmingly women's spaces. More than 80 percent of market suppliers are women, and women who are in charge of the daily shopping for their families make up the primary customer base. Even when market participants were criticized as sellouts to capitalism, women went to work. It helped that their role in official organi-zational life was marginal. Illegal or marginal behavior by women was less likely to attract serious political criticism than that by men. The gender norm viewing women as responsible for housekeeping was also advantageous for the production, exchange, and processing of *jangmadang* supplies by women, as most goods were related to the domestic consumption of food, clothing, and shelter.

Women who were discriminated against in the official sector gained self-confidence and a sense of accomplishment as they became the family bread-winners. As women confirmed their survival skills at *jangmadang*, many of

Figure 3.2. Women are the drivers of the domestic economy: women working in the "grasshopper market" in Seosong-gu, Pyongyang. Yasunobu Shirouchi

their husbands were still entangled in the organizational life of the formal sphere and did little to help with domestic life. Women began to joke about how little their husbands contributed to the family livelihood, calling them "lightbulbs of day time."

A North Korean refugee from Chongjin told me that she supported her entire family by running a business making and selling potato noodles and blueberry liquor at a *jangmadang*. She proudly explained how, using money she had earned in the market, she had succeeded in changing all of the bad class background records for her children by bribing officials. Thanks to his improved records, her son was able to attend college and become a party member.

As a person who had adapted well to the system in North Korea, the digitalized credit system that she encountered in South Korea offered new challenges. While she was enjoying her relative freedom in Seoul, she had to work hard to meet the needs of the competitive society and felt as though the future was bleak. Watching people dashing along the subway platform, she would mumble to herself, "It's a pity. People here don't have it easy either."

DREAMS UNREALIZED

"Everyone will enjoy a prosperous life eating white rice with beef soup and wearing silk clothes in a tile-roofed house."

This is the slogan that Kim Il-Sung announced in 1962 based on the success of the First Chollima Movement (1957–1961). This was a time when North Korea was being lauded as having achieved a "Korean miracle" through speedy postwar restoration and remarkable economic growth; in international socialist circles, its performance was widely viewed as exemplary. However, as the Cold War turned hot in Asia, especially in Vietnam, North Korea focused its resources on strengthening its military power. Half a century after Kim Il-Sung's promise, the dream of enriching people's lives feels more remote than ever.

"Let's Turn Grass into Meat!"

I had the opportunity to eat a variety of foods during my visits to the North for relief efforts. The problem of hunger, however, was too serious for me to savor the fine foods that I was sometimes presented. Still, I would like to share a few thoughts on the polarization of food culture and the problem of food self-sufficiency.

I remember the first breakfast I had at a hotel in Pyongyang during the height of the famine. I was taken aback by the expansiveness of the buffet in front of me. "I don't need all this," I mumbled, but perhaps not quietly enough, because a colleague gave me a poke in the ribs. In reality, it was a standard breakfast buffet of the kind that one would expect at any international hotel for the money we had paid. Encountering North Korean culture was as much a struggle with my own preconceived notions as it was a struggle with the particularities of the culture itself. Looking closely at the food in front of me with the eyes of an anthropologist, I noticed that familiar dishes had been presented in quite unusual ways. The ingredients had been used parsimoniously, but trimmed with tremendous skill and craftsmanship. The abundance of skill and dedication made up for the lack of substance.

"The ice cream here is delicious!" a high-ranking party cadre suddenly opined. Dressed in a dark blue Mao suit, he was a veteran negotiator, and we were in the middle of a serious conversation about children's nutrition problems over a meal. Despite the gravity of the topic of discussion, the expression on his face when he made this statement was so guileless that I had to laugh. Indeed, people did not subsist on bread alone. We on the outside are obsessed with a monolithic image of North Korea, unaware of the multifaceted lives and desires of those inside the country.

Okryugwan is not only the culinary icon of Pyongyang but of North Korea itself. I was taken there on nearly every trip I made to Pyongyang. Not only was the food delicious, but the building was impressive too. The two-story traditional gable building built on the banks of the Daedong River is said to be "a treasure of the people and the pride of Pyongyang." I did not notice the size of the restaurant at the entrance, but once inside I realized just how huge it was.

Okryugwan serves ten thousand bowls of noodles each day. Pyongyang citizens receive one ticket per year to enjoy a meal at the restaurant. A socialist practice indeed—or so I thought. Actually, about half of the tickets are distributed to powerful government agencies, and the other half go to specially selected enterprises and private citizens.

Anyone who has visited North Korea is likely to have experienced feasts that were too elaborate considering the overall food situation. Treating guests to elaborate meals is a universal phenomenon. In North Korea, however, guests are often pressured to hold banquets. Some infer that the regime is attempting to earn foreign currency by inducing visitors to spend money. In addition, my interpretation is that my hosts, too, wanted to enjoy a good meal whenever there was an opportunity. It provided them with a chance to consume dishes ordinarily unavailable under their planned economy. It seemed that, as individuals, they were not prone to suppressing such a desire. It reminded me of the common cultural practice in which members of certain societies go through long periods of time saving and hoarding food, only to consume them by binge eating on the day of a festival or special occasion. Nevertheless, the amount of food we consumed at Okryugwan during the famine still makes me uncomfortable to this day.

It would be difficult to achieve Kim Il-Sung's "white rice with beef soup" dream with a closed, self-sufficient economy. In South Korea, where rice is superabundant, the food self-sufficiency rate—that is, the percentage of food that is produced internally—is only 47 percent (as of 2018, the grain self-sufficiency rate was 23 percent). In the same period, it is estimated that the food self-sufficiency rate in North Korea was 92 percent, twice that of South Korea. However, a high rate of self-sufficiency does not guarantee enough food for everyone. North Korea would have to import huge amounts of food if everyone was to eat white rice and beef soup.

During the 2005 Arirang performance in Pyongyang, hundreds of people wearing masks in the shape of cows, pigs, goats, chickens, and eggs came out and danced during the mass games. In the background, twenty thousand students in the stands flipped over cards to create a massive message: "Let's turn grass into meat!" I understood that this scene represented a desperate dream. Yet I could not help feeling sorry for their pitiful and unrealistic portrayal of the future. Ten years later, in 2015, goats raised in North Korea were still being smuggled into China for rice and beans. The reality was that the number of people needing grain was greater than the number needing meat.

In May 2019, the UN Food and Agriculture Organization (FAO) and the WFP announced the results of a joint investigation into the North Korean food problem, informing the international community that 1.36 million tons of food aid were needed to assure subsistence for the population. The study predicted that eleven million people—about 40 percent of the population—would suffer from malnutrition due to food shortages that year. The UN then redesignated North Korea as one of thirty-nine food-deficit countries in the world, placing it in the company of Yemen, Syria, Iraq, and more than thirty countries in Africa.

There has recently been much coverage in the media of Pyongyang's new dining culture. Daedonggang beer and foreign fast food were introduced as symbols of a shift in food culture under Kim Jong-Un. This is important political propaganda for the leadership. These are foods that people in North Korea had only seen in the foreign dramas they secretly watched. The message is that those who are successful within the system do not have to risk crossing the border in order to enjoy such delicacies. Yet millions continue to face hunger.

A Uniform Society

In March 2000, the first time I visited Pyongyang, the streets seemed bereft of color. It did not help that the concrete buildings were gray and the roads mostly empty. More than anything, the people walking along the streets were dressed in drab uniforms. It almost felt as if I were on the set of a black-and-white film.

Pyongyang is only 120 miles north of Seoul, but everyone there was still bundled up in coats and scarves as if it were still winter. We then came across a child dressed in red walking hand in hand with her mother. It was the first colorful outfit we had seen since arriving in Pyongyang two days earlier. Everyone in our group was delighted. The only times we saw brightly colored clothes, they were worn by children.

There were a few colorful figures who stood out on the dreary streets of Pyongyang, such as the policewomen controlling traffic. Typically young and slim, they wore conspicuously large white hats, white uniforms with relatively short blue skirts, and white socks. Passersby could not but gaze at the striking young women making sharp, disciplined gestures.

Suddenly, it began to rain. The policewoman who had been controlling traffic on the road left. When she returned soon afterward wearing a transparent plastic raincoat, the men on our bus let out exclamations. In this drab guerrilla state, it seemed that a charming young woman in a colorful uniform was a welcome sight.

Pyongyang is still a uniform society. In a uniform society, one has to adapt to the weather with one's body, not with one's clothes. During the inter-Korean summit in 2018, hundreds of thousands of citizens lined the streets to welcome the presidential motorcade in downtown Pyongyang, all of them dressed in formal attire. College students wore school uniforms, the men in Western-style suits and ties and the women in *hanbok*, the traditional formal dress. The colors and designs were not identical, but all were outfitted in strict observation of the occasion's dress code. The farewell parade reconfirmed these rules. On that rainy daybreak, citizens lined up without umbrellas to bid farewell to the South Korean president. They would have had to wait for the motorcade for many hours in the rain in their Sunday best.

In a collectivist culture with strict political norms such as that of North Korea, one risks being called "bourgeois" or "decadent" for wearing clothes with colors or designs that stand out. Everyone takes steps to ensure that they are wearing clothes similar to those around them, and even small differences are immediately apparent. If such differences are noticed, one risks being branded "liberal" or "selfish" at the minimum; if the breach is serious, one can face accusations of being a "counterrevolutionary." Anyone courageous enough to express one's personality and style may try to push the limits, but it takes an acute sense of strategy to challenge where the line is.

Even minor changes in the fashions of the leaders and members of the elite are a pretext for those seeking transformation. Popular men's fashion in the capital during the Kim Jong-Il era was quite unusual. In the mid-2000s, sunglasses suddenly became fashionable, all thanks to Kim Jong-Il, who wore sunglasses during many of his public appearances. His unique jumper-style clothes also became fashionable among men. Men replicated Kim's style of dress as semiformal attire. But, within only a few years of his death, no one could be seen wearing such styles. As unnoticeable as it is to undiscerning eyes, North Korea has fashion trends of its own.

Toward the end of Kim Jong-Il's reign, bottom-up changes had already begun to occur in the country's fashions. The clothing culture we see today in North Korea is the result of the official acceptance of changes during the Kim Jong-Un era and their consequent rapid spread. After the closure of the Kaesong Industrial Complex with its South Korean companies, Chongjin and Hyesan near the Chinese border became leading fashion capitals, thanks to covert and informal economic exchanges between these two cities and the outside world. In these two northern cities, tactical self-expression is relatively easier than in Pyongyang, where the dress code is more vigilantly enforced. But self-expression still remains dangerous.

Collective Housing and Fancy Apartments

Our guide in Pyongyang pointed to a towering high-rise apartment building on Tongil Street. "We built that when we were in college." He told us that college students from all over the country had come and constructed the building in preparation for the 1989 World Festival of Youth and Students. He spoke as though reminiscing on fond memories of summer camp.

Along with soldiers, college students are still being mobilized to construct apartment buildings in Pyongyang today. Rumors circulated that some students spent so much time on construction sites that they have to repeat an entire school year. One would think that the students and their parents would complain. However, recollecting the expression on the face of my guide, I would not jump to such a hasty conclusion. If I am not completely mistaken, students mobilized for such construction efforts would relish the cultural significance as well as the camaraderie involved in participation in such projects.

Why are soldiers and students mobilized to build housing? What compensation do they receive for their labor? The answers are simple. They are mobilized because such construction work is viewed as part of a "national project." Naturally, there is no pay. The logic seems to be that the students cannot ask for money for the work since the state provides them free education, and the participation is required as an honorable duty.

Mass mobilization of labor has a long tradition in North Korea as a means of accomplishing major national projects. It began with a project to restore and protect flood-prone areas adjoining the Botong River in central Pyongyang immediately after the liberation of Korea in 1945. Then there were the postwar restoration projects and the Chollima Movement, to name just a few. There is an enduring sense of pride in the country at having achieved the "Korean miracle" within a short period of time through such large-scale public mobilization. Whether a road or a residential complex, each completed project was given a name and received public recognition. Participants are said to be proud because they dedicated their youth to the completion of historically significant projects. I cannot be certain that all participants share this sentiment. However, if one's work is recognized and celebrated as socially significant, one is likely to feel appreciated for one's hard labor.

Who lives in these apartments built in the name of a national cause? At first glance, it would appear that the situation must have been ripe for jealousy or complaints about who had or had not been granted residency. To put to rest any controversy over preferential treatment, the regime waged a massive propaganda campaign, insisting that the apartments were a social reward in recognition of the tenants' contributions or their loyalty to the nation. For example, athletes who had won Olympic medals as well as long-term political prisoners returning to the North after decades in South Korea were examples of those announced as tenants. The authorities also paid attention to the size and the location of the apartments, which varied greatly. They stressed that such differences were not to be interpreted as signs of inequality among tenants, emphasizing again that the apartments were gifts from the leader in return for the important contributions made by the occupants.

In the case of the apartments on Mirae Future Scientist Street and Ryomyong Avenue, which were constructed relatively recently, priority was given to professionals, such as scientists and professors, in order to induce feelings of appreciation rather than jealousy among the public. Of course, apartments were also distributed to people of privileged classes and family backgrounds.

These days, most of the high-rise buildings and apartments in Pyongyang and other major cities are built with investment funds from *donju*. However, in order to carry out construction in a system in which labor and the means of production cannot be privatized, investors cannot but mobilize state-organized labor, such as soldiers and students. The buildings and apartments are first allocated to those who contributed to the public/national cause. The remainder are distributed among military or party officials and private investors, the former for making the project look official and the latter for having actually funded their construction. Instances of these apartments being traded have also been on the rise in recent years.

The right to residential space created using social labor for a national cause is nothing more than a "right to occupy" such space. Of course, because inheritance is permitted, some argue that it is functionally indistinguishable from the right to ownership. However, there is an essential difference. This "right" can be rescinded whenever the nation requires. Societal control of land, buildings, and real estate is still possible in North Korea.

The apartment buildings in Pyongyang and other major cities exemplify socialist urban planning. They also embody the priorities and personal tastes of the leaders. For instance, the apartments on Tongil Street and Gwangbok Street from the Kim Jong-Il era were the first high-rise apartment complexes intended to create a new skyline for Pyongyang. In preparation for the World Festival of Youth and Students in 1989, the government focused on quickly creating a facade for each building, paying less attention to the quality and functionality of the interiors. The elevators in these high-rise apartments frequently broke down due to unstable power supplies, and the water supply and sewage networks were riddled with problems. In some cases, a single communal restroom was installed per floor rather than per unit. Communal

Figure 3.3. High-rise apartments and harmonica houses: (top) Ryomyong Street and high-rise apartments featuring solar panels and geothermal heating system; (bottom) old low-rise harmonica houses in Pyongyang hidden behind walls and not easily visible from the streets. Top, source: North Korean Calendar 2019. Bottom: Byung-Ho Chung

bathrooms of course reduced the time and cost of construction for the high-rises but also affected the daily experiences of residents.

The high-rise apartments on Ryomyong Street which opened in 2017, with their colorful lights, are said to be a sight to behold at night. They stand tall enough for the regime to advertise them in such a way. But my first thought upon seeing them was one of concern regarding electricity and heating for the buildings. I had heard in Dandong that the newer buildings were fully or partially equipped with geothermal heating and solar hot water. New technologies, including ones harnessing natural energy, had probably been adopted initially simply as a means of overcoming energy shortages.

However, residential spaces where most people actually live are lower-level multiunit buildings. In the 1950s, North Korea rebuilt its cities in the ruins of the war. Construction emphasized the efficiency of collective labor and cooperation. In particular, with active support from the Soviet Union and socialist brother countries in Eastern Europe, North Korea began to build multistory apartments. This type of housing relied heavily on prefabricated components, allowing for the effective utilization of a largely unskilled labor force, and postwar urban reconstruction progressed rapidly. Kim Il-Sung famously prevented the indiscriminate introduction of Western-style elements, making sure that the traditional *ondol* floor heating system was installed even in Western-style multistory, multiunit buildings.

In the early 1960s, a nationwide campaign was waged with the goal of collectivizing rural villages into agricultural cooperatives accompanied by newly built "cultural housing" complexes. It was a massive reform project to collectivize not only labor but the lives of farmers through the construction of people's units (*inminban*). The long, low houses built during this period were called "harmonica houses." The standard home had two rooms: one bedroom and one kitchen. Units with two bedrooms sometimes housed two families. Communal toilets and bathing facilities were usually shared among several units.

Social relations among residents are the glue of collective residential life. Mobility, in both geographical and social terms, is limited in North Korea. Local communities—one's neighbors—are important bases not only politically but also in terms of socioeconomic relations. Oftentimes, neighbors live next door to each other for an entire lifetime. Local units, such as the *inminban*, meaning "neighborhood units" or "people's units," have often been thought of as parts of a peer-monitoring system whose sole function is to deliver political messages from the top down. In reality, their primary function is as a mutual aid network among neighbors, whereby local problems are expected to be solved cooperatively. In particular, after the collapse of the distribution system during the famine of the 1990s, local residents frequently responded by pooling informal resources and survival knowledge. For example, the traditional credit rotation system, *gye* or *durae*, was revived among those trading at *jangmadang*. Many learned business skills from their neighbors, raising seed money through traditional and informal forms of cooperation.[6]

In the early 2000s, I had several opportunities to get close-up views of neighboring apartments in Pyongyang and other types of housing in provincial cities. The difficulties in living conditions faced by residents were immediately apparent. I saw houses with broken windows covered with plastic sheeting or wooden planks. Some houses had verandas that had been enclosed using plastic stretched over wooden frames. Others had thick bars over the windows, presumably to ward off thieves.

In the spring of 2003, Pyongyang got a makeover. Gray cement walls were washed and newly plastered, while faded surfaces were scraped and repainted in brighter shades. It was a time when inter-Korean exchanges were beginning to pick up, and I heard that a South Korean conglomerate had supplied paint for the beautification efforts. Each time I heard about Pyongyang's streets being spruced up, I could not help thinking about those broken windows with their plastic sheets.

In the fall of 2005, the Chinese government funded the construction of the Daean Friendship Glass Factory for the manufacture of sheet glass in North Korea. As a country all too familiar with socialist hardship, China well understood what North Korea needed. The following year, I visited the factory with South Korean businessmen. After a look around, one of the businessmen loudly remarked, "I don't see what the big fuss is." It seemed that those who had donated paint to brighten up the facades of buildings did not understand what a difference sheet glass would make to the daily lives of ordinary North Korean people who needed protection from the cold winter winds as well as light in their apartments.

Recent Pyongyang visitors say that the city landscape has changed dramatically. The state is concerned with the appearance of the city, and it has prioritized the maintenance of building exteriors. Living is the responsibility of the people. It is they who have to manage the reality of residential spaces. Changed though the urban landscape may be, people's living conditions are unlikely to have transformed as uniformly as appearances would suggest.

LEISURE AND LAUGHTER

Pyongyang is proud of children who display talent at a young age. They play musical instruments of all kinds, sing, dance, paint, and even do calligraphy, all with expertise paralleling that of much older artists. The state identifies their talents early and enrolls them in special education. In other words, they are selected and trained for their skills. While viewers of the outside world may marvel at the amazing talents of these children featured in the media, their extraordinary performances often seem very artificial.

Not all children in North Korea spend their days training at such privileged facilities. Whenever I visited Pyongyang, children were always present on the streets, many of them preoccupied with one form of play or another. Everywhere I went, I saw them on roadsides, in vacant lots, and in parks playing slap-match (*ttakji*), hopscotch, or jumping over elastic strings (*gomujulnori*).

I once saw four little rascals placing nails on the tracks to be flattened by the train, only to scuttle away when scolded by an adult. They were mischievous and full of life. Children many times more vibrant than those proudly show-cased by the state were coming of age in Pyongyang's windy alleys.[7]

The World of Children's Play

International visitors have few opportunities to glimpse the daily lives of people outside of Pyongyang. Still, on every occasion when I passed through a smaller city or village, I saw children playing. Every time I came across such a sight, I pressed my nose against the window, curious to see what they considered fun.

Children in the provinces seemed to play more vigorously and independently than those in the capital. Regardless of the season or temperature outside, they could always be found playing a great variety of games. In addition to *gomujulnori*, the form of play involving jumping over rubber strings mentioned above, I also saw girls playing a sort of snake game in which they lined up and held on to one another as if doing the conga, then tried to catch the tail end of the other group's "snake." In a vacant lot, I saw boys playing mock-horse, rock-paper-scissors, leapfrog, and the traditional *jachigi* game using sticks, shooting marbles, and spinning tops.

Figure 3.4.   Rubber string play: girls playing on the streets with rubber strings and a naughty boy on the run after breaking off the rubber string. Jong-Jin Lim

They were always playing in groups, as I had done when growing up. I saw children swimming naked in streams during the dog days of summer and sledding across frozen streams on chilly winter days. Some of them ran with wooden sticks between their legs, as if mimicking a pack of wild horses. Out of breath, they stopped now and then, their young faces drenched in sweat and bursting with excitement.

I could immediately recognize many of the games the North Korean children were playing, as I too had played most of them as a boy in South Korea. Many of the games I saw being played were traditional games common in both the North and the South. Although I did not see one personally, I was told that children in North Korea also held full-fledged mock battles, where a group of children from one neighborhood would fight with another from a neighboring community, throwing gravel and wielding sticks. I recall also playing such war games growing up.

From the Chinese side of the Tumen, I caught on camera a group of kids sitting around a bonfire across the river, laughing and talking loudly. When I showed the footage to young North Korean refugees in South Korea, their eyes twinkled as they all started chipping in with comments.

"They're roasting corn, aren't they?"

"No, no. Potatoes!"

"Gosh, I miss hanging out like that!"

Just moments ago, these youth had been taking turns singing plaintive songs in a basement karaoke room in Seoul. Now, their faces suddenly lit up. The memories of how they had entertained themselves as kids seemed to make them come alive.

Leisure and Holidays

Children are not the only ones who know how to have fun in North Korea. Adults play just as much as the youngsters. This may sound strange, considering their harsh lives. However, weighed down by our strict image of the regime, we overlook the fact that North Korean people enjoy a variety of games on a daily basis, and sometimes even draw upon the spirit of play in their formal routines.

The most common adult game is the card game *jupae.* Just as chess is often played in North Korean parks, this card game is widely played in public places. In Pyongyang, one can easily find small groups gathered in parks playing the game. It seemed likely to me that *jupae* games often involved an element of gambling. North Korean refugees said that in the past, penalties for losers had involved buying cigarettes, drinks, or food for the winners. Nowadays, in the era of active market transactions, the stakes are said to be more substantial.

Figure 3.5. Costume dancing party: grandmothers gather at Moranbong Park every weekend to dance in various costumes (scout uniform, Egyptian pharaoh, etc.). Takashi Ito

On a hillside along the Daedong River, I saw groups of people scattered about, enjoying picnics at Moranbong Park. The groups, made up of families, friends, and coworkers, were eating, drinking, and enjoying themselves. Excitement was in the air. Some of them sang and danced together. While they would ordinarily be wary of outsiders, some of them now beckoned us to come and share a drink with them. I readily took up one of the offers, joining one group's circle. The guide, who had smiled at first, gestured at me to return to our group. Many years ago, people enjoying themselves outdoors and sharing food and drink with passersby had been a common scene in South Korea. That is no longer the case. Perhaps, during the rapid cultural changes of the past twenty years, the joys of the previous era have been lost in the headlong rush into the digital era.

My encounters with children and adults at play in North Korea always filled me with joy. Play itself is like a crack in a society tightly bound by discipline, and those at play are like green plants that have somehow managed to grow in the cracks between gray cement blocks. In the spirit of play and laughter, they strategically turn from their social responsibilities and daily routine tasks, entering private space and time.

Johan Huizinga, who introduced the concept of "*Homo ludens,*" explored the nature of play in culture. In his book *The Autumn of the Middle Ages*, he called the late Middle Ages in Europe, commonly known as the Dark Ages, an age of prelude to the future, rather than an age of decline and fall. While it was difficult for medieval people to denounce the social world of the time, dominated as it was by doctrines and rituals, and while the earthly reality they faced was often a miserable one, they were able to achieve temporary relief by entering the world of play.[8]

New Year's Day (*seolnal*) in North Korea is also called "Alcohol Day" (*sulnal*). For New Year's Day and other major holidays, such as Kim Il-Sung's birthday, the state distributes pork and alcohol as gifts in the leader's name. While the supply of pork has run dry since the famine, alcohol—one bottle of *soju* per family—is still distributed. Of course, such official distribution alone does not account for all of the alcohol and food consumed during the holidays. It generally takes several months to prepare a New Year's party, and even longer if one is raising a pig for the occasion. Rice cakes, pancakes, dumplings, vegetables, meat soup, rice, and noodles are prepared, along with plenty of homemade alcohol, and the whole family gathers to pay tribute to the ancestors and enjoy a feast. At the workplace, too, drinks are poured even as workers listen to a formal New Year's address. These are ritual drinking occasions. After the rituals, the "proper" drinking starts, accompanied by dancing and games. This also happens with members of peer groups and *inminban* neighborhood groups. People move from house to house for drinks. "On Alcohol Day, we drink all night. But it's not drinking at just one house. Normally, it's at least five or six houses. . . . We hop from house to house, because it's Alcohol Day," said one North Korean.[9]

Heavy drinking does not exactly exemplify the socialist lifestyle, which emphasizes frugality and moderation. However, given that the expression "Alcohol Day" is accepted for usage in state media, New Year's Day can be interpreted as a socially accepted day of transgression. Paying respects to elders and informal exchanges of gifts are indispensable components of the holiday. The most common gift to bring on such visits is alcohol. Gifts of alcohol thus received are circulated to other persons of importance. An abundance of alcohol will then be shared to strengthen social bonds. "In the series of rituals over the New Year holiday in North Korea, alcohol comes down from the leader, then goes up to the ancestors, then travels to family and neighbors, ending up with the boss at work, and is finally consumed rakishly in a playful binge," as South Korean anthropologist Choe Hak-Nak writes.[10]

Humor and Satire

Mikhail Bakhtin, who was exiled from the Soviet Union during the Stalin era, argued that festivals and laughter can be revolutionary. "Laughter as an emancipatory play, which is considered a waste, a debauchery, or decadent at first glance," he writes, "is an active and transformative ability. It moves a stagnant reality and breaks the existing order of hierarchy."[11] Furthermore, laughter is said to be a creative act that demonstrates that a new world can be lived here and now. The ruling power of the feudal era attempted to provide relief to the subjugated class by having grievances released through festivals. However, festivals and laughter can leave a lasting image of liberation from having shaken and overturned formal norms, albeit temporarily.[12]

Guides who accompany foreign visitors have one of the most high-tension jobs in North Korea. They are the face of the republic and its spokespersons. As such, they cannot make any mistakes. Also, because they can be easily corrupted ideologically, they usually operate in twos, each pair consisting of one senior and one junior guide. At least once every two days, they must conduct rigorous criticism sessions in relation to themselves and their partners.

On one occasion, a young guide stumbled and fell as he was climbing the stairs of our tour bus. As he came up, blushing and flustered, his partner joked in a loud voice, "You fell while looking at a pretty woman. Women, they're the problem!" He made this remark with a smile as he glanced at a young woman from South Korea sitting in the front row of the bus. Everyone in the bus burst out laughing, including the guide who had fallen. A South Korean feminist sitting in the back seat laughed and, imitating the Pyongyang accent of the older guide, chided: "The problem is with the man who fell. Why blame women?" Another round of laughter broke out.

A few years later, by chance, I ran into the same young guide. He was wearing a dark blue Mao suit and was mixing with high-ranking party leaders. He must have become a very high-ranking cadre himself, for people around him were extremely courteous toward him. The young man was of the so-called Baekdu line, a scion of Kim Il-Sung's anti-imperialist guerrilla group. It was then that I understood another layer of meaning in the incident that had happened years earlier. The senior guide in that incident had made a joke in order to help relieve the embarrassment felt by the younger guide—his junior by profession but his superior in social standing—when the latter made a mistake. His gesture was an example of the effective use of age and position to prevail over class status.

Those who visit Pyongyang on official business are accorded a ceremonial meal with North Korean officials. Such meals usually start in a formal manner with official welcoming remarks and toasts. However, once there are a few rounds in and the atmosphere is ripe, North Koreans are prone to asking provocative questions, and one cannot always tell whether they are being friendly or sarcastic.

North Korean jokes can be disconcerting, especially for those who are not fine-tuned to that gray area between tension and ease, the territory of humor in which North Koreans often operate. Sometimes their ribbing can even seem insulting.

They reminded me of my childhood visits to relatives in the country. They would greet me warmly at first, only to later taunt me for being a city boy. For example, they would ask, "I hear dogs walk around in Seoul with cash in their mouths. Is that true?"

I was actually asked a similar question in Pyongyang. "Byung-Ho *seon-saeng*," they said, using the respectful but friendly appellation of "teacher" to refer to me. "You said you grew up in Seoul. Do you know how many bridges there are on the Han River?"

I was not sure. "Well, I guess they numbered them for a while. . . . But, now there are ten, maybe twenty?"

"You mean you don't even know how many bridges there are in the city you grew up in?"

A veteran activist from South Korea came to my rescue.

"Comrade, if you know such things off the top of your head these days, they would call you a spy in Seoul."

Everyone around the table clapped and laughed. The North Korean official laughed along with the rest of us, albeit sheepishly.

In the early days of the famine, Kim Jong-Il paradoxically began to emphasize smiles and laughter. The most dramatic example occurred during the preparation of the funeral portrait of his father, Kim Il-Sung. Until that point, the portraits of the leader that hung in every home and public venue featured him wearing a stern expression. The appearance of a huge new portrait of Kim Il-Sung at the funeral smiling brightly puzzled many. Kim Jong-Il had personally instructed that Kim Il-Sung be portrayed with an extra toothy grin in order to emphasize hope for the future at a time when the daily reality faced by many North Koreans was a desperate one.[13] In the era of tragedy and hardship that continued thereafter, Kim Jong-Il himself embarked on field guidance tours, always beaming and laughing, in an attempt to overcome the limitations of the situation through displays of boundless optimism.

His son, Kim Jong-Un, also appeared laughing and surrounded by people at a missile launch site, a location with the potential to provoke a state of crisis in the rest of the world. The more a country emphasizes discipline, the greater the need to promote an image of the leader laughing when meeting with the people. It is easy to interpret this laughter as being contrived. However, leaders in disciplinary societies are not the stern and stony commanders they are stereotyped to be. At least for the people who personally interact with them, they must put on a human face and be able to lighten the mood. Spontaneous gestures that break the conventional boundaries of formality promote bonding and elicit empathy.

The official emphasis on optimism and laughter has led to an "excess of laughter" in state-produced movies and TV dramas.[14] In recent years, the new dramas show misunderstandings and mistakes made by ordinary people in their daily lives being responded to with laughter, adopting a light touch in their portrayal of the minutiae of everyday life. This approach marks a significant departure from earlier productions with heavy themes, such as feature films and dramas portraying the heroic anti-imperial struggle or moving stories about the nation's leader. Introducing lightheartedness in the official media was perhaps the least the state could do in the face of an undercurrent influx of new foreign entertainment flooding the country.

Stealing Time

I once came across a group of people filling a pothole on the street near my hotel. The pothole itself was not very big, but more than twenty people had gathered to work on it. Upon closer observation, I realized that only five or six of them were actually working, and only intermittently at that. The rest stood around, talking and laughing. I first saw them in the morning. By the time I came across them again in the afternoon, little progress had been made on the road.

Michel de Certeau, who studied the culture of resistance in everyday life, observed that if power regulates and monitors like a "regular army that occupies the space," the weak resist like "guerrillas who steal time" with tactics of "pretending to obey," "pretending not to know," and "pretending to do."[15] In a similar vein, James Scott, who studied resistance among Malaysian peasants, described misconduct such as stealing, lying, slandering, and fleeing as the "weapons of the weak."[16] In North Korea, after the authority of the ruling power was shaken by the famine, instances in which institutional coercion was rendered ineffectual or deliberately subverted in order to suit the interests of the actors involved became commonplace.

People who traveled to China to secure necessities during the famine began to bring back South Korean dramas, movies, and music, which were already widespread among members of the ethnic Korean communities in China. The regime, vigilant about the infiltration of capitalist culture, responded by making South Korean dramas and music politically taboo and subject to a heavy crackdown. However, once curiosity has been triggered, that which has been proscribed often becomes even more enticing. For North Koreans, watching these forbidden dramas wasn't just fun; it was thrilling.

Buying and watching South Korean dramas are acts that involve the violation of official social norms. As such, they are already significant as examples of "time stealing." Because they involve furtive transactions in the pursuit of personal pleasure, a sense of complicity in secretly sharing forbidden activities with others, and a sense of victory in enjoying them with others, such acts themselves have deep significance as emblems of a culture of resistance occurring in everyday life. South Korean popular culture first spread via CDs and DVDs and then via flash drives. These have now given way to iPads and laptops. Such rapid changes in technology and culture will bring about considerable changes in North Korea. It gives me hope that such changes are likely to bring diversity, yet at the same time I am concerned that they may widen the already persistent gap between those who have access to such forbidden culture and the many who do not.

FROM IDEOLOGY TO DEVELOPMENT

On a dark night in December 2015, three North Korean seamstresses jumped from a third-floor window of their dormitory to escape from a small factory on the outskirts of Dandong, China. North Korean security officers stationed there kept watch through the night at points where they thought the women might attempt to defect. The next morning, employees at the North Korean consulate in Dandong found the three women at the gate of the consulate, shivering from the cold. The workers said they had walked all night to reach the consulate in order to appeal directly to General Kim Jong-Un concerning the injustices they were experiencing at work. They worked hard for the fatherland, they said, but their families back home were suffering because someone was snatching their wages before they reached their intended recipients.

The "comrade-in-charge" responsible for the local supervision of workers dispatched to Chinese companies was summoned back to Pyongyang, undoubtedly to be punished. But a few days later he returned unscathed, having been found not guilty. It turned out that a senior bureaucrat in Pyongyang, not the comrade in Dandong, was the embezzler of the workers' wages. Rumor had it that the real culprit was executed, but this cannot be confirmed. What is certain is that North Korea's *sinso* ombudsman system was at work.[17] The workers believed that their country would protect them, that they could rely on an impartial system of justice, and that even though they were workers selling labor in the capitalist labor market abroad, they could still appeal to the North Korean system for justice.

This story, which was told by one of my informants in Dandong, leaves many questions unanswered concerning, for example, the details of the women's labor conditions as well as their rationale for choosing the risky option of escaping from their dormitory rather than going directly to the comrade-in-charge. It also begs the question of why they did not simply defect to South Korea rather than appeal to the leader of their home country. These questions can help us understand the social changes taking place in Kim Jong-Un's North Korea.

"Don't Tell Her to Come Back Home"

A few years before the above incident took place, I had an opportunity to visit a number of sewing factories in Dandong. I was passing by the area with a Korean-Chinese businessman who dealt with factories that employed North Koreans. He needed to stop by one of them and asked if I would like to come with him. The people at the factory seemed to think that I was a South Korean on a business trip to China.

The factory was a four-story building without any signage, standing alone in the middle of a field. Once we set foot inside, it was as if we were back in Pyongyang. "Our great comrades Kim Il-Sung and Kim Jong-Il are forever with us. Loyalty is the first principle of life." Slogans written in red lined the staircase, while a military march played in the background. On paper, it was a Chinese company owned by a Chinese national. However, the fifty workers and three managers were all North Koreans. The comrade-in-charge I met on the second floor was a bespectacled man in his late forties who had the air of a public official about him. He introduced himself as "Mr. Park," the CEO of the company. A mid-level Pyongyang bureaucrat who had worked in a finance-related ministry in Pyongyang, he had come to Dandong with his wife.

Mr. Park asked if I would like a tour of the factory. Perhaps my Chinese entrepreneur friend had told him that I might open doors to new markets for him through my many contacts in Seoul. Whatever his reason for asking, my eyes almost popped out with joy, but I hid my excitement and followed him.

The factory was surprisingly well lit and clean. One could see the entire production line at a glance, from the garment-cutting station to the area used for the inspection of finished products and the ironing stations. The walls and columns of the hall were lined with militant slogans.

"Let us build a strong and prosperous socialist country!"

"Save, and save again!"

"Absolute, credo, unconditionality!"

North Korean marches played in the background, in odd juxtaposition to the decorative clothes for Japanese teens hanging in the finished-product section. The Chinese entrepreneur jokingly asked Mr. Park why he wasn't playing K-pop music as usual. Mr. Park's face stiffened as he responded, "We like to work to songs from the fatherland."

Figure 3.6. Foreign currency–earning workers working at a sewing factory in Kaesong Industrial Complex. Jean-Kyung Chung

The third and fourth floors served as the workers' dormitory. When not working, the women spent time here, sleeping, eating, and relaxing. I was told that sometimes a worker would go down to the second floor to work "voluntarily" at night. I imagined a worker toiling away alone or with a few others on a sewing machine in the wee hours of the night. Confined to collective living inside the building over an extended period of time, these workers had nowhere else to go.

Once a month, the workers were permitted an outing to Dandong. On such occasions, they were required to travel in groups of five and return before curfew. If late, they were severely criticized and grounded for the next month. If this happened frequently, "repatriation action" was taken. I was told that the workers feared nothing more than hearing the words "You're going home." This was in part because they were only able to work overseas as a result of "stuff money," usually bribes. A worker at the factory was a family investment, a source of income for those back home. Mr. Park related to me that in the past year, he had been informed of the death of a worker's parent on three separate occasions. He said that each time the family had begged him, "Please don't say anything. We don't want her to be childish and come back." Mr. Park said that he had felt bad but had done as he had been asked.

Most of the women working at the factory were from the countryside of the greater Pyongyang area. About two-thirds of them were single and in their twenties, the others being married and in their thirties. All of them were there on three-year contracts. They each received about $300 per month in wages, plus a $50 meal allowance. By comparison, North Korean workers at the Kaesong Industrial Complex run by South Korean companies earned a total of approximately $150 per month at the time. In Kaesong, the state took 40 percent of the wages, with the workers receiving the remaining 60 percent.

From the perspective of the Chinese company, apart from the fact that the wage was only two-thirds of what they paid Chinese workers, the worker turnover rate was almost zero, providing a high degree of workforce stability. Also, what the comrade-in-charge said was considered law at the factory, so labor management was headache free.

When we were about to leave, a rather young woman walked in and started yelling at Mr. Park while pointing and shaking her finger at him. She was the Chinese owner of the company. I could not tell what was wrong, but Mr. Park was no longer the dignified and relaxed self that he had been minutes earlier. I felt sorry for him, a bureaucrat from an ideological state sent overseas to deal with the logic of money in the international labor market.

Nationality over Ethnicity

Why do they not defect to South Korea when they must endure such humiliation in China? North Koreans are well aware that South Korea has become a rich country. They know that defectors from the North receive settlement funds and an apartment. So what stops them from going?

The primary reasons are probably fear of severe punishment and retribution in the case of failed escape and constant surveillance by neighbors and peers. In addition, defection means severing ties not only with one's family but with all of the meaningful social contacts that make up one's world.

There is another aspect to consider that has to do with self-identity and values. To facilitate understanding, it will help to recall the South Korean students, miners, and nurses who went to West Germany in the 1960s and 1970s. At the time, North Korea was doing much better than South Korea in terms of economics and world presence. For South Koreans living in West Germany, it would have been relatively easy to cross over to East Berlin and defect to North Korea. Why didn't they?

The South Korean government was well aware of this situation and thus on guard. It sent armed intelligence operatives to Germany and France to catch those seeking to go to North Korea, arresting, transferring, and incarcerating them without due process. It is true that, to an extent, fear of surveillance and punishment deterred South Korean students and workers from defecting to the North. However, their self-identity as South Koreans had become firmly ingrained throughout their Cold War education, and most of them did not give defection much serious thought. Instead, they sent money to their families back home, taking pride in their roles as members of a foreign-currency-earning vanguard working to make the fatherland more prosperous and powerful than North Korea. Among today's North Korean overseas workers, one can find similar values and a similar sense of self-identity as citizens of a developing nation.

Under Kim Jong-Un, North Korea began emphasizing *national* identity over *ethnic* identity. In other words, there are now public narratives that foster rivalry with South Korea, despite the shared ethnicity. North Korean state TV repeatedly broadcasts stories about those who defected to the South only to later return to the North. Most were teachers or engineers, skilled professionals. The returnees testify that they experienced social discrimination in South Korea and that their livelihoods were unstable as they worked as domestic helpers, caregivers for the sick, or unskilled laborers. They confess, choking back tears, that no matter how hard they worked at such menial jobs, there was no future for them in the South. They confess that the General heard their repentance and "has accepted [them] back with love and forgiveness," and they pledge allegiance with gratitude and loyalty to the fatherland and its leader. These "reentry" stories of the North's prodigal sons and daughters are broadcast to households across the nation.[18]

What we are witnessing here is a North Korean media blitz on "identity politics" in response to the South Korean media blitz on "defection politics."[19] The North Korean broadcasts emphasize how its people are discriminated against and looked down upon in South Korea despite their shared ethnicity. These stories connect economic discrimination with the issue of national identity; the subtext here is that North Koreans cannot enjoy the wealth of South Korea or other places in the outside world without paying a heavy price. Furthermore, the media blitz is a campaign of symbols that evokes the pre–World War II anticolonial national liberation narrative. In this narrative, the evil sympathizer with Japanese imperialism is replaced by the rich South Korea of today, a proxy of US capitalism. Conversely, the poor and persecuted Korean sharecropper of the colonial period is overwritten by the down-and-out North Korean defector in South Korea.

The goal of building a "civilized socialist nation" is to overcome capitalist discrimination. The category of national identity has now shifted from Korean ethnicity to North Korean nationality, the national goal having changed from liberation of the Korean people to the development of North Korea.

A CIVILIZED SOCIALIST STATE

Skinny jeans and designer handbags. Fried chicken and draft beer. Pizza and spaghetti. Mobile phones and taxis. High-rise apartments and neon signs. Theme parks and ski resorts. These are key symbols of social and economic change in North Korea under Kim Jong-Un. What is utterly ordinary anywhere else becomes world news when found in North Korea. Why are we so shocked to see these things in North Korea? Such a reaction stems from an incongruency with what the outside world is used to hearing about North Korea.

Books such as *North Korea Confidential* written by Daniel Tudor and James Pearson and *Pyongyang Jabonjuui Baekwa* (Encyclopedia of Pyongyang capitalism) by Ju Seong-Ha have introduced the changes taking place in North Korea. According to the authors, North Korea is already a "quasi-capitalist" country.[20] However, former communist countries, such as China and Vietnam, argue that they have developed "market socialism" or "postsocialism," led by their respective ruling parties, and that in doing so they have demonstrated alternative models of development from those taken by Japan and South Korea. In short, there are many cases of developing countries with a socialist ideology embracing the capitalist market system. Why should a comparable phenomenon in North Korea be ridiculed and criticized? Perhaps we can find the answer if we consider the issue of how the regime has managed to survive in spite of the many forecasts of its impending collapse. It will soon become clear that the assumptions upon which such predictions are made are based on a fundamental misunderstanding of the way in which the North Korean power structure operates.

The North Korean Developmental State

The changes that take the world by surprise in the Kim Jong-Un era are primarily cultural changes in everyday life. If we compare North Korea to a computer, the main operating system—the state ideology of socialism—is still the same, but a few capitalist programs have been added and are expected to produce various changes in content. A program for dramatizing the power of the theater state, which is embodied by the Supreme Leader, is also still running. Naturally, the operating system is old and rigid, meaning that it cannot run high-capacity programs. Nor can it effectively control virus-contaminated content. However, so long as the computer itself is not abandoned, it is unlikely that North Korea will completely overhaul the operating system; it is more likely to mobilize all of its resources in order to continue being able to use the old computer, albeit cautiously.

Kim Jong-Un is the third-generation leader of a nation founded by his grandfather and defended by his father. For now, the old bureaucrats and the people, who went through thick and thin with his grandfather and father, and have pledged their allegiance to him. However, with its poor economic situation and obsolete governance, the future of the nation is anything but clear. His father defended the regime, obstinately clinging to the old ways of prioritizing nuclear weapons as the key to security. In the meantime, the nation lost many allies, its credit rating plunged, and it was cut off from receiving outside investment. Pulling itself up by its bootstraps—"self-rehabilitation" as they call it in North Korea—is no longer feasible. The only assets it still has are its disciplined labor force, the land on which it stands, and, as Trump mentioned during the Singapore Summit, its excellent location. Its neighbor South Korea has grown stronger and is trying to shut down or buy out the country, constantly coaxing its people to cash out for prosperity. If you inherited a nation in such a state, to what lengths would you go to keep it standing?

The North Korean nuclear arms program was an interim survival strategy, a display of firm resolve, at home and abroad, to keep the regime intact and thereby have the power succession recognized as legitimate. As the situation stands, however, the regime cannot be sure of its own future to assure the economic and technological development that will ultimately determine its fate. Lacking money and technology, and without significant foreign investment, the only resources available to it are land and labor. In the absence of any large-scale flows of investment funds from outside, North Korea has already begun pursuing "self-rescue" measures in a diverse range of areas.

For example, it rented out its land and labor to companies in adjacent countries, opening areas such as the Kaesong Industrial Complex (South Korea pulled out in 2015) and the Rason Special Economic Zone to the outside world (mainly through the highway built by China) and trying to collect "canal tolls" on road and rail connections between South Korea and Russia and China (it failed to complete the links). It built hotels in prime tourism locations (e.g., Mount Kumgang and the Wonsan-Galma Resort that failed to open), gave long-term land leases to members of its own inner circle for the development of high-rise residential and commercial buildings, and sold some of its stakes (the rights to sell cell phones and imported goods) to small- and medium-sized foreign enterprises, not major global companies. It sells labor-intensive products (as an original equipment manufacturer [OEM] in electronic parts and apparel) to other countries and sends workers overseas in order to earn foreign currency and provide them with the opportunity to develop their knowledge of new technology while working in the construction and manufacturing sectors. With such a range of strategic countermeasures, North Korea is steadily seeking to strengthen its capacity for self-reliance, thus far with scant results, not least because of sanctions and pressure from outside as a consequence of its shows of military might.

The changes that have taken place in North Korea during the Kim Jong-Un era are not particularly unique. North Korea is merely seeking to adopt the general strategies of East Asian developmental states.* South Korea, under comparable conditions, also mobilized similar early-development strategies. Now a model development state of East Asia, the South pursued development strategies based on strong state intervention and control, where formal and informal sectors were wildly mixed, rather than on the adoption of undiluted capitalist market economic principles. North Korea has tried similar strategies, but it faced a US- and South Korea–led total blockade of any funds or technology coming from outside.

Under Kim Jong-Un, North Korea has had to adopt a revised development model because widespread changes had already taken place at the grassroots level. When rations were cut during the Great Famine, people began organizing their own markets in order to survive. By 2019, there were four hundred such *jangmadang* (field markets) nationwide, according to the official count alone. The public distribution system now exists in name only, and people depend entirely on *jangmadang* for everyday sustenance. However, all spheres of market activity are subject to state surveillance and regulation, as practical transactions are always regulated in the liminal space between formal and informal, legal and illegal, and spontaneous and planned. Under such abnormal circumstances, it is difficult for any semblance of market "order" to take root. What *is* in operation is an economy based on regulations, bribery, and contraband. Government regulations are routinely overridden with bribes to officials, from the lowest to the highest in rank.

Certain characteristics of Kim Jong-Un's North Korea—conspicuous consumption, urban development, speculative investment in real estate, state surveillance and control, bribery, and smuggling—are typical features of nations at the early stage of development, when they are accumulating capital. Outside observers often interpret such irrational economic behaviors as signs of imminent regime collapse in North Korea. However, some studies have pointed out that in the early stages of development, even corruption, graft, and bribery may strengthen unity among members of the elite, concentrating capital domestically and helping these developing countries overcome the inefficiencies of bureaucracy.[21]

---

* "Developmental state is a shorthand for the seamless web of political, bureaucratic, and moneyed influences that structures economic life in capitalist Northeast Asia. This state form originated as the region's idiosyncratic response to a world dominated by the West, and despite many problems associated with it, such as corruption and inefficiency, today state policies continue to be justified by the need to hone the nation's economic competitiveness and by a residual nationalism." Meredith Woo-Cumings, *The Developmental State* (London: Cornell University Press, 1999).

"Forward with the Speed of Masikryeong!"

On January 1, 2012, Kim Jong-Un announced his plan for North Korea in his first New Year's address. His vision of a "civilized socialist state" is a country where everyone would enjoy "a high level of socialist culture and the best form of civilization."[22] As promised, he began large-scale construction projects building fancy high-rise apartments, up-scale restaurants, department stores, and amusement parks in Pyongyang for North Koreans to enjoy a more affluent lifestyle.[23]

While the goal is now to become a developmental state, the resources at the disposal of the ruling power are limited to the mass mobilization system, a vestige of the previous era, in which socialism was the be-all and end-all. To secure a labor force without the necessary capital and technology, the state sends troops to construction sites and other industrial sites run by private interests. Soldiers are mobilized as free labor in the construction of various recreational, cultural, and welfare facilities as well as high-rise apartment buildings attracting private investors. In addition, North Korea recruits and manages the large-scale workforce that it sends abroad at the state level. If for no other reason than to manage such a large workforce, one that receives controlled wages or no wages at all, the ruling power still employs the political

Figure 3.7. A night opening at an amusement park: citizens and soldiers enjoying rides during the night opening of an amusement park in Pyongyang. Benoit Cappronnier

slogans and the dramaturgy of the theater state from an earlier era in which ideology reigned supreme.

It was during the construction of the Masikryeong Ski Resort that Kim Jong-Un gave his debut "on-site guidance." It may seem odd that the construction of a mere ski resort, using troops as free labor at that, should have been selected as the national project heralding the new leader. However, the nation soon went on a political and arts propaganda blitz, portraying the ski resort as the symbol of the advent of a new era. Soldiers who had participated in its construction gave testimony to the worthiness of carving a ski slope out of "a jungle," stating how proud they were to have been part of the project. In essence, it was the symbol of "a civilized state." In Pyongyang and throughout the country, giant banners were hung with the exhortation "Forward with the speed of the Masikryeong Ski Resort!" Skiing symbolized the speed with which they would build their "socialist civilization."

The Kim Jong-Un era demands high speed. The Chollima Movement of the Kim Il-Sung era, named after a mythical horse that could fly one thousand *li* (about three hundred miles), has given way to the "Mallima Movement," denoting a tenfold increase in speed. The Young General believes in, and emphasizes, the importance of new technology and science. Old recreational parks and swimming pools have been fully refurbished and reborn as dazzling theme parks complete with zipping rides and glittering neon signs. The city, formerly as dark as a wartime blackout exercise upon sunset, began to dazzle with the glow of neon lights. Fast-sprouting skyscrapers, stores selling never-before-seen goods, and new restaurants are changing the urban landscape. The central district of Pyongyang, where commemorative sculptures and monumental towers and buildings were once all there was of note, has taken on new life as an everyday space for people to enjoy leisure and cultural consumption. Such spatial and temporal reconfiguration has taken place not only in Pyongyang but extensively in major cities around the country. The "civilized socialist state" underscored by Kim Jong-Un is emerging at a rapid pace, glowing brightly, ironically with the help of the informal market economy.

A Leap in Technology

A more important "civilizational" change took place when state control over the distribution of cell phones for security reasons was eased and the spread of the new technology began to compress spatial and temporal distances nationwide. As of 2020, it was estimated that six million cell phones were in use in North Korea. Considering the issue of multiple phone ownership, it can be estimated that approximately 20 percent of the population now uses a mobile phone.[24] North Korea entered directly into the age of the wireless telephone, bypassing copper-wired telephone lines for every home. One must assume that North Korea is now experiencing transformational changes that are similar to (or much greater than) the changes South Korea experienced in the wake of the 1997 IMF bailout crisis, when it leaped full speed into the advanced IT industry.

Yuval Harari mentions that with technological developments in artificial intelligence and biotechnology, North Korea could develop a sophisticated surveillance system and control the thoughts and behavior of its people in more fundamental ways than what has been familiar to us so far.[25] He also suggests a number of scenarios for the possible fate of North and South Korea as this technological revolution plays out.[26]

The efficiency of "market socialism" has already been proven in large-scale urban development projects and infrastructure construction projects (e.g., roads and railways) in China and Vietnam. It makes a difference when the state has nationwide ownership of land. In fact, it has been reported that the new high-rise apartment buildings in Pyongyang utilize alternative energy sources, such as solar panels for electricity and geothermal technology, on a massive scale for heating. The underdevelopment of infrastructure in North Korea could actually act as an advantage when drastic changes are made.

In this respect, the theory that nations develop in successive stages is a stereotype, an ideologically driven notion from the Cold War era. Not every country has to take the same road to development, climbing the ladder one rung at a time. A country may pave its own path forward, achieving in one fell swoop what other nations took decades of incremental change to accomplish.

A New Reality

To outside observers, North Korea seems to remain largely unchanged. Military parades are still held in Kim Il-Sung Square next to the high-rise buildings going up on brighter streets. The Supreme Leader still sometimes wears a Mao suit and provides "field guidance" at missile launch sites, though he is a young man accompanied by a fashionable wife. The power elites in military uniforms still vote unanimously by holding up identical pocket note-books, but women's attire has become colorful on the streets of Pyongyang. People still bow down before statues of their leaders and sing songs of loyalty, but musicians play cheerful pop-style songs and dances. Underneath the unchanging appearance of the official system, steady changes are taking place at the level of ordinary daily life.

These changes are taking place informally. The structure of the formal system is left intact, while informal strategies create cracks and fissures. Since the famine, people have combined the resources, information, and experience they accumulated in the informal sector to overcome the institutionalized barriers of discrimination that remain in the official domain. These people are creating a new reality in the country. The changes have disturbed, and sometimes reversed, hitherto strict boundaries between center and periphery, between pure and polluted, between those with relatively more and those with relatively less favorable family backgrounds, and between men and women.

As the informal economy began triggering social change, the polarization that existed between center and periphery became less absolute. In particular, border cities such as Sinuiju, Chongjin Hyesan, and Nampo began showing a vitality unseen in Pyongyang, which is under the direct control of state power. With the spread of mobile phones and the increase in private means of transportation, state control over the population via geographical separation is weakening. While Pyongyang still receives preferential treatment, in reality, the privileges at work there are being undermined in various ways.

With the resources accumulated in the informal economy, more and more people are transcending the social barriers of class and *songbun*. Strategists with relatively low *songbun* achieve progress—through marriage, admission to the "right" schools, and business deals—elevating themselves to important positions, or raise their status by establishing ties with members of the privileged group.

Informal economic activities led by women in the *jangmadang* and in other emerging markets are substantially changing the existing patriarchal gender hierarchy in the country. Reflecting this change, even the official media has encouraged husbands to help with the housework.

Based on notions of purity and pollution, the formal system still makes rigid distinctions—"in" versus "out," "us" versus "them," and "normal" versus "abnormal." However, markets are flooded with foreign goods even as foreign popular culture is still officially considered contaminated and decadent.

Despite such widespread changes in the daily lives of the people, vested interests in North Korea still enforce political regulations and institutional discrimination in order to preserve privileges based on blood, class, region, and gender. They occasionally use the legal system, far removed from changes on the ground, as a political tool to exploit informal economic activities.

Some international observers interpret the changes taking place in North Korea as signs of a regime on its last legs. Others focus on the regime's theatrical shows of power and displays of military strength, denying that changes are taking place at all. What we need to understand is that although the gap between the formal system and informal strategies is growing, both are real, and they in fact function complementarily. Changes in North Korea are creating new realities throughout the country, born in the spaces between formal and informal spheres, each interacting with and influencing the other.

NOTES

1. See Ju-Won Kang, *Naneun Oneuldo Gukgyeongeul Mandeulgo Heomunda* [Today, I am still making and breaking the border] (Seoul: Geulhangari, 2013); *Amnokgangeun Dareuge Heureunda: Munhwaillyuhakjaui Nuneuro Bon, Gukgyeonggwa Gukjeogeul Neomeo Aungdaung Salgo Osundosun Jinaeneun Saramdeul Iyagi* [The Amnok River flows differently: The story of people quarreling and living in harmony beyond the barriers of national borders and identities, seen through the eyes of a cultural anthropologist] (Seoul: Nulmin, 2016).

2. Abito Ito, *Kitachosen No Jinmin No Seikatsu* [The lives of the North Korean people] (Tokyo: Koubundou Publishers, 2017), 434–35.

3. Caroline Humphrey, *The Unmaking of Soviet Life: Everyday Economies after Socialism* (Ithaca, NY: Cornell University Press, 2002).

4. Min Hong, "Bukhan Sijang Ilsangsaenghwal Yeongu: Geuroteseukeuwa Bujorigeug 'Sai' Eseo" [A study of daily life at a North Korean market: "Between" the grotesque and the theater of the absurd], in *Bukhanui Ilsangsaenghwal Segye: Oechimgwa Soksagim* [The world of everyday life in North Korea: Shouts and whispers], ed. Sun-Seon Park and Min Hong (Seoul: Haneul, 2010).

5. Abito Ito, *Kitachosen*, 434–36; Heonik Kwon, "'Seeking Good Luck' in North Korea," *Asia-Pacific Journal: Japan Focus* 20, no. 9 (2022), https://apjjf.org/2022/9/Kwon.html.

6. Abito Ito, *Kitachosen*, 387–404.

7. Byung-Ho Chung, "Preface: Namgwa Buk Aideul Eotteoke Kiulkka?" [How are children raised in the South and the North?], *Gaettongine Noriteo* [Gaettongi's playground], 2007.

8. Johan Huizinga, *The Autumn of the Middle Ages* (Chicago: University of Chicago Press, 1996).

9. Oral statement on New Year's Day by a woman from a city in Jagang Province. From Hak-Nak Choe, "Bukhan Seollarui Sobiwa Seonmul Yeongu: Uimuwa Wibanui Maegaeroseo Sul" [A study on New Year's Day consumption and gifts in North Korea: Alcohol as a medium of duty and transgression] (symposium proceedings, Korean Society for Cultural Anthropology, Fall 2019).

10. Hak-Nak Choe, "Bukhan Seollarui," 5.

11. Jin-Seok Choe, *Minjunggwa Geuroteseukeuui Munhwajeongchihak Mihail Baheuchingwa Saengseongui Sayu* [The cultural politics of *minjung* and the grotesque: Mikhail Bakhtin and generative speculation] (Seoul: Grinbi, 2017), 322–23.

12. Mikhail Bakhtin, *Rabelais and His World* (Bloomington: Indiana University Press, 1984).

13. Hyeon-Cheol Oh, *Songun Ryeongjanggwa Sarangui Segye* [*Songun* Leader General and the world of love] (Pyongyang: Pyongyang Publishing House, 2005).

14. Myeong-Ja Yi, "Kim Jong-Il Tongchi Sigi Gajok Mellodeurama Yeongu: Bukhan Geundaeseongui Byeonhwareul Jungsimeuro" [A study on family melodramas during the reign of Kim Jong-Il: With a focus on changes in modernity in North Korea] (PhD diss., Dongguk University, 2005), 117–21.

15. Michael de Certeau, *The Practice of Everyday Life* (Berkeley: University of California Press, 1984).

16. James Scott, *Weapons of the Weak: Everyday Forms of Peasant Resistance* (New Haven, CT: Yale University Press, 1985).

17. For further discussion on the mechanism of the *sinso* ombudsman system, see Sung Kyung Kim, "Bukhan Jeongchichejewa 'Maeumui Seupsok': Juche Sasanggwa Sinso Jedoui Jakdongeul Jungsimeuro" [The North Korean political regime and the "mind convention": With a focus on *juche* ideology and the workings of the Sinso institution], *Hyeondai Bukhan Yeongu* [Review of North Korean studies] 21, no. 2 (2018): 191–231.

18. Byung-Ho Chung, "North Korean Refugees as Penetrant Transnational Migrants," *Urban Anthropology and Studies of Cultural Systems and World Economic Development* 43, no. 4 (2014): 329–61.

19. For a quick survey of various media programs showcasing North Korean defectors in South Korea, see Elise Hu, "South Korea's Newest TV Stars Are North Korean Defectors," NPR, January 31, 2016, https://www.npr.org/sections/parallels/2016/01/31/464798910/south-koreas-newest-tv-stars-are-north-korean-defectors (accessed March 6, 2020).

20. Daniel Tudor and James Pearson, *North Korea Confidential: Private Markets, Fashion Trends, Prison Camps, Dissenters and Defectors*, 2nd ed. (Clarendon, VT: Tuttle, 2020); Seong-Ha Ju, *Pyongyang Jabonjuui Baekgwasajeon: Ju Seong-Ha Gijaga Jeonhaneun Jinjja Bukhan Iyagi* [Encyclopedia of Pyongyang capitalism: Real North Korea stories as told by reporter Ju Seong-Ha] (Seoul: Bukdodeum, 2018).

21. Su-Il Jeon, *Gwanryo Bupaeron* [Theory on bureaucratic corruption] (Seoul: Seonhaksa, 1999), 70–74, 81–85.

22. "Gongdong Saseol [Joint editorial]," *Rodong Sinmun*, January 1, 2012.

23. Sung Kyung Kim, "Change and Continuity: North Korean Society at a Crossroads," Global Asia 16, no. 3 (2021): 55.

24. Min-Kwan Kim, "Choegeun Bukhan Smatupon Iyong Hunhwang Mit Sisajon" [The current condition and implications of the usage of smart phones in North Korea], in *Weekly KDB Report* (Seoul: Korean Development Bank, 2020).

25. Yuval Harari, "Introduction to Korean Edition," in *Homo Deus: Miraeui Yeoksa* [Homo deus: A brief history of tomorrow], translated into Korean by Myeong-Ju Kim (Paju: Gimm-Young Publishers, 2017), 6–11.

26. Harari suggests that North Korea could potentially achieve a new breakthrough technology ahead of South Korea by taking advantage of the fact that it is an authoritarian developing nation with a centralized power system. He argues that North Korea could potentially bypass a legislative conundrum and quickly implement a total system change. China has already taken advantage of authoritarian centralized power by starting a nationwide digital surveillance system. Harari, *Homo Deus*, 8–10.

Chapter Four

A Bold Class Society

A socialist state is not necessarily a state that preserves social equality. The difference lies only in the structure and content of the inequality. People in many countries throughout history have learned that many regimes that advocated justice were not just and that other regimes that called for freedom and democracy delivered neither. The same is true for North Korea. The state ideology espouses an equal society without discrimination, but the reality is that people experience all sorts of inequality. In this chapter, I discuss the social hierarchy and the five types of discrimination that are most prevalent in North Korea: discrimination between center and periphery, discrimination based on *songbun* (family background), discrimination based on purity and pollution, discrimination based on education and class, and discrimination based on gender. Let us start with the "Pyongyang Line," the line between Pyongyang and the periphery, where all forms of discrimination collide.

CENTER AND PERIPHERY

Pyongyang is very different from the rest of the country, though the state is reluctant to admit it. Thanks to the extended period of my engagement in relief activities in North Korea, I was able to crisscross the provinces on several occasions. On my visits to North Korea, each journey to a provincial city was inevitably accompanied by a fierce negotiation over the itinerary and a grueling process involving making arrangements with the proper authorities.

Pyongyang and the Provinces

Checkpoints were stationed on all roads leading into the capital city. The clearance process was not as simple as merely checking IDs and then letting travelers through. I saw various people—from middle-aged women with heavy rucksacks to service men and women and youths in uniform—anxiously pacing about, waiting their turn. The tension was palpable, as it is at most international border checkpoints.

The first time I passed through a checkpoint to leave the city, I immediately understood why the authorities were so reluctant to open other areas to foreign visitors. Not only the roads and buildings but also the clothes people wore, the expressions on their faces, their gait, and their attitudes were all different. While a material difference existed in living standards, a visible gap also existed at the level of sociocultural welfare.

Naturally, many North Koreans want to live in Pyongyang. In many metropolitan cities around the world, housing prices continue to rise due to a population influx from rural areas and smaller municipalities; urban shantytowns and slums have become a universal feature of the world's metropolises, in large part due to such inflows of people. Pyongyang's border control system, unmatched in the world, makes it an exception to this phenomenon.[1] So far apart are the two realms that residents of Pyongyang carry a "Pyongyang citizen's card" that differs from the ID used by those dwelling in the provinces.

Not only is entry into Pyongyang controlled, but the regime also started to evict people from Pyongyang during the famine. The regime called this an "evacuation," resurrecting a historical term used by the colonial authorities of Imperial Japan when they forcibly transferred urban residents to provincial areas toward the end of the Asia-Pacific War. Doing so showed that the North Korean government conceptualized the severe famine as a crisis tantamount to war. At first, the authorities even held farewell ceremonies for those ordered to evacuate, framing evictions using such phrases as a "foray into the provinces" or a "relocation to support rural communities."

The question then arose of who should be sent. Those with impure *songbun* and those considered a threat to the regime had already been expelled from Pyongyang in the 1970s and 1980s on several occasions, making the task of selecting more people to evict from the remaining pool difficult. Nevertheless, under the duress of the crisis, potential lines of division surfaced, becoming yardsticks for eviction. Those with less prestigious family backgrounds became the first targets. Next came those who had caused trouble in their neighborhood units or at their workplaces, those who had been caught committing minor offenses during daily inspections, and even those who had irritated their bosses.

Figure 4.1. Defend unto death! A sign reading "Let us become the fortress and shield for defending, unto death, Pyongyang where the revolutionary leaders live." Byung-Ho Chung

In *Purity and Danger*, anthropologist Mary Douglas argues that a society's mainstream could actually invent deviation.[2] To define someone as "matter out of place," she wrote, the mainstream can simply move the boundaries of the place itself. In other words, the mainstream need not wait for perpetrators to break rules, because it can change the rules in order to make certain groups deviants or to render them subversive or impure elements. The widespread crisis presented by the famine meant that the rules used to discriminate center from periphery in North Korea were constantly shifting.

Dispatch Order to a Province

In August 1997, Choe Jini, a woman writer in Pyongyang, was ordered to move to the provinces. Her family was being expelled due to a misdemeanor committed by her husband and was given five days to pack—a death sentence for her and her family, she thought. Among those forced to leave Pyongyang due to the actions of their spouses, many applied for divorces for the sake of the rest of their families. In response, the authorities issued an emergency order prohibiting divorces for evacuees. As she left Pyongyang, she feared for her safety among the "vulgar people" outside the capital because they had "no moral sense and there was venom in their manner of speech."[3]

The writer had been banished to Chongjin, North Hamgyeong Province. Upon her arrival, she found it to be less hellish than expected. An unexpectedly lively atmosphere shone through the immiserated cityscape. In part due to its proximity to the Korean autonomous prefectures in China and the Rason (Rajin-Sonbong) Special Economic Zone in North Korea, Chongjin was one of the few cities where one could make ends meet in accordance with the policy of self-sustainment after the collapse of the distribution system. In 1998, before the official introduction of markets in North Korea, a huge number of *jangmadang* markets cropped up, and various processed foods and goods from China as well as local seafood circulated around the region. Because of its geographical distance from Pyongyang, the grip of central government control was relatively loose in Chongjin. The city took advantage of the circumstances and was rapidly growing into a new base in the country's informal economy. The writer was impressed by the vitality of the local city compared to Pyongyang, which was still clinging to the collapsing distribution system. The then up-and-coming Sunnam Market in Chongjin still sets fashion trends for North Korea to this day.

The writer, an alumna of a prestigious university in Pyongyang, started contacting her college friends in a bid to survive by relying on her network. Most of them had also been banished to the provinces after being targeted for revolutionary reeducation. Those like her who had been relocated maintained personal ties with their relatives and college cohorts in Pyongyang, dreaming of the day when their children, if not they themselves, could return to the capital as a result of excellent achievement in work and education. In short, even the elites in the periphery oriented their values and priorities around Pyongyang.

The Pyongyangers

In 2008, when the Kaesong Industrial Complex was up and running and it was possible for South Koreans to tour the city, souvenir shops, restaurants, and pop-up shops selling local products sprung up to cater to tourists.

After a meeting in a restaurant at the center of the city, I perused the souvenir shops selling local specialty goods. Young women dressed in *hanbok* were selling goods in a parking lot with a few cars with Seoul license plates. Upon talking to the women, I realized they were speaking in the standard Pyongyang accent. At first I thought these "cultured" accents were put on, but this was not the case. The women had come from Pyongyang, as did most North Koreans charged with interacting with South Koreans.

Wanting to buy some souvenirs, I turned to the pop-up stores lining the parking lot. Just then, my guide from Kaesong asked me in a low voice if I would follow her. I saw a small stand in an out-of-the-way spot nearby. Our counterparts from Pyongyang were ahead of me. I asked the Kaesong guide why she was taking me to these stalls in particular. "Over there at the parking lot are the tables set up by the Pyongyang blighters," she replied. "Over here in the alley we have tables run by people from Kaesong."

"Pyongyangers" even got first pick of the spots at every tourist site in Kaesong, giving them an advantage over the locals in earning money from South Korean tourists. Sympathizing with the Kaesong people, I made my way to the Kaesong stand.

There I bought some liquor made with genuine Kaesong ginseng. Evidently, no bottles or bottle caps were available for the bottling of liquor in Kaesong. Instead, merchants sealed the ginseng and liquor by melting the open ends of glass tubes, adopting a technique used for vials of liquid medicine used for injections. To borrow a North Korean motto, the spirit of the historically famous merchants of Kaesong was undergoing "self-sustainment" in an ingenious way. To this day, I have yet to open the liquor I bought there.

Center Orientation

In early 2001, I was invited to give a lecture at Hanawon, a governmental acculturation training institution established to assist North Korean refugees as they settle in the South. On the first day of class, I ran into a violent protest at the entrance to the building. The protest was so intense that the riot police were called in. It had been organized by those who had been assigned to live in cities outside of metropolitan Seoul via a lottery-type selection process. Their complaint was that they had come to South Korea expecting freedom and were angered to be relegated to the provinces once more.

Staff in charge explained that there was a shortage of government-subsidized rental apartments in Seoul to assign to them, meaning that some people would have to be settled in the provinces. They remained unconvinced. They asked, "Why me?" firmly believing that once "pushed out," it would be a Sisyphean task to make their way up the rungs to Seoul.

Officials from the Ministry of Unification insisted that Seoul, located in the "free Republic of Korea," could not be compared to Pyongyang. But the refugees seemed to intuitively recognize the reality of discrimination based on the distinction between center and periphery in South Korea, about half of the nation's population being concentrated in the Seoul metropolitan area with political and economic power consolidated in the capital. Among those refugees who had been assigned to the provinces, many refused to settle in those areas, choosing to lead itinerant existences in Seoul instead, leaving their apartments in the provinces empty.*

Young refugees also opted for a capital-centered adaptation strategy. During the Cold War era, a policy was instituted granting North Korean refugees admission to universities without requiring them to take the notoriously difficult entrance examinations. Many took advantage of this system and were admitted to prestigious universities in Seoul, regardless of their academic achievements. Most eventually dropped out after several leaves of absence, having failed to adapt to the ruthlessly competitive university environment. The consequences of their failures were complex. A diploma from a prestigious school is a crucial standard for evaluating a person in South Korea. It has powerful symbolic value, and school connections sometimes make or break deals. Conversely, for those who cannot withstand the level of competition, failure to secure such qualifications is a source of anxiety and frustration.

When international interest in North Korean human rights issues peaked, some young refugees who had failed to navigate the South Korean education system "defected" a second time, seeking refugee status in the United States, Canada, Britain, or Germany. "It's where everyone wants to go, isn't it?" asked a young refugee who had successfully made it to one of the countries that many South Korean middle-class youths aspire to reach.[4]

---

* Sociologist Kang Joon-Mann analyzes how Seoul-centered politics and education reproduce the power structure in South Korea. See Joon-Mann Kang, *Seouldaeeui Nara* [The country of Seoul National University] (Wonju: Gaemagoweon, 1996).

FAMILY BACKGROUND AND SOCIAL HIERARCHY

"Are You from a Landlord Family?"

While chatting with guides in Pyongyang one day, I mentioned that my mother's family was from Suweon but that she had attended a school for women in Seoul during the colonial era. The supervisor looked me straight in the eye and asked: "Were they landlords?" I was taken aback by his cold look and the change in his tone. My mother's family did own a vineyard, and moreover, they had been Christians for generations. I realized then, "Ah! It would have been difficult to live here under such a gaze."

The North Korean state was founded immediately after the peninsula's liberation from Japanese rule, and socialism was its guiding ideology. In the course of building the state, premised on the Marxist view of class struggle, its founders gave preferential treatment to the exploited classes, namely the laborers and poor peasants, while suppressing landlords, wealthy farmers, merchants, and entrepreneurs. Former independence fighters received preferential treatment, while collaborators who had assisted the imperial government, army, or police force were punished. In other words, the founders attempted to realize social justice in their postcolonial nation by inverting the hierarchy of the colonial era.

In the process, considerable coercive force, both physical and otherwise, was mobilized to deprive pro-Japanese collaborators and various elites of their former privileges. Measures were taken to prevent collaborators from returning to their previous positions of social dominance, the founders being wary of the possibility that these individuals might utilize their sociocultural capital even after their property had been confiscated.

National liberation and the completion of the socialist revolution were the purported goals of the North Korean state, the foundation of its political legitimacy, and its raison d'être. A person's political status was thus defined in accordance with both their prerevolutionary social class and their qualifications, as well as their ability to serve the state's goals. The terms *songbun* or *chulsin songbun* (the makeup of one's family background) are generally used to refer to the political status of individuals. *Songbun* classification serves as the basis on which important administrative decisions, including those concerning education and food distribution, are made.[5]

Family backgrounds were defined according to one's social class at the time of national independence, that is, the social class of the grand- or great-grandparents of the current generation. The hierarchy ranked the following groups in order of decreasing prestige: industrial workers, tenant farmers, poor farmers, office workers, middle-class farmers, craftspeople, merchants, entrepreneurs, rich farmers, and landlords and capitalists. Since the founding of the nation, individual contributions to the socialist state (or loyalty to the Leader) have determined the social class of one's descendants.[6]

Reverse Discrimination and Hereditary Hierarchy

In addition to the official classification of individuals based on family background prior to the revolution, the state also distinguishes people by "class" or "group," claiming that the revolution is a process of struggle and that it is necessary to clearly distinguish the "core [*haeksim*] class" driving the revolution from the "hostile [*chokdae*] class" it targets and the "agitated [*dongyo*] class" in the middle.[*]

The party further divides these three major classes into as many as fifty-one subclasses. The categories change depending on changes in party line or policy, with classes being newly added or deleted. It is hard to confirm the details with any certainty, no official documents having been released on policies pertaining to the groups. However, what is clear is that resource allocation and social discrimination are based on this detailed, as yet unofficial, classification system. The public is not privy to the specific details of the classification system. However, as the widespread use of terms such as "good family background" and "bad origins" shows, it is well known that such a system exists and that it has a significant impact on people's lives.[7]

What needs to be pointed out with respect to social classification by *songbun* is the problem of guilt by association, which punishes not only the perpetrators but their family members and descendants across generations. After independence, landlords, pro-Japanese collaborators, defectors to the South, and Christians were persecuted under the guilt-by-association premise. This phenomenon is not unique to North Korea. In South Korea, a similar system was applied to family members of left-leaning political prisoners and defectors (and abductees) to the North. In the South, family members of those deemed guilty were barred from government office or employment at most companies, many of which required a certificate of ideological position (*sinwonbojeung*). Such undesirables were restricted from traveling abroad, the rules only being relaxed in the late 1980s following democratization. The regimes in both South and North Korea have used guilt-by-association systems to monitor and suppress social groups deemed to be threatening.

---

* According to CIA analyst Helen-Louise Hunter, the North Korean *songbun* system was highly successful in turning the prerevolutionary social structure upside down, and the "preferred (core) class" consists of 30 percent of the population, the "ordinary (agitated)" make up the middle 40 percent, and the "undesirables (hostile)" make up the bottom 30 percent. Helen-Louise Hunter, *Kim Il-song's North Korea* (Westport, CT: Praeger Publishers, 1999).

The hereditary succession of power in North Korea solidified and justified a system similar to the Confucian status system and social hierarchy of the Chosun dynasty. The nascent socialist state legitimized discrimination based on family background as a "revolutionary" measure. Turned on its head, such discrimination has become institutionalized as a formidable tool for exclusion as well as the preservation of privileges. Over the past seventy years, privileges gained in such a manner have been passed down between members of three or four generations of elites.*

The principle of discrimination based on guilt by association was also applied to regions. Political infighting and *songbun* reclassification were all practiced as power became concentrated around the Leader. In the process, many were expelled to remote areas, while those deemed loyal and competent by the regime were brought to Pyongyang.

The hereditary succession of power by the Supreme Leader's kin takes place in the name of the "Baekdu bloodline." The families of the other founding fathers of the nation—that is, anti-Japanese armed fighters—are collectively called the "Mount Baekdu Branch." They, too, pass down their ranks and privileges to succeeding generations via a hereditary system. The families of war heroes are collectively known as the "backbone of revolution," forming an extended network of families and relatives who inherit and pass down their status. These groups form a community bound by a common destiny, sharing not only blood ties but also various other forms of social connection with each other, all centered around Pyongyang. Often the graduates of the most elite schools in North Korea, they are bound together by blood, school network, and residence in Pyongyang.

Strategies for Upward Mobility

Despite the existence of a strict hierarchy related to family background and rank, class "migration" does take place in exceptional cases. An individual with outstandingly high exam scores or one whose loyalty is particularly exemplary can move up the ladder, regardless of family background. However such exceptions are exceedingly rare. As a result, recipients often believe their social promotions to be "special gifts from the Leader." A North Korean refugee I met in Seoul told me that, in spite of her bad family background—a product of her parents' past as landlords who moved to the South—she had

---

* The social impact of the guilt-by-association system was also grave in South Korea. Particularly hard hit were people from Jeju Island involving the 4.3 incident, the Yeosu-Suncheon area, and areas occupied by the North Korean forces during the Korean War. Many from these regions fell behind or were excluded from the benefits of postwar national development, which led to their becoming the target of further social discrimination.

studied hard, trusting only in the Leader. "The Leader granted me the honor of becoming a doctor by allowing me to enroll in medical college," she said. Even after defecting to the South, she was still thankful.*

In North Korea, an individual is not free from the regime and the Leader; individualism and liberalism are moral sins that could hurt one's family for generations to come. Thus, when one's spouse commits a political fault, one publicly blames the ex-partner for the divorce and remarries, all to protect the children. Amid the epidemic of family suicides during the Great Famine, it was common to find suicide notes placing sole blame on the incompetence of the family itself rather than on the actions of the Leader or the regime. Such notes were clearly composed in a way that would help to safeguard surviving family members from negative ramifications involving their family background.

For the same reason, most North Korean refugees are reluctant to publicly reveal their names and faces in South Korea, and many of them (35 percent of married women) claim to have been divorced in North Korea. In the North, defection is viewed as such a betrayal of the Leader and the regime that it would result in the downgrading of the family status of one's (ex-)spouse, children, and relatives. For this reason, many refugees are racked with guilt and gripped by concern for the safety of the families they left behind in North Korea.

The Great Famine wreaked havoc on social order, disturbing the *songbun*-based system of discrimination. Those already active in the *jangmadang* and other venues of informal economic activity were not elites endowed with good *songbun*. With the resources they had accumulated in the informal economic sector, they were able to buy social rank or otherwise overcome the limitations they had encountered in the past due to their backgrounds.

Individuals deployed various strategies in order to clandestinely raise their rank and status. Destroying or falsifying one's family background records was a risky but quick solution. When tampering with *songbun* documentation became too rampant, in 2010 the regime began digitizing records, starting with the new citizen cards carried by Pyongyang residents. But paths to higher status remained. Marriage to a party member allowed those of lesser status to dilute their bad *songbun*. Many such unions began to appear, allowing those of lower rank newfound access to the capital. In terms of education,

---

* The doctor, who had defected from the North during the famine with the help of her family in the South, said that she had been successful in North Korea because she had trusted *opoi suryeongnim* ("Great Leader, the Father"), worked hard, and lived by his words. Now, she thought that she had to "believe in and obey God, the Father, [in order] to be blessed and well-off in South Korea." She mentioned the "Ten Principles for the Establishment of the Monolithic Ideological System," which are considered sacred in the North. She then asked me: "Aren't they and the Ten Commandments of Christianity the same?" (from an interview by the author, June 2000).

students with low *songbun* bribed teachers and party officials in order to gain access to universities in Pyongyang. Such people are changing the present and future composition of Pyongyang.

The socialist countries that emerged from victorious revolutions in the twentieth century promised to eradicate social discrimination and inequality. However, they failed to prevent the advent of new privileged classes and the revival of previous ones. North Korea undid the existing order of social hierarchy, replacing it with a new order based on *songbun*. Today, the country still adheres to the postrevolutionary class order. Only, this order has evolved into a system that further solidifies existing boundaries and reproduces class hierarchy. The regime calls this "Korean-style" socialism, claiming that its elites are still engaged in a revolutionary fight against imperialism and that the logic of postcolonial liberation from more than seven decades ago is still valid. These are its justifications for maintaining a system that perpetuates rampant new forms of social inequality and discrimination today.

PURITY AND POLLUTION

This type of system, in which individuals are included or excluded based on their social backgrounds, is not unique to North Korea, with variants found in many socialist countries. It stems from the Soviet psychological theory that claims that the environment in which a person matures significantly influences the formation of identity, also determining a person's ideological leaning. In the case of North Korea, the socialism-rooted principles of classification and exclusion were combined with traditional concepts of "purity" and "pollution," becoming much more rigid and intense in the process.

"My Family Background Is Clean"

"I come from a poor peasant family, and because of my family background [*songbun*], I served as the head of my neighborhood unit [*inminban*]."

As the female refugee spoke, an old man, also a refugee from the North, responded, "I come from the landlord class, and I was accused of having rotten thoughts all the time."

"My grandfather went down to the South, and I couldn't go to college because of that blemish."

"My uncle's family was kicked out of the party as a sectarian. We were suspected of having been infected with the same bad thoughts and were barred from becoming party members."

"The families of revolutionaries had the purest *songbun*, and they had advantages in gaining admission to colleges and becoming party members."

Once one person started, others rushed to recount how their *songbun* had determined their quality of life in North Korea. Many refugees said that they had faced discrimination due to their bad *songbun* or the political misdeeds of family members or relatives. Still, a significant number of refugees boasted of the preferential treatment they had received for the opposite reason. Regardless of their position, they used terms like "clean," "dirty," "rotten," "pure," "blemish" and "infection." Social occupations and behaviors are seen from a political perspective and classified as "pure" or "polluted"; these categories were transmitted along family lines.[8]

In this cultural system, not only those accused of being "polluted" but also those associated with undesirables are shunned due to assumed contamination. People suspected of being polluted meet hurdles when it comes to marriage, college admission, career choices, and promotions. They make up a lower rung of society.

The hierarchical class system, combined with the concept of purity and pollution, makes marriages across class lines difficult. A marriage, especially with someone belonging to a polluted class, is not simply a matter of personal choice. It is a dangerous affair that could taint oneself and one's family down the line. Refugees I spoke to lamented the social discrimination that they and their families had experienced due to marriages across the boundary between pure and impure.

Only the Leader can "cleanse" those socially stigmatized by their family backgrounds or misdeeds. "Virtuous vignettes" featuring Kim Il-Sung and Kim Jong-Il depict them pardoning and reinstating talented people whose competence was ignored because of their backgrounds. The leaders did not abolish the discriminatory system itself. Thus, the individual granting of pardons by the Leaders remained exceptional and special events.

Racial Discrimination

"Are you an anthropology professor?" A young guide asked me this question, his eyes twinkling, as I was climbing Mount Kumgang. "Have you researched the earliest origins of our people?" He said that he had picked up an interest in anthropology while studying the origins of the Korean nation. Judging by his words, it seemed that he equated anthropology with the fields of ethnology and eugenics from the old days.

A few years later, in 2007, at a hotel bookstore in Pyongyang, I found a book titled *In Search of Our Ancestors from Very Long Ago*, published by the Social Science Press in Pyongyang. The book claimed: "From the dawn of human history, our ancestors were not only at a higher stage of evolution in comparison to their contemporaries, but they were also at a higher level by far spiritually." In particular, "incomparably more neoanthropic fossils are found along the Daedong River in the Pyongyang area than in any other region of the world." It further elaborated: "Our ancestors, who were still evolving at the time, were remarkably wise and effective, and they were the first people to evolve into the complete form of the modern *Homo sapiens* in the East."[9]

Scholars in North Korea were trying to "scientifically" link Korea's Tangun creation myth to the origins of humanity itself. One of the book's authors, Chang U-Jin, frankly admits that "the matter of human origins is a political rather than a scholarly issue," selectively introducing findings of the latest excavations of human fossils worldwide in the text. He concludes that "our ancestors who have lived in the land of Chosun since a very long time ago were at the forefront to lead" the evolutionary process of all humanity.

Regardless of where they were born, the author argues, the Korean people are "the direct descendants of the Tangun Chosun people who founded the first ancient state [of Korea] in Pyongyang and achieved the community of the nation."[10] As for evidence, he claims that morphological traits in skulls found around Pyongyang distinguish Koreans from neighboring peoples.[11]

Such logic bears similarities to the rationale for claims about the mythicized Tenson tribe in Japan. Historians of Imperial Japan sought to establish as historical facts the origins of the emperor system and its "one lineage of ten thousand generations," and physical anthropologists, focusing on eugenics, attempted to prove that Japanese people were superior to neighboring ethnic groups, such as the Ainu, Okinawans, Taiwanese, Koreans, and Chinese. Nazi Germany, which was championing eugenics in Europe at the time, went one step further, identifying the physical characteristics of the Aryan people and outlawing marriage between Aryans and "polluted" ethnic groups, such as Jewish and Romany people, in order to protect ethnic purity.*

The United States and Britain, which accused their German and Japanese enemies of racism, had their own deep-rooted prejudices and practiced their own forms of discrimination and eugenics against ethnic minorities. The book *Race* by Ruth Benedict, published during World War II, analyzed and criticized racism in the United States as well as its enemies. Its argument—that

---

* The Nazi obsession with eugenics, purity, and pollution had an impact on people with mental disorders and genetic illnesses through the enactment of the "sterilization law," and even the massacre of such people at the end of the war. In Imperial Japan and colonial Korea, people with Hansen's disease (leprosy) were forcibly isolated, castrated, and sterilized. Due to the eugenics-based prejudices and ethnic discrimination that were widespread from the onset of modernity, there are still people who shun social contact with other ethnic groups, to say nothing of marriage with them, in their belief that "the blood of other people is dirty."

ethnicity was associated with the notion of pollution in American society—was so provocative at that time that the US military banned the book.[12]

According to testimonies by North Korean refugees during the famine, the most extreme example of discrimination based on the concepts of "purity" and "pollution" took the form of forced abortions performed on women caught in China and sent back to North Korea. These women were not only forced to abort their pregnancies but were scolded and humiliated for carrying "dirty foreign blood." Some pleaded that their sexual partners had been ethnic Korean Chinese, but to no avail. Those possessing foreign nationalities were also considered to be dangerous and polluted.[13]

I shuddered while listening to their accounts of the outrageous violations of human rights that had taken place in the name of purity. At the same time, I recalled the numerous "children of mixed blood" in postwar South Korea of the 1960s and the signboards of ob-gyn clinics known for performing illegal abortions that I came across on the streets of Itaewon near the largest US military camp in Seoul. *Honhyeol*, the word used to denote mixed ethnic background in Korean, already had the connotation of "abnormality" as well as that of "mixture with heterogeneous blood" as opposed to "pure blood."*

On April 27, 2006, the North Korean newspaper *Rodong Sinmun* carried an article warning: "Recently, South Korea has been playing a bizarre game of pursuing a 'multi-ethnic, multicultural society,' while obliterating the essential character of our people." The article called homogeneity "the pride of our people that no other people in the world have," and "the spiritual fountainhead of national unity essential in the struggle to achieve our people's everlasting advancement and prosperity." Blaming the US military occupation, the paper claimed that the debate concerning a "multicultural" and "multiethnic" society in the South was "an intolerable discourse on annihilating the Korean people, a negation of the homogeneity of our people, and an attempt to make South Korea heterogeneous, mixed up, and Americanized."[14]

After the inter-Korean summit in June 2000, there was an increase in the number of South Korean visitors to the North as well as growth in inter-Korean exchanges. Given that South Korean visitors wield far greater socioeconomic power than the North Koreans they meet, the North Korean regime presumably had to clearly define the in/out boundary again. The image of South Korea as heterogeneous and polluted was underscored around this time. Contrasting with North Korea, self-portrayed as a country that

---

* Nobel laureate writer and human rights activist Pearl Buck established the Sosa Opportunity Center in 1967 in order to provide care and education for about two thousand biracial children after observing that they were discriminated against even by beggars in South Korea. See Peter J. Conn, *Pearl S. Buck: A Cultural Biography* (Cambridge: Cambridge University Press, 1996).

safeguarded the "purity" of the Korean nation, South Korea was maligned as a "polluted" multiethnic and multiracial country.[15]

In the early twentieth century, the ideal of the Socialist International was to realize equality and working-class solidarity that transcended borders. Today, the socialist North and the capitalist South have inverse official positions on ethnicity and equality.

Discrimination against the Disabled

"Pyongyang is the face of our country. As people judge people by their faces, foreign visitors judge the level of the development in our country by the looks of Pyongyang. That is why we must keep Pyongyang clean. Keeping Pyong-yang in good order is like cleaning the face of our country."[16]

So said Kim Il-Sung in 1987. His directive was implemented, as "only physically and spiritually healthy people must be allowed to live in Pyong-yang," becoming a principle that is still strictly maintained.[17] The deaf, the physically disabled, and the mentally ill were forcibly relocated to the prov-inces, along with their families. Disabled people—not only in Pyongyang but also in Nampo, Kaesong, and Chongjin, the other cities most exposed to the eyes of foreign visitors—were relocated to mountainous areas and remote islands. Disabled war veterans and accident victims, even those from the higher rungs of society, were no exception. As a matter involving saving the face of the nation, the supreme task was to make such people "invisible" on the streets of Pyongyang.

According to Erving Goffman, who studied social stigma as a mechanism involving exclusion and discrimination against those with features that a society considers to be undesirable, there are three types of stigmatization. The first is based on physical flaws and disabilities, the second on character flaws such as treasonous beliefs, unnatural feelings, mental illness, and lack of willpower. The third is tribal or collective stigmatization based on, for example, race, ethnicity, or religion. Such traits are transmitted along family lines and can taint entire families when stigmatized.[18]

People cannot be cleanly divided into either "normal" or "stigmatized" groups; such division is a matter of perspective. In the course of a lifetime, anyone can encounter situations that cause them to become either "stigma-tized" or perceived as positively. Nonetheless, once individuals or a group of people are stigmatized, they are subject to defamation and shame, suffering discrimination that robs them of opportunities. It is rare to find a modern nation-state that has formulated a system that officially segregates and dis-criminates against all types of stigmatized people. However, North Korea has maintained such a system for decades.

A disabled person belonging to the "core class" would be sent alone to facilities for the disabled located in the vicinity of Pyongyang. Their family could pay them visits, but they themselves would not be allowed to visit Pyongyang. Ito Abito, a Japanese anthropologist who studies daily life in North Korea, has cited an exception to this in which a Japanese woman disabled by polio was allowed to live in Pyongyang.[19]

The woman was a famous painter who went to live in Pyongyang after marrying a *zainichi* Korean in Japan. She was expelled from Pyongyang to the provinces because of her disability. Thanks to the efforts of the pro-Pyongyang General Association of Korean Residents in Japan, which used financial pressure to plead with the authorities on her behalf, she was finally allowed to live with her family in the outskirts of Pyongyang. However, not allowed to leave the house, she was unable to attend the opening of her own exhibition in downtown Pyongyang.

In the mid-2000s, a South Korean woman who had battled childhood polio visited Pyongyang. On the streets of Pyongyang, she made a rare sight, as the city had not seen anyone with a visible disability in decades. Citizens of Pyongyang saw a handicapped woman smiling brightly and engaging in lively conversation with other people. Instead of showing wariness toward a person who must have seemed "abnormal" by their standards, many actively expressed curiosity and goodwill toward her. In this case, a system of public order imposed from above could not suppress the natural expression of human emotion.

The woman's NGO group visited a research institution. There, she introduced herself as a college professor. The North Korean women there immediately started whispering: "Wow! She's a professor!" "Married, at that!" "You know, we've only heard about women married to disabled heroic veterans." When the official visit ended, a woman came up to her. Her eyes were wet, and falteringly she said, "Goodness. Thank you." Another veteran researcher at the institute, older than his colleagues, took her hand in his, his face full of emotion and appreciation.

EDUCATION AND CLASS REPRODUCTION

"A Professor's Son Becomes a Professor, and a Farmer's Son Becomes a Farmer"

Nearly every high-ranking Korean Workers' Party (KWP) member I met in North Korea was a graduate of Kim Il-Sung University. When I asked one party cadre that I spoke to about his son, he beamed, saying that the boy was attending his alma mater and majoring in political economy, just like his

Figure 4.2. Children pushing handcarts to help fix potholes in a rural road in North Hamgyong Province. AP Photo, David Guttenfelder

old man. "He seems to have done OK," the man said. While his words were modest, his pride was unmistakable. Upon being asked about his son's plans, the man said: "I suppose he will become a party worker like me. Isn't that natural? Isn't it best for the son of a professor to become a professor, the son of a farmer a farmer, and the son of a party worker a party worker?" At first I doubted my own ears. How could he be so confident, and so explicit, in stating that class reproduction was natural and good?

"Are there not complaints of inequality?"

"No, that is the story in capitalism," he rebutted. "In our society, occupation has no hierarchy. Everyone is equal, so it is better, more efficient, for children to succeed their parents [in their careers]."

I wanted to ask him if a farmer, a miner, or an assembly line worker might think the same. But I held my tongue. He was only speaking *his* mind. It was an opportunity to understand the principles and the values at work in reality.

TV broadcasts in Pyongyang often show model farmers, researchers, and workers who followed in their parents' footsteps career-wise. Among athletes, artists, circus troupers, and writers, a good portion inherit the career of one of their parents. It occurred to me that regime succession is also justified in this context. Or, rather, it seemed that, thanks to the power succession of the Supreme Leaders, career "succession" was encouraged, even for elite positions at the core of the power structure. The prevalence of occupational inheritance is comparable to that of wealth inheritance in other societies. In order to understand class hierarchy in a particular nation, and how it is maintained or changed, the cultural norms of equality, as well as their real-life consequences, must be examined.

The proclamation of socialism or revolution alone guarantees neither an equal society nor a society in pursuit of equality. The question is how inequality and social class differ in capitalism and socialism. That is to say, which inequalities are accepted by socialists as natural consequences of their system, and which ones are accepted as natural consequences of lawful competition in capitalism?

Helicopter Moms in Pyongyang

I had rare opportunities to meet with mothers in Pyongyang who spoke candidly about their children's education and preparation for college admission. While neither home visits nor personal contact with local residents were allowed during my visits to Pyongyang, such windows of opportunity miraculously opened now and then.

As a cultural anthropologist in Pyongyang, I was so excited and curious that I often woke up in the middle of the night and found myself unable to go back to bed. Leaving the hotel was not an option, and neither was waking up my colleagues. I wandered around the hotel to see if anything was open, but to no avail. Then I saw a woman coming out of a door above which hung a sign that read "Karaoke" in English. It seemed that the bar was closing for the night. As I lingered at the door, I heard a voice from inside the bar telling me it was OK to come in. I was the lone customer, and there was no way I was going to sing. I ordered a beer instead. But I had piqued the staff's curiosity. Who was this lanky outsider sitting in their midst?

Having been to a number of child-care and educational facilities that day, I broke the ice by telling them what I had seen and heard. I caught one of the employees by surprise when I mentioned the name of the very kindergarten her child was enrolled at. She was delighted. I casually repeated what I had heard earlier in the day. "So you have an excellent piano teacher there at the kindergarten, right? I heard that she even authored a lesson book!" The woman clapped her hands with glee, saying that her son was taking piano lessons. I told them that I was a professor at Hanyang University in the South but that I had also been a nursery director. That was when I truly captured their attention.

"Isn't Hanyang University known for protest rallies? What's it like?" "How can a man run a nursery?" They peppered this strange professor from a strange land with all sorts of questions about education in the South. Sitting there in the dead of night, engrossed in a debate about education in the

North and South, I lost track of time. More than once, I became aware of the time, asking them if they needed to close the shop for the night. Each time, they brushed off my concern, clearly wanting to continue the conversation. That late-night talk in the hotel bar provided firsthand insights into the typical expectations and concerns of North Korean parents. It also provided me with an understanding of common long-term strategies employed by parents in relation to their children's education.

When they aired their concerns about their children's education and career paths, or about pressure from their husbands and parents-in-law, I would tell them about South Korea's own competitive version of keeping up with the neighbors. As we talked and laughed, they would occasionally clap their hands and shout out, "Us too!" Other times, they would cock their heads and ask, "Why is that?" or "How so?"

In short, I met the Pyongyang version of helicopter moms. The woman I first ran into introduced herself as Kim Yoon-Ok.[20] Yoon-Ok was in her mid-thirties and had studied music and played accordion. Her son was taking piano lessons at Gyeongsang Kindergarten, and her husband was a university faculty member. The other woman introduced herself as Pak Song-Suk. She said that she too had been a student at Kim Il-Sung University, where she had majored in science. Her daughter had graduated from Changgwang Kindergarten and was now in fourth grade at the elementary school affiliated with Pyongyang No. 1 Middle School, where I had sung in one of the classes. When I lit a cigarette, she ragged on her husband as "a chain-smoking journalist." She had met him in college. The following is a summary of what I learned from our midnight discussion about education in North Korea.

First, generational succession involving careers and positions, which the party cadres I met took for granted, was possible but not automatic. For such succession to become a reality, mothers had to get started while their children were still little, diligently pooling all their resources. In other words, North Korea had its own system of competition and selection for career and social positions. The women worked every other day at the karaoke bar and spent at least three hours every day supervising their children's study, regardless of how exhausted their work had left them.

Second, fierce competition and selection started from an early age. The chances of long-term success increased the earlier a child was selected for admission to special schools for gifted children. The facilities I visited were all special schools that were open to international visitors. Children had to compete to enter these schools at every stage, from nursery to upper middle school. Furthermore, students did not automatically advance to the next grade at the end of the school year but had to fret about failing their level. As long as a child survived the competition to graduate from one of these gifted schools, he or she was almost certain to be able to pursue further studies at one of the national-level universities, such as Kim Il-Sung University, the Pyongsong College of Science, the Kim Chaek University of Technology, or Pyongyang Medical University.

Third, the mothers related that when the children were young, education had been based on mastery (i.e., rote memorization) of instructions by the Leader. Women with education had "no problem" helping their children back then. However, children's education now depended much more on reasoning (i.e., debates and question-and-answer activities) that emphasized autonomy and creativity, with children having to learn to think for themselves. This made it difficult for the mothers to help their children at home. Apart from their regular school curricula, children also had to do well in extracurricular activities in order to increase their chances of entering prestigious schools. Such activities included organizational activities such as engaging in self-criticism sessions or performing good deeds in Young Pioneers and Youth League and participating in extracurricular activities at school. The mothers also said that solid ethics lessons at home were a must.

Students had to successfully make it through all these stages with good scores in order to receive recommendations for their college applications. At this point, *songbun*, physical fitness, and talent were taken into consideration. However, unlike in South Korea, there was less hoopla about the entrance examination itself. By the time students were preparing for college, the pool of peers competing for entrance to the most prestigious schools had already been whittled down through a selection process that had begun when they were still in elementary school.

In the early days of North Korean statehood, special education for gifted children was criticized on the grounds that it violated the principle of equal education. However, starting in the late 1960s, at the initiative of Kim Jong-Il, educational institutions were established with the goal of discovering and training gifted children in the fields of music, art, dance, and foreign languages. Since 1984, North Korea has established special science schools and implemented a consistent system of gifted education from kindergarten to higher education.[21] These special kindergartens and schools for gifted children were far better endowed than regular institutions in terms of facilities, teachers, and curricula. The children of the elite living in Pyongyang had an absolute advantage when it came to admission to these early-childhood institutions for the gifted due to their proximity. Competition for admission to these institutions in Pyongyang was similar to that for admission to arts, language, and STEM high schools in Seoul's privileged enclaves. The difference was that competition started at a much earlier age and within a much smaller elite group in Pyongyang.

Figure 4.3. Education for gifted children: gifted students are selected from a young age to receive special education. Eric Lafforgue

Yoon-Ok said that she had not been as good a student at school as her husband but that she had received musical training from an early age. Her son was now studying piano at Gyeongsang Kindergarten, a school well known for its musically gifted children. I asked her if she planned to raise him to be a pianist. "I should, since the state provided education for him from an early age," she replied. "But he is a boy, and so I think I'll send him to Pyongyang No. 1 Middle School." She said that doing so would be the surest way for her son to get into Kim Il-Sung University and study political economy, just as the Dear General had done. For this reason, she was making sure her son dedicated ample time to studying subjects other than music. I asked what she would do if her child were a daughter. She replied that a girl would be better suited to studying the arts and marrying well. "Like myself," she added, with a laugh.

We all chuckled along as I pointed out that sentiments were similar in South Korea. However, I had the distinct impression that in the North, people in the arts, entertainment, and sports enjoyed higher social esteem and more respect. Song-Suk said that she only had a daughter and no child (son) afterward, poking fun at her choice as "selfish." Her daughter, who was in fourth grade, was interested in science. Eventually she hoped to send her daughter to Kim Il-Sung University, the alma mater of both Song-Suk and her husband.

When I told them that my wife was a year older than me, they were startled. "How could that be?" they asked. "What went wrong?" They seemed to consider such a state of affairs to be immoral. "She must be very beautiful!" they said nodding. I told them that my wife was also a university professor and that since we did similar work I would try to bring her along on my next trip to Pyongyang. Their eyes grew wide as saucers, and they made me promise to bring her so they could meet her. I have yet to fulfill that obligation due to complications in North-South relations.

It was two years before I made it back to that hotel. Still working there, the women welcomed me heartily as if I were a long-lost family member. They were surprised and delighted when I presented them with school supplies from the South for their children. As expected, Yoon-Ok's son was now in elementary school, and Song-Suk's daughter was in middle school. Song-Suk said her daughter was active in her school's science club. I gave her a simple electronic calculator that I had brought especially for her daughter.

By the time I made it back to Pyongyang, North-South exchanges had ramped up considerably, as evidenced by the greater number of guests at the hotel. A third woman was now working at the bar. Trained as a singer of classical music, she had a daughter at Geumsong No. 2 Middle School, famous for its arts education. She said her child was especially talented and that she was scheduled to perform at Mangyongdae Children's Palace. When I told her I was scheduled to go there the next day, she said to look for her daughter in the second row, in the fifth column from the left. I teased her, saying that parents in the North and the South were the same in bragging about their children too much, causing her to chuckle.

In the meantime, five South Korean men came in. They ordered drinks and became quite rowdy, loudly boasting about their time as student activists as if for everyone to hear. After a few drinks, they beckoned the women over, calling them "*agassi*" (miss) and "pretty." The men wanted the women to sit with them. I was so angry and embarrassed that I could not bear to look at the women. But I decided to quietly observe the scene from my corner of the bar. The mothers initially took the situation in their stride as the men's actions crept perilously toward the realm of sexual harassment. Soon, however, they glanced my way, clearly uncomfortable. As an anthropologist, it was a golden opportunity to observe the vivid reality of North-South exchanges, so I restrained myself from intervening. Fortunately, something urgent must have come up, for the men all scuttled off in a hurry.

After their departure, in part to lift the women's spirits and in part out of curiosity, I asked them who the cockiest person they had met from the South was. Seemingly having put the incident behind them, they laughed as they said in unison: "Men from the South are all the same." Be they from the big companies or small ones, bureaucrats or former student activists, they were all the same, the women said. "But don't you think the men from the big businesses [*chaebol*] are a little bit more restrained?" one asked another. The discussion did not last long, but I felt the sharpness of their analysis.

I could understand the North Korean regime's calculus in dispatching these women to be hotel karaoke hostesses. In times of economic crisis, it was OK for these women to have contact with outsiders because they were core workers from inner-circle families, and the regime could therefore trust them with no reservation. The women themselves must have felt a sense of pride and duty; they were working at the front lines of the revolution dealing with dangerous outsiders. The job may have entailed difficulties of its own, but it also came with much prestige. It was a special honor to perform such work, and to have the opportunity to earn foreign currency.

In the fall of 2007, during the height of tourism to Mount Kumgang, I stayed at Kumgangsan Hotel, a North-South joint venture. The main restaurant business was under the direct control of the North Korean side. During a meal there, the waitresses gave a performance. Once on stage, the clumsiness they had shown while waiting tables gave way to a mastery of their instruments and a charismatic command of their audience.

After the performance, they returned to the job of delivering dishes to tables. I said to one of them, "You were great on your instrument. By any chance, did you attend Gyeongsang Kindergarten?" She stopped what she was doing and looked at me, her eyes wide.

"How did you know that?!" she asked in a clear Pyongyang accent.

I told her that I had visited the kindergarten a few years back and had been greatly impressed by the children's performance. She pointed to a waitress across the room, saying that the comrade had attended the same school. According to the woman, the restaurant's waitstaff were all from Pyongyang and Wonsan, but only those from the capital performed. Wide-eyed colleagues in South Korea asked me how I knew her kindergarten. One need not be clairvoyant to ask such things if one understands the North Korean education system.

In 2016, toward the end of the Park Geun-Hye administration and shortly before the April general election in South Korea, a whole group of North Korean waitresses in their twenties working at a state-controlled restaurant in China defected to the South. Upon hearing the news, I thought that things must have changed significantly in the North, because from what I knew of the system, this would have been no easy feat.

However, it later came to light that, having been won over by South Korean intelligence agents, the restaurant manager had tricked the waitresses into thinking they were moving to another city in China, only to bring them to South Korea. To this day, the women's parents and families continue to entreat the South Korean government and the international community to return their daughters. If one knows the North Korean education system, one can understand who they are, what kind of middle-class families they are from, what kind of mothers would have raised them, and the amount of attention and care each of them must have received from their parents while they were growing up. They remain in the South, however, joining a long line of separated families.

Elite Tracks and Alternatives

Since Kim Jong-Un took power, apartment buildings reaching seventy stories high have gone up along Ryomyong Boulevard and the Avenue of Future Scientists. In celebration of the completion of this project in April 2017, Kim Jong-Un had professors move in first to the new apartment buildings in recognition of their contributions to scientific and technological advancement. Of the 4,700 new units on Ryomyong Boulevard, 1,200 went to faculty members at Kim Il-Sung University; on the Avenue of Future Scientists, teachers and scientists from Kim Chaek University were given priority. While his father, Kim Jong-Il, had given special privileges to writers, artists, sports players, and professional soldiers, Kim Jong-Un was changing the direction in accordance with the times. These veritable gated communities of Pyongyang are now reportedly booming with restaurants, hair salons, bathhouses, and other amenities of the kind typically found in luxurious apartment complexes.

There are rumors that in Pyongyang, the provision of supplementary education at home by educated mothers is already a thing of the past, having been replaced by lessons given by college prep professionals. It is also reportedly possible to find early-start private education programs for "gifted children," materials for private home lessons, rampant bribery, and corruption—all familiar features of South Korea's education game.

Simultaneously, the cultural shift in North Korea seems to have given rise to an alternative direction. In November 2002, in the aftermath of the Great Famine, the poet Ryom Hyong-Mi published the following poem:

As soon as he returns from kindergarten,
Like an unbridled kid goat,
He runs out to the hills and creeks.
My mother-in-law and husband both chastise me.
Tell me I should tie him down to teach him something,
Like children in other households.

I pretend not to have heard them,
As I rub his darkly tanned body with soap bubbles.
What do they mean, I am simply letting him be.
He rolls like a football on our sweet homeland, to his heart's content.

Go ahead and become a snowman when it snows,
Get dripping wet like a flower petal when it rains.
Go ahead and catch the dragonflies and grasshoppers,
Get stung by pricking pine caterpillars.

Take everything beautiful from the green land of ours
To your heart that is as clean as a white paper
Etch them there indelibly and preciously.
I gave birth to your heart,
But the blood that must run a lifetime there
Must be made by no one other than you.[22]

A great many people overcame the crisis on their own, with no protection from either the state or the regime. Individual experiences of human tenacity and resilience became important. This gave rise to a breed of people who began looking for alternative ways of life, or at least maximum autonomy within the system.

Of course, it is also true that more people turned obsessively to competition in the wake of the crisis. On Ryomyong Boulevard in Pyongyang, there must certainly be many parents eager to have their children emerge successful from the competition for elite education. However, even within such an education system, there are also parents who realize that their children are, first and foremost, human beings who must uncover and pursue new possibilities on their own terms. Which of these approaches is more likely to produce an "autonomous" and "creative" future generation in North Korea?

THE TWO WHEELS OF THE REVOLUTION

One of my visits to Pyongyang coincided with observance of International Women's Day. Our guide joked that he should have been home making breakfast for his wife as it was International Women's Day. The implication was that his duty to us prevented him from doing so and that he was sorry about this. However, his expression indicated that he was quite glad to get out of the task. As a man married to a feminist, I asked him, smiling, "Only today?" Hesitating for a moment, he asked back: "What do you mean? Do you, Mr. Chung, prepare meals on other days, too?"

We carried on a conversation about men's housework. After listening to me for a while, he announced his conclusion: "Ha! Men in South Korea lead a pitiful life."

"Women Are Flowers"

Since the foundation of North Korea, its official position has been that women are "one of the wheels of the revolution," proclaiming that the revolution has transformed the traditional family into the "red family" of socialism. However, everyday life and relations among family members are apparently not so different from the old days of the patriarchal family system. Our guide shared that although his wife also had a job, she was the one who prepared breakfast before they both went to work in the morning, and she was also the one who took care of household chores after returning from work. The man boasted about the traditional role his wife played, seemingly unsympathetic. The principle of male dominance was still strong. He taught me a song that was popular in Pyongyang at the time, as if to show off to a poor wife-whipped South Korean man.

Women are flowers, flowers of living
A flower taking good care of the family
Dear wives and sisters, without you
A part of our lives would remain empty
Women are flowers, flowers of living.

The song was cheerful, but its lyrics were far removed from the image of revolutionary women projected by socialist thought. The sentiment was also different from the ideals of women's liberation from the early days after the founding of North Korea. When did these ideals change? And how does the regime explain such a change?

From immediately after liberation until the 1960s, North Korea pursued a gender revolution, calling for "revolutionizing women" within the framework of socialist ideology. It focused on women's education, campaigned against illiteracy, and tried to eliminate discrimination in formal educational and social activities. In particular, it remarkably expanded opportunities for women to advance in public office. One such example was the *inminban*, units of about twenty to thirty families that were often led by women.[23] Women also took on leadership roles in every kind of political organization at the national level and were appointed to symbolically important offices from the very inception of the nation.* Women entered the professional workforce,

---

* Women do hold one-third of the representative positions in the lower echelons of power, but with not much sway over major decisions. "As one examines the more powerful organizations such

becoming doctors and judges. Many also participated in postwar restoration projects and socialist industrialization, in the process receiving technical training in various industries and becoming expert technicians. Between 1963 and 1989, the number of female professionals and technicians grew 10.6 times while male professionals grew only 2.5 times.[24]

A conspicuous manifestation of the more recent patriarchal family culture is related to the establishment of the Leader-centered "Monolithic Ideological System" under Kim Il-Sung in 1972. Traditional ways of family life were revived as integral to the argument that "Korean-style socialism" was unlike socialisms elsewhere. Similar attempts were made in South Korea in the same year. The Yusin constitution of Park Chung-Hee, which virtually accorded the sitting president a lifelong term, emphasized "loyalty and filial piety" while calling for a "Korean-style democracy" that was different from the Western liberal version. Divided by the Cold War, the North and the South upheld opposite ideologies politically. However, they evolved along surprisingly similar trajectories, fostering authoritarianism in social relations and reviving patriarchy in everyday culture.

In the 1980s, as the North Korean economy began to stagnate and Kim Jong-Il's succession became official, the concept of the "socialist extended family" emerged. Mirroring the blood ties of family, the Leader was the father who gave political life to the nation, with the party as the mother. The people were to "serve" them as such. This precept was reiterated through various everyday rituals, and the home was no exception. With such a thorough emphasis on loyalty and piety toward the Supreme Leader and the party, the traditional patriarchal family order also came back, taking hold even more strongly than before. *Chosun Nyosong* (Korean women), a North Korean magazine issued during this period, asserted as follows: "When women are revolutionized and gain class consciousness as workers, they will respect their husbands more and manage their households better, and ultimately the family will find harmony."[25]

Changes in women's policy have affected not only family relationships but also various rituals, marriage being one example. For women, marriage means moving in with one's in-laws; the husband is responsible for providing the house, while the wife is responsible for making this house a home. Most of the elite North Korean women I met lived with their in-laws, although some had divorced due in part to conflict with their mothers-in-law.

The burden of contraception also fell entirely on women. Male use of contraceptives accounted for only 0.4 percent of total cases, and women mainly

---

as the Central Committee and the Politburo of the Korean Workers' Party Congress and the Cabinet, it becomes apparent that very few women have held positions of power." Kyung Ae Park, "Women and Revolution in North Korea," *Pacific Affairs* 65, no. 4 (1992): 540.

used intrauterine devices.[26] North Korean women I met in China complained of the painful side effects of IUDs.

"Women in Pants Not Allowed"

On my first visit to Pyongyang, I found that, without exception, women on the streets wore skirts, even when the weather was quite cold. It was early March 2000, and the temperatures often dropped below freezing. When I asked why this was the case, the guide's reply was: "Women wear skirts in Pyongyang, the capital of the revolution." He spoke as if this were a law of nature. Because the capital is where outsiders are allowed to peer into North Korea, it must maintain its smart appearance for the sake of the republic's image, the guide elaborated. For women, skirts are formal dress, while pants are casual or work clothes. I later learned that, in 1986, Kim Jong-Il had given an instruction banning women in the capital from wearing pants. However, it would take more than just a recommendation to ensure that all citizens adhered to such a dress code. Every morning, on the roads entering Pyongyang, young party inspectors checked the clothing of those entering the city.

Figure 4.4.   The first woman to wear pants: Kim Jong-Un's wife, Ri Sol-Ju, wearing pants during a field guidance of the Wonsan-Galma Coastal Tourism District. Source: Chosun Central News

A few years later, members of a South Korean famine relief group visited the Samjiyeon Grand Monument near the summit of Mount Baekdu. A giant statute of Kim Il-Sung and large sculptural works depicting partisan struggles stood in a clearing next to the lake. The artworks were part of "works that turn mythologies into history," Mount Baekdu as a mythological symbol being intertwined with stories of secret bases used by partisan fighters in the struggle for independence and official government claims that the mountain was also the birthplace of Kim Jong-Il.*

A woman in our group from South Korea, looking at a sculpture of anti-Japanese guerrilla fighters, asked the guide, who was dressed in the military uniform of the guerrillas, "Do you think the anti-Japanese guerrilla women fought in pleated skirts in the cold of the winter mountain?" She seemed to have momentarily forgotten that one cannot ask too serious a question at a sacred place such as this one. The guide, dressed in a pleated skirt and leather boots, a pretty handgun at her waist, had clearly never heard such a question before; she did not know what to say and became very uncomfortable. As the awkward silence dragged on, I chipped in with a lighter take:

"Let's call it an artistic rendering."

The North Koreans visibly relaxed, one of them responding:

"That's right. We have expressed historical facts artistically."

Art can always overpower facts. That was already common knowledge among North Koreans.

In the summer of 2009, I watched a documentary showing a middle-aged woman in pants trying to enter Pyongyang and quarreling with young male inspectors in armbands.[27] What made an impression on me was that there was a woman protesting. In September 2012, Kim Jong-Un's wife, Ri Sol-Ju, made her first appearance at an official function wearing pants. By that time, the wearing of pants by women had presumably made the shift from provocative act to irreversible reality. The young leader and his wife were showing off their people-friendly image by demonstrating their capacity to adapt to this new reality.

In an extremely collectivist society, changes in fashion arise and spread in the subtle gap between everyday self-censorship and tactical self-expression. In the fall of 2012, I visited Kaesong again, five years after my previous visit. A woman in a blouse with lace on the shoulders was walking along an unpaved road near downtown. She stood out because her clothes were

---

* Based on various sources, including eyewitnesses, Wada Haruki, Dae-Sook Suh, and other scholars estimate that Kim Jong-Il was born in February 1942 in a Soviet military camp near Khabarovsk. See Haruki Wada, *Kitachosen: Yugekitaikokka kara Seikigunkokka e* [North Korea: From guerilla state to regular army state] (Tokyo: Iwanami Shuppan, 1998), 59. The historical revolutionary sites around Jong-Il Peak, including the Samjiyeon Grand Monument and the Mount Baekdu secret military base, were newly created and constructed beginning in 1979. Today, the area has become a revolutionary pilgrimage site receiving over two hundred thousand visitors every year.

different from what others around her were wearing. There were also many women in high heels, perhaps an indirect consequence of the cultural influence of South Korean companies in the Kaesong Industrial Complex. Given that the dirt road had many rainwater-logged potholes, their high heels looked uncomfortable, but fashion prevailed. In the years since my last visit to the country, the colors and styles of the clothes have become ever more diverse.

Southern Men, Northern Women

It wasn't in the North but rather in the South that real revolutionary changes in culture took place in the 1980s. Democratization opened a floodgate of cultural changes. In addition to industrialization and urbanization, political democratization not only upended political power but also dramatically transformed all aspects of social relations, including labor and gender relations.

Social psychologist Chung Jean-Kyung conducted a study comparing the gender-role characteristics and values of men and women in North and South Korea. The results revealed that North Koreans are more gender typed in their personality characteristics. With regard to gender egalitarianism, North Koreans showed more conservative attitudes, and men were more discriminating than women. In particular, South Korean women actively embraced gender equality, thus widening the gap with the North.[28]

In fact, a significant proportion of male North Korean refugees who settle in the South find it hard to give up male privileges in family life. On the other hand, North Korean women were relatively quick to adapt to new gender relations. The difference in the pace of change in gender-role consciousness has also been the cause of domestic violence and divorce in refugee families.

On our way back to Seoul from a meeting held in downtown Kaesong, we made a stopover at the Kaesong Industrial Complex, which was run by South Korean enterprises. At the entrance to the complex, we ran into a crowd of tens of thousands of workers heading home from work. Dozens of buses with different destinations in Kaesong snaked down the roads, paralleled on the sidewalks by lines of workers waiting to board their rides home. It was a spectacular scene to behold. Most of the workers were young women. I was in a car with a North Korean guide and two South Korean men: an entrepreneur and a government worker. The entrepreneur remarked from the back seat: "So many pretty women here in the North! *Namnam bugnyeo* indeed!"* The rudeness and insensitivity of his comment made me cringe. The North Korean guide glanced up, visibly holding his tongue. I felt sorry for the only Northern man among us, who kept his eyes locked forward and his jaw clenched.

---

* *Namnam bugnyeo* is a Korean saying that (handsome) Southern men and (beautiful) Northern women.

NOTES

1. China's *hukou* control system has also denied most rural people access to living and working or having an apartment in the cities since the 1950s, with some changes in recent years.

2. Mary Douglas, *Purity and Danger: An Analysis of Concepts of Pollution and Taboo* (London: Routledge, 2002), 114.

3. Jin-I Choe, *Gukgyeongeul Sebeon Geonneun Yeoja* [The woman who crossed three national borders] (Seoul: Bookhouse, 2005), 73–155.

4. Byung-Ho Chung, "Naengjeon Jeongchiwa Bukhan Ijumineui Chimtuseong Chogukka Jeollyak" [Cold War politics and penetrant transnational strategies of North Korean migrants], *Review of North Korean Studies* 17, no. 1 (2014): 49–100.

5. Robert Collins, *Marked for Life: Songbun, North Korea's Social Classification System* (Washington, DC: Committee for Human Rights in North Korea, 2012), 4.

6. Jae-Ung Kim, "Yeonjwajewa Chulsinseongbunui Gyujeongnyeokeul Tonghae Bon Haebang Hu Bukhaneui Gajokjeongchaek" [Family policies in North Korea after the liberation considered through the influence of the implicative system and family classes], *Journal of Korean Studies* 187 (2019): 313–41.

7. Abito Ito, *Kitachosen No Jinmin No Seikatsu* [The lives of the North Korean people], (Tokyo: Koubundou Publishers, 2017), 42–46.

8. Journalist Barbara Demick also recognizes this "class structure" as an updating of the hereditary "caste system" and reports that a bad family background, called "tainted blood," lasts for three generations. Barbara Demick, *Nothing to Envy: Love, Life and Death in North Korea* (London: 4th Estate, 2010), 26–28.

9. U-Jin Chang, *Adeukhi Mon Yennarui Uri Sonjodeurul Chajaseo* [In search of our ancestors from very long ago] (Pyongyang: Social Science Press, 2009), 133, 48, 207.

10. Chang, *Adeukhi Mon*, 147.

11. Chang, *Adeukhi Mon*, 145.

12. See Ruth Benedict, *Race: Science and Politics* (New York: Viking, 1964); Tae-Han Jang, *Heugin: Geudeureun Nuguinga* [African Americans: Who are they?] (Seoul: Hanguk Gyeongje Sinmunsa [Korea Economic Daily Co.], 1993).

13. Pollution, wrote Mary Douglas, "is a type of danger which is not likely to occur except where the lines of structure, cosmic or social, are clearly defined." Douglas, *Purity and Danger*, 114.

14. According to Myers, North Korean propaganda portrays South Korea as a land polluted by foreign domination, particularly by the permanent presence of the US military. He argues that the guiding ideology of North Korea is race-based far-right nationalism derived from Japanese fascism rather than any form of communism. B. R. Myers, *The Cleanest Race: How North Koreans See Themselves and Why It Matters* (London: Melville House, 2010).

15. In South Korea, too, as the number of North Koreans in the country increased, one began to see an increase in the number of TV programs creating and disseminating images portraying North Koreans as different and strange. Such programs serve the interest of those who wish to reinscribe and preserve the existing lines of the

North-South division. See Christopher K. Green and Stephen J. Epstein, "Now on My Way to Meet Who? South Korean Television, North Korean Refugees, and the Dilemmas of Representation," *Asia-Pacific Journal* 11, no. 2 (2013), https://apjjf .org/2013/11/41/Stephen-Epstein/4007/article.html.

16. Il-Sung Kim, *Inmin Jeonggwongigwan Ilkundul Apeseo Han Yeonseol* [A speech delivered to the workers of the people's government organs], Kim Il-Sung Jeojakjip [Anthology of writings by Kim Il-Sung] 33 (Pyongyang: Chosun Rodongdang Chulpanbu [Workers' Party of Korea Publishing House], 1987).

17. Abito Ito, *Kitachosen*, 52.

18. Erving Goffman, *Stigma: Notes on the Management of Spoiled Identity* (Englewood Cliffs, NJ: Prentice-Hall, 1963), 1–5.

19. Abito Ito, *Kitachosen*, 54.

20. Pseudonym.

21. Man-Gil Han, ed., *Bukhaneseoneun Eotteoke Gyoyukhalkka: Bugnyeokkeseo Salda on 16* [*Simnyuk*] *Inui Saengsaenghan Gyoyuk Cheheomgi* [How do the North Koreans educate? The vivid educational experiences of sixteen people who have lived in the North] (Seoul: Urigyoyuk, 1999), 207–8.

22. Hyong-Mi Ryom, "Aireul Kiumyeo" [Raising a child], *Chosun Munhak* [Korean literature], November 2002.

23. Andrei Lankov, *The Real North Korea: Life and Politics in the Failed Stalinist Utopia* (Oxford: Oxford University Press, 2013).

24. Kyung Ae Park, "Women and Revolution in North Korea," *Pacific Affairs* 65, no. 4 (1992): 537.

25. *Chosun Nyosong* [North Korean women] (a monthly), April 1989, 5.

26. Medical Aid for Children, "Bukhan Yeoseongeui Imsin Mit Chulsangwa Geongange Gwanhan Bogoseo" [A report on pregnancy, childbirth, and health among North Korean women] (Seoul: Medical Aid for Children [an NGO based in Seoul], 2005).

27. Yong-Chul Gong and Hun-Mo Chung, "3[*Sam*]-Dae Seseup Jigeum Bukhaneseo Museun Iri Ireonago Inna?" [The third-generation succession—What is happening in North Korea now?], in *KBS Special* (South Korea: KBS-1 TV, June 28, 2009).

28. Jean-Kyung Chung, "Bukhansaramdeului Seongyeokhal Teukseonggwa Gachigwan: Talbukja Jaryo" [The gender-role characteristics and values of North Koreans: Data from North Korean refugees], *Korean Journal of Psychology: General* 21, no. 2 (2002): 163–77.

Chapter Five

Guns and Rules

MILITARY-FIRST POLITICS

According to *juche* ideology, independence is the lifeblood of human beings, the lifeblood of the people, and the lifeblood of a nation and a state. In order to preserve independence while suffering pressure from counterrevolutionary forces, it is necessary to prioritize the army and "carry the gun with a firm grip," as North Koreans say.

The political elites in North Korea would argue that Kim Jong-Il's *songun*, or "military-first," politics was the way to overcome the failures of the Soviet socialist suzerain. Furthermore, they would argue that the North Korean way is the more orthodox socialist solution, contrasting it with the degenerate "economics-first socialism" of neighboring China.[1] However, in reversing the pecking order of party and military, *songun* politics disturbed the power balance fundamental to the principle of state management in a socialist system. It also overturned the premise of orthodox Marxism, which emphasizes the importance of the material and class foundation as the driving force of revolution.*

Kim Jong-Il was conscious of the criticism that his military-first politics was an example of a militaristic authoritarianism that contravenes socialist principles. He rebutted such arguments, saying, "We are building socialism while being besieged by imperialism and constantly threatened militarily.

---

* The *juche* idea emphasized by *songun* politics is the idealistic argument that puts human agency ahead of material conditions and emphasizes "correct thoughts and ideological disposition." In this respect, the "socialist revolution" that North Korea advocates is combined with the neo-Confucian tradition of Chosun in emphasizing ritual causes and ethical principles. Heonik Kwon and Byung-Ho Chung, *North Korea: Beyond Charismatic Politics* (Lanham, MD: Rowman and Littlefield, 2012), 120.

Under these circumstances, there can be no people, no socialist state, no party without a strong army. In this sense, the army is the people, the state, and the party."[2] The assertion that "the army is the people" signifies that people must also arm themselves mentally with militant spirit, as they share a common destiny with the military, and live in a social reality in which the military always comes first.

The book *Songunshidae* quotes Kim Jong-Il as having said the following in the fall of 1999 when the famine was at its worst: "The Yankees are afraid of us even though they know fully well that our people do not have enough to eat and we are suffering."[3] The book then claimed, "Why are the Yankees so scared of us? Is it because we have a large territory? Or is it because we have a large population? Of course not. It is because our military and our people are ready to unite, follow their leader, and sacrifice their lives without hesitation. There is no country in this world that can stand up to the unity of a people centered around its leader."

A History of Defeating Evil

The exhibitions at the Korean Revolution Museum in Pyongyang explain that US aggression is a product of American imperialism, which has intervened at every historical moment of Korean national suffering. They explain that the war between Japan and the United States was a territorial war between imperialist forces and that the US occupation of South Korea (meaning the US military presence and its retention of wartime operational control) is proof that Korea is not fully liberated—that the old invader had merely been replaced by a new one. Throughout the "Fatherland Liberation War," as North Korea calls the Korean War, the US military bombed the North indiscriminately, reducing much of the country to rubble while killing and injuring countless civilians.[4] The actions of the United States, the "demon" and the "sworn enemy" that plagued the Korean people during the entirety of its modern history, are on display at the museum, accompanied by photographic proof.

To my surprise, one of the historical artifacts that I encountered in the first exhibition room was the Wijeong Cheoksabi, a stone monument to "rejecting heterodoxy and protecting orthodoxy": "When Western barbarians invade, not fighting them is equivalent to making peace with them, and making peace with them is equivalent to selling out the country."[5] The inscription on the side of the stone reads, "A Warning to All Posterity." The message was written in 1866, and the monument was erected in 1871. The dates correspond to the respective defeats of French and American expeditions at Ganghwa Island, near Seoul, but the inscriptions also reflect the North Korean attitude toward the outside world today.

In South Korea, the same monument is viewed in a completely different light. It is seen as a symbol of an anachronistic policy that had the country shutting its borders at the turn of the century at a time when it urgently needed to open its doors to modern Western civilization. Had Chosun welcomed Western powers at that time, history teachers in South Korean schools explain, Korea would have modernized faster and not suffered annexation by Japan. While South Korea has set globalization as the rationale for development, North Korea, on the other hand, has taken a different course, stressing that driving away "foreign forces" and living "our way" is the right thing to do.

In the museum hung a painting titled *The Brave Battle of the Pyongyang People*, depicting the sinking of the *General Sherman*, an American merchant ship that came up the Daedong River in June 1871. The event is seen as the starting point of Korea's modern history of resisting external forces.

A monument commemorating the sinking of the *General Sherman* stands on the banks of the Daedong River to this day. At the river bend nearby where the ship was destroyed, the USS *Pueblo* is on display. This is a US Navy spy ship that was captured after crossing into North Korean territorial waters in 1968, about a hundred years after the sinking of the *General Sherman*. Those visiting the ship see a picture of a solitary North Korean sailor of short stature jumping onto the state-of-the-art US Navy warship and threatening dozens of towering US soldiers with a single gun, prompting them to surrender. After visiting the *Pueblo*, children, used to seeing and hearing such David-and-Goliath-type tales, express their faith in mind-over-matter victories via drawings and songs.

Ideological significance, not objective facts, is emphasized at such sites of historical education. In other words, facts that must be believed and lived by from the *juche* (self-reliance) ideological standpoint are conveyed through a plausible narrative structure. From the *juche* perspective, the role of history is to foster national pride by making people accept as fact the meaning of such a long and arduous struggle, which "made the impossible possible."

In this context, actions involving taking liberties with historical details are viewed not as fabrications but as part of a pragmatic and instrumental approach to how history is presented and understood. In fact, such a constructivist approach lies behind the histories of most nation-states. The North Korean version is an extreme case, showing how far such an approach can go. It is worth noting that various groups in postcolonial nations, thirsting for a subjective liberation narrative, circulate such stories and accept them culturally as logical. The factuality of specific details is never important in these stories because people want to believe they are

Figure 5.1. A heart to hate the enemy: children running a race on a kindergarten sports day. AP Photo, Kwang Hyon Kim

true. What is important is the meaning of the story; it must be instructive and compelling, imparting a moral lesson that reinforces the contemporary ruling power.*

This is true not only of stories related to the leaders and state power, but also of various lesser heroic tales. Myths and heroic tales are disseminated through state-controlled institutions, from day-care centers and schools to workplaces and the military. Hungry for heroic stories in their information-controlled society, adults and children alike endlessly consume a set of variations of such tales of liberation.

From a very young age, children in North Korea learn through stories that hostility toward strong and evil foreign powers is legitimate moral rage. I once came across five-year-old children in a kindergarten class learning a story that Kim Il-Sung, in his childhood, developed a heart to love the country and to hate Japanese imperialists and resolved that he would grow up and take back the country. The children also learn that they should study hard and

---

* North Korea is criticized as an extreme case of using and abusing postcolonial rhetoric. When a revolutionary anticolonial movement evolves into revolutionary state politics, and when this state mobilizes militant postcolonial rhetoric in order to reinforce its legitimacy, the rhetoric can turn into hegemony that cuts out diverse voices and interpretations. Postcolonialism then degenerates into an instrument of power. Kwon and Chung, *North Korea*, 15.

become strong so that they can go to the People's Army and hold guns in their hands to smash the Yankees.[6]

In the book *Politics and Songs of the Great Man of the Songun Era* (written in Korean), Kim Jong-Il argues as follows: "We must not be praised by our enemies. We must be hated by them. Hatred from enemies means that what we are doing is just and that we are doing it well."[7] According to the book, a heart to hate the enemy, an active will to fight, and self-esteem are essential virtues to cultivate from an early age.

"Without Chosun, There Is No World!"

A few days before the new millennium, I visited Tumen, a city on the Chinese side of the Tumen River, in order to understand firsthand the border-crossing situation and meet North Koreans hiding in China. The sky was clear and the air felt icy in my lungs. The temperature was -24°C. The river was frozen solid and covered with snow, its surface marked here and there by footprints as well as the occasional bicycle track. Despite being the middle of the day, not a soul could be seen on the river; all was quiet. It was too cold to stand still, even for a short while, so I went into a concession store on the riverbank.

As I was talking with the couple that owned the store and warming myself, I glimpsed a man treading warily outside the window and shivering from the cold. The shop owners said he must be from North Korea. I told them to call him inside so that I could buy him something to eat. They didn't seem to understand why I was going to the trouble but called him in all the same. He entered the store, a young man frozen blue from the cold and quaking in his threadbare clothes. After gulping down his second cup of hot noodles, he turned to me and offered his thanks.

The man said he had come to find food, but having failed he was planning on returning home that night empty-handed. After some back-and-forth, the store owner told the man he should come up with a plan to flee the country with his family before the regime collapsed. At that, the man's face suddenly hardened, and he swore that he was going to keep to, and live by, "our-style socialism." The couple looked at each other and said, scoffing, "We tried that sort of thing here in China in the old days. It's all useless." The man then said, "If it were not for the sanctions by the Americans. . . . Our socialism is right, isn't it?" The store owner replied that in that case North Korea should not have pursued nuclear arms, to which the man replied, "I can't say we do or don't have nuclear bombs. But should the US attack North Korea, that would be the end of the world. As far as we North Koreans are concerned, life is difficult either way. If a war comes, at least we will all die a heroic death."

With that, the man clenched his teeth and added with a fierce glare, "Without Chosun [North Korea], there is no world!"

In the era of *songun* politics, one often comes across the phrase "Without Chosun, there is no world!" As if to emphasize that this is not mere rhetoric, the phrase is accompanied by specific codes of conduct, such as "Defend unto Death," "Let's Become Bombs," and "Suicide-Bomb Spirit." Will the world really disappear without North Korea? Assuming all North Koreans became bombs, it is unlikely that the world would go anywhere.

This amazingly self-centered assertion emerged in the 1990s in the wake of the collapse of the global Cold War order. "When the flag of socialism was lowered in the former Soviet Union and the Eastern Bloc countries and those who yearned for socialism found themselves at a loss, our fatherland raised the red flag of socialism even higher without any policy change, demonstrating high dignity as a bastion of socialism," writes one North Korean scholar.[8] In other words, while the Soviet Union collapsed and China made compromises with the global capitalist system, North Korea "took the lead in the collective struggle to resist incorporation into the new world order led by the imperial hegemony of the United States and became the driving force that ignited the spirit of independence of Third World people."[9]

The outside world has interpreted North Korea's stubborn refusal to change as a self-isolating and dangerous decision. However, by claiming to be the only unchanged revolutionary state in a changing world, North Korea seems to have found a new mission and a sense of pride in its circumstances. Given that the Soviet Union, the nation that laid claim to being the center of socialism, has disappeared, a socialist state on the periphery of East Asia wants the world to know that it is willing to step up and become a global hub for socialism. This dovetails with the liberation narratives of the legendary anti-imperial guerilla (partisan) fighters, in which the heroes found themselves surrounded by hostile forces. The moral of such stories is that the heroes overcame such bleak objective conditions through the sheer force of their subjective will. Such narratives make the assertions in North Korean propaganda almost believable.

While internally such assertions may have boosted pride, providing North Koreans with a sense of mission, externally they led to self-isolation and national crises. Since the end of the Cold War, North Korea has become one of the United States' most dangerous enemies. As such, it is the target of intensive international sanctions, with Washington taking the lead in their application.

In the thirty or so years since the fall of the Berlin Wall and the collapse of the Soviet Union, the United States and other world powers have been waiting for the collapse of the North Korean regime. They have not considered the possibility that North Korea might reform and shift to market socialism, as China and Vietnam have done. At the same time, the United States has continued to work to isolate and weaken North Korea. In the meantime, the North Korean regime has conducted six nuclear tests, developed hydrogen bombs and intercontinental ballistic missiles, and smoothly completed two successions of power. Rather than collapsing, the regime has become an even stronger guerilla state, armed with weapons far more threatening than those it had thirty years ago. Let us look at the reality of North Korea's military-first politics and how this can be understood in relation to the lives of ordinary people.

"You Have to Listen to the Man with the Gun"

The party cadres who were guiding us suggested that we visit the American spy ship, the *Pueblo*, anchored on the Daedong River. The spring breeze was still cold, but it was a sunny Sunday afternoon. Smoke rose from the banks of the river. Children, apparently on a school trip, were carrying out their annual springtime grass burning, controlling the fire with their small brooms and shovels. Only the teacher and a few students were paying attention to the fire, with the rest playing, screaming, and chasing each other around.

As our party descended the stairs on the riverbank on our way to the ship, the armed guard in front of the bridge of the *Pueblo* screamed out: "Stop!" We halted in our tracks, startled. The children paused their activities to see what was going on. What the guard wanted to convey was that the *Pueblo* was closed on Sundays.

After glancing around, our guides grasped the situation. They adjusted their party cadre uniforms and stepped forward. One of them explained that they were there with foreign visitors and asked if he could speak to an officer inside. Shifting into port arms position, the guard immediately shouted back, "Don't bother! Go!" The gray-haired party cadre looked at the boyish guardsman, dumbfounded. When the guides turned back to face us, they were embarrassed. One of them took the first step to leave, saying, "You have to listen to the man with the gun." In the five years since Kim Jong-Il had announced his *songun* politics, the pecking order between party and military had changed, as had the way in which this change played out in daily life. The children playing on the riverbank watched the scene with curious eyes.

Regardless of the "-ism" advocated in a particular country, the sight of a civilian cowering in front of a man with a gun is a sad one. I witnessed party cadres shrinking in front of men with guns every time we passed through the checkpoints at the city boundaries of Pyongyang. Young men with guns would speak curtly, and the aging party cadres would try as much as possible to preserve their dignity.

In fact, we visitors from the South understood the situation immediately. Roadside inspections were common in South Korea during the long military dictatorship. At checkpoints installed at city borders, military policemen, their helmets low on their faces, would board buses armed with bayonets, dragging out anyone deemed to be suspicious. I remember trying to avoid eye contact with those armed military police. Now, at roadside checkpoints going into and out of Pyongyang, I adopted the naive expression I had trained myself to wear back in those days as I felt the sharp glare of the guards fall upon me.

"Let's Become Bombs and Defend until Death"

Signs on every tall building on the streets of Pyongyang bore slogans boosting this claim: "Unity with One Heart!" "Let's Become Bombs!" "Suicide-Bomb Spirit!"

Every bayonet in our grip
Shines with the oath to protect our General.
The revolutionary center is aflutter with the red flag.
Let's become bombs of ten million [people] to defend until death.[10]

This macabre song played on the television in my hotel room in Pyongyang in 2005. The phrase "Let's become bombs of ten million" caught my attention. The lyrics called on not only the military but the entire nation to "defend until death" for the revolutionary core—that is, the political leadership in Pyongyang. The grisly slogans on the streets were imperatives that applied to the entire nation. Did they involve simple exaggeration? Were they merely examples of propaganda containing emotional appeals? Did people really believe their words, and would they follow through on them with actions? I was curious and afraid at the same time.

As members of a family-state, the leader and people of North Korea have a parent-child relationship, and they are said to be parts of one family, united by affection and loyalty. Still, it is difficult to understand a logic in which the people are expected to become "bullets and bombs" and be willing to sacrifice themselves in order to protect the leader. The more common ostensible logic in a modern nation-state is that the state's leader and military forces should risk their lives to protect the people. The latter resonates better with the common logic of parents making sacrifices for their children. It is rare for children to sing that they will sacrifice themselves for their parents.

However, a historical precedent does exist in the case of the relationship between the emperor of wartime Japan and his subjects. All subjects in the empire of Japan pledged to give their lives to protect the emperor, the "national body" (*kokutai*). Here, the emperor was not simply a state leader but a symbol of the state itself, and not simply an individual but an entity symbolizing the identity and permanence of the collective body of the nation. Accordingly, for citizens, each one a finite entity, protecting the emperor meant a readiness to give one's life in order to make the life of the group—the state or nation—everlasting.*

The North Korean regime was premised on a personality cult, portraying the charismatic leader Kim Il-Sung as a father figure. In the process of Kim Jong-Il's accession to power following the death of his father, the logic of inheritance by the eldest son was emphasized. When Kim Jong-Il's third son, Kim Jong-Un, in turn succeeded him, the "head family" logic of the "Baekdu bloodline" was underscored, inculcating people's loyalty to the family that was spearheading the revolution. Currently, North Korea seems to have institutionalized this cultural logic of inheritance within a political system.

In Imperial Japan since the Meiji Restoration, a national strategy encouraging children to equate piety toward one's parents with loyalty to the emperor (or the state system) involved having them memorize the "Imperial Rescript on Education" via the public education system. In South Korea, too, the Park Chung-Hee regime in the 1970s introduced the "National Education Charter" for every student in school to recite every day, the goal being to encourage them to equate personal destiny with the "endless glory" of the state and the nation.

During the same period, North Korea institutionalized the Monolithic Ideological System, formally establishing a socialist dictatorship and spreading the idea that filial piety within one's family and loyalty to the Leader (state) constitute "one and the same heart." The people were to cherish the "political life" of the nation provided by Comrade Kim Il-Sung, the father-leader, repaying him with loyalty and serving the revolutionary cause, generation after generation.[11]

In human societies across the globe, there are many examples of religious belief systems that lead people to believe that mind can overcome matter. Koreans experienced it during the Japanese occupation, when the idea of

---

* Masao Maruyama states that the fundamental characteristic of the Japanese national structure is that it is an extended family. Specifically, in this structure, the emperor is the head of the family, while the imperial family is the head house and the people are the offshoots of the head house, all of which make up an extended family; Masao Maruyama, *Thought and Behavior in Modern Japanese Politics*, ed. Ivan Morris (New York: Oxford University Press, 1969). Imperial Japan is not the only example in history. Hannah Arendt, who experienced Nazi Germany, wrote that blurring and dismantling the boundaries between public collective relations such as the state and private collective relations such as the family is an important feature of modern politics and the origin of totalitarianism; *The Human Condition* (Chicago: University of Chicago Press, 1958).

the kamikaze, or "divine wind," and the notion of "breaking like jade" (in a suicide mission) were forced upon them. Toward the end of the Pacific War, when Japan's fighting capacity had declined and it began losing battles, negotiations proceeded for surrender to the Allied powers. However, Japan's leaders refused to surrender unconditionally in order to protect the emperor system.[12] In the meantime, the leadership sought to prepare the Japanese people to die fighting to the last man, and the military trained tens of thousands of pilots for kamikaze suicide squads and built bombers without landing gear.

Thousands of young Japanese, and even some Koreans, volunteered (or were institutionally coerced) to join the suicide squads. It was more than patriotism; it was a collective ritual based on shared religious beliefs. Their sacrifices were glorified by the state in both religious and artistic terms. They sang as they headed for the battlefield: "Let us meet as falling cherry blossoms at Yasukuni Shrine, where we will be enshrined as heroes who died protecting our country." Official data record that 3,500 suicide bombers died during the war. They died in a desperate effort to secure a guarantee of the emperor's life.

Listening to the song that North Korean children sang in the era of military-first politics, I could not calm my trembling heart:

My country, where happiness blooms
Is targeted by an evil enemy.
Let us line up, the Young Pioneers of Chosun,
For the Dear General,
We will become bombs of three million.[13]

In a system that champions socialism, how does the system plant such fanatical beliefs in people, beliefs befitting religious zealots embarking on a holy war? During the post–Cold War era, North Korea evolved into a more rigidly militaristic nation. I feared that the state could turn political ritual and power theatrics into real-life tragedy.

We can find historical resonances in the study of a theater state. Negara, the theater state in nineteenth-century Bali, did not surrender in response to a siege by Dutch forces. Instead, the king, the nobles, the priests, and the soldiers formed a final ritual parade, adorned with splendid decorations, before walking in orderly fashion into the fire of Dutch soldiers to meet their deaths.[14]

Overlooking the fact that the other party may make decisions different from one's own based on a value system that differs from one's own can lead to tragic results. In the case of North Korea, a theater state with nuclear arms, its suicide will not involve one-sided mass self-destruction. What is certain

Figure 5.2. Marching with the National Flag: Children parading in the streets of Wonsan on International Workers' Day. Eric Lafforgue

is that, in a theater state that systematically reproduces a self-centered belief system, the influence of the outside world is bound to be limited.

External pressure of the kind that North Korea is currently facing is not effective. It only reinforces a belief system that is based on the premise of crisis. A physical attack may partially destroy the social system and cause a disturbance, but it will only serve to reinforce the legitimacy of its symbolic belief system, which is grounded in the notion of resistance to external aggression.

The ideal solution would involve helping the troupe of the theater state to stop acting from within. Ultimately, there is always the possibility that they will change their cultural act as soon as they see a new position they can accept, just as actors can instantly change roles if there is a new script. To wit, the Japanese emperor's declaration of surrender led Japanese soldiers on all fronts to disarm instantly. The Japanese people had been ordered to fight until the last subject died, even if arming themselves with nothing but bamboo spears if necessary. However, it was as if the short statement from the emperor roused them from the effects of black magic, particularly when it is recalled how they even welcomed the US troops, their mortal enemy, during the occupation of Japan. In this case, a dramatic change took place because the emperor, the center of the symbolic system, shifted course.[15]

The Flower Girl

North Korean officials guided us to the East Pyongyang Grand Theater to see a live performance of the famous revolutionary musical *The Flower Girl*. We entered the modern, dome-shaped theater. The auditorium was dark and cold, making us feel as if we were inside a huge refrigerator, and reminding us of the difficult electricity situation. It was a cold evening in early March 2000, and everyone in the audience was dressed in thick military coats, scarves, and gloves.

Once the doors had closed, the orchestra began playing the introductory score as the curtains rose to reveal a brightly lit stage. Enormously wide and deep, it was decorated with layers of spectacular three-dimensional sets, the technicolor musical world contrasting starkly with the gray reality offstage.

The Flower Girl is the tragic story of a poor tenant farmer's family. In the story, the father of the heroine, a girl named Kkotbun-i, or "flower," dies in Manchuria during the Japanese colonial period. The family continues to live in poverty, suffering exploitation at the hands of the Japanese rulers as well as abuse by pro-Japanese landlords. Despite Kkotbun-i's efforts to support her family by selling flowers, the family is torn apart. Eventually her mother dies, her younger sister is blinded, and her brother disappears.

The theater was just as cold as the poor family in the story. My hand, recording the sad drama on video, kept going numb. Actors in delicate costumes ran barefoot across the ice-cold stage. As vocalists of great capacity sang, their breath condensed into white steam. Sitting with an audience dressed in dark khaki coats, it felt as if I were sitting in a field theater during wartime. The mood, both on and off the stage, was resolute and determined.

When the vicious landowner and his wife blinded Kkotbun-i's younger sister, a voice from the back row shouted, "Oh no! Can't somebody beat that wicked landlord to death?" Others cried out here and there, "Strike down that bitch!" One person behind me mumbled loudly, "If the people had awakened then, they'd have beaten the Japanese soldiers to death, taken their weapons, and fought!"

Kkotbun-i's brother, thought to have been killed by the Japanese police, escapes from prison. Now an anti-Japanese guerilla (partisan), he returns to the village to punish the exploiters. Kkotbun-i then goes out into the streets to sell flowers to support the larger revolutionary family, singing, "I sow flower seeds of the revolution."[16] In the final scene of the musical, Kkotbun-i and the whole village welcome the glorious guerilla leader. When the leader slowly appears on the stage, the sun rises in the background, and Kkotbun-i politely offers him wildflowers. With the love of a benevolent father, the guerilla leader gives the orphans and the dispossessed diaspora a new sense of belonging within the revolutionary family.

North Korea claims that its revolutionary history begins with the Korean diaspora living in Manchuria during the Japanese colonial period. This narrative is repeated in various works of art and cultural products. Well-known revolutionary musicals such as *The Flower Girl* and *Sea of Blood* as well as the Arirang Mass Games portray Korean tenant farmers being exploited by Japanese colonial authorities and pro-Japanese landlords. They follow their leader, joining the guerilla struggle for national independence. The underlying aesthetics of salvation here are reminiscent of the Exodus in the Old Testament.

Seeing the audience gathered in the frigid theater immersed in this revolutionary drama, I realized that I was witnessing a convergence of the guerrilla state, the family-state, and the theater state. North Korea insisted that it was under siege by hostile forces and that the nation had to endure an "arduous march" of the kind endured by the anti-Japanese guerillas during the colonial era. Yet the splendid revolutionary theater productions did not stop during the dire days of the famine. Millions of people were going hungry, and the reflections on an "arduous history" that such performances aimed to elicit among their audiences evoked the ongoing reality faced by the country.

After the performance, the audience left the theater quietly, like the sea at low tide. People fastened their collars and covered their heads with hats and shawls, walking home down the unlit streets as if in a wartime blackout. The bus carrying us traveled along empty roads, its headlights picking out the red letters of slogans emblazoned on huge signboards along the way: "Defend unto Death," "Let's Become Bombs" and "Spirit of Self-Detonation."

"Seoul Is Not Far from Here"

"Seoul is not far from here. Should war break out, it will become a sea of fire," a North Korean representative once said during one of the inter-Korean talk sessions at Panmunjom, stirring outrage in South Korea. While it was only a provocative threat, it is true that Seoul is less than fifty miles from the DMZ, and more than twenty million people live within range of North Korean long-range artillery.

The international community often has a hard time understanding the hostile coexistence of the North and South Korean regimes. North Korea's long-range missiles are a diplomatic tool as well as an offensive weapon. The sense of crisis in Japan and the international community, which began with the launch of the Daepodong-1 missile that flew over Japan in August 1998, reached its peak with Pyongyang's launch of an intercontinental ballistic missile (ICBM) in July 2017. But while the international community was shocked by the prospect of imminent war, people in South Korea remained relatively unperturbed. They had been living with this threat for decades.

North Korea's cannons, not its ICBMs, are the biggest threat to South Korea. If North Korea dared to risk war, it could destroy South Korea's information and communication networks using long-range artillery guns and short-range missiles. They could also disable nuclear power plants peppered across the South. South Korea runs on an organically and delicately networked system, which is to say that even partial destruction of its economy and infrastructure would lead to serious damage. On the other hand, North Korean society is relatively mechanical and independent, meaning that even if attacks from the outside devastate most of the country, it may not be enough to break the system.

At a time when North-South military tension was particularly high, a columnist for a leading South Korean newspaper wrote, "If our fellow citizens would put up with it for three days only, we could bomb the core targets of North Korea and lead the way to victory."[17] This statement is ignorant and dangerous. It may have brought catharsis to some readers, but it is seriously misleading. It reveals a lack of understanding of the essence of North Korea as a guerilla state. We cannot rule out the possibility that a single bomb dropped on Pyongyang would prove to the people that everything they had been told by the regime for decades was true, and they would then "defend until death" with "a spirit of self-detonation." What would be the meaning of victory in such a war?

ORGANIZATIONAL LIFE AND ROLE PLAY

North Koreans live a ritualized life. They live according to a tightly woven schedule of rituals, and each important event in the life cycle is accompanied by socially defined rites of passage.

Mornings begin with the sound of revolutionary music booming from loudspeakers. Whether in the gloom of a winter's dawn or in the glow of daybreak in summer, people in every neighborhood can be seen moving about with brooms in their hands, sweeping the streets.

At home, before breakfast, families in North Korea must pay respect to the leaders in front of their portraits, which must hang on the cleanest wall in the house. This hanging of portraits is reminiscent of the hanging of crosses and portraits of Jesus in Christian households. It is hard to know how many people actually observe this ceremony every morning. However, families with school-age children need to follow this social norm.

Routines concerned with organizational life differ slightly depending on occupation, age, and class. However, political education is a common element of everyone's daily and weekly routine. They include a thirty-minute "reading assembly" for reading government newspapers and "instructions" every morning before the work. And every Wednesday after the work, a "learning assembly" for studying revolutionary classics or a "lecture assembly" for listening to propaganda and political instigation is organized. As with all ceremonial acts, they can easily become formalistic when repeated daily. Nevertheless, they have the effect of internalizing a collectivist lifestyle, as each day starts and ends with everyone coming together in a meeting.

The "Communal Assembly" and the Culture of Confession

The most remarkable rite in the ritualized life of North Koreans is the weekly communal assembly, *saenghwal chonghwa* (literally meaning "life harmonization"). At this event, one reflects upon one's own life ("self-criticism") and those of others ("mutual criticism") in front of an assembly of people from one's organization.

One is usually criticized for one's failure to live up to the revolutionary ideals or for one's "liberal" attitudes (individualism or egoism) in light of the words of Kim Il-Sung and Kim Jong-Il as well as the "Ten Principles of the Monolithic Guidance System."[18] People must confess their errors and be criticized by others. In this way, by regularly reflecting on one's own life and the lives of others in line with social values, each individual checks his or her place in society and establishes himself or herself as a social being.

Several North Korean refugees in South Korea remembered the communal assemblies they had in North Korea and made a few episodes into role plays.[19] In one of those episodes, a woman confesses that she was criticized by the unit for not doing a good job of cleaning the portraits of the Great Leaders at home. She says that it was because she lacked loyalty to the Great Leader. "Every morning, without fail, I will carefully serve the portrait of the leader, and not only myself but my entire family will serve it with loyalty and enthusiasm." She then points out one person and renders her criticism. "Comrade Bongsun has been influenced by revisionism and her hair is too long. Is that hair or a wig? Such long hair is not appropriate at a time when you need to take the lead in building a strong and prosperous nation. We must be neat and tidy in accordance with the socialist lifestyle." The leader then says: "Comrade Bongsun, cut your hair today. And everyone should serve the portrait of the Leader with loyalty at this monsoon season."

In another episode, a woman confesses, "I missed morning reading time three times because I was sick. I'm sorry for making the comrades wait because of me. My revolutionary resolve was not firm and I became complacent. I regret my mistake and will take good care of my health not to get sick." Next, she points out one person and criticizes her. "A few days ago, comrade Youngmi missed work and got a perm at the hair salon. I think she is too selfish to care about grooming herself rather than being faithful to her tasks. We must get rid of such liberal habits and remain faithful to the revolutionary tasks." The leader asks, "Is it true?" Youngmi says, "I was lying down at home and felt a little better, so I went to the hair salon." The leader interrupts, "Comrade, that is so wrong. Do you think that makes sense? If that's the case, you should come to work." Youngmi then says, "I'm sorry. It won't happen again."

From the perspective of the ruling power, this is an effective means of social control through which everyone constantly self-censors and monitors other's daily lives. The weekly assembly at the local or basic unit of an organization is expanded to a monthly assembly at a higher level, then to an annual assembly at the highest level. Assemblies at the highest level sometimes turn into scenes of high-tension political drama, as those accused of having committed serious mistakes may be publicly criticized or even publicly executed in order to set an example.

The stakes are high in these tense political rituals. The participants therefore preemptively confess mistakes that can be passed over easily in a bid to avoid criticism for mistakes that may lead to heavier punishments. Some collude with others on what to say or reveal in order to reduce the risk of severe punishment. One who inadvertently criticizes another participant too harshly might later visit the home of their target and apologize. Often, last-minute collusions are attempted in order to stop a vicious cycle of revenge.

In the wake of the famine that shook North Korean society to its core in the years from 1996 to 1999, the assemblies transformed into distinctly ceremonial group rituals. Preoccupied with trying to survive, many began to miss these weekly gatherings. When the meetings did take place, they often ended with only a few people having spoken for the sake of ritual formality. There were even instances of sabotage, in which the participants deliberately failed to maintain the ritual, undermining respect for the assembly as well as its authority.

Although they have been transformed, communal assemblies still exert a strong influence on the psychology and behavioral patterns of North Koreans. With their emphasis on confession, criticism, reflection, correction, and a new start, they carry strong religious overtones. They act as sites of purification that presuppose a belief that if one first confesses one's failures, one will then be forgiven and become clean again. It is a confessional culture similar to Catholic rites of reconciliation, whereby one voluntarily confesses one's sins to an omnipotent god and asks for forgiveness.

The state leadership itself, which forced participation in these sessions on the people, seems to have internalized this confessional culture. During the 2003 North Korea–Japan summit in Pyongyang, Kim Jong-Il confessed and apologized to Junichirō Koizumi, the then Japanese prime minister, for the abduction of Japanese citizens by the North during the late 1970s and early 1980s. The world was shocked at this unexpected confession by the North Korean leader, and in South Korea, the United States, and Europe, this confession was interpreted as a conspicuous show of sincerity and willingness to change in the future.

Japan responded to North Korea's confession and apology in an unexpected way, however. The relationship between the two countries sunk to a historic low. Japan insisted that North Korea return all abductees and punish those responsible, calling the abductions an indelible insult to the Japanese people. The anthropologist Ruth Benedict described Japanese culture as one sensitive to honor and shame, one very different from a culture based on guilt in which one accepts the other's confession and apology and then forgives the other and starts anew.[20] It is interesting to note here that Japan has its own cultural reasons for refusing to admit its own past war crimes against Asian countries and for avoiding official apologies.

Social Cultivation and Rites of Passage

In North Korea, the term *gyoyang* refers to the "cultivation of a refined and amicable character that is the basis for a proper social life." More specifically, a person with *gyoyang* is well trained to distinguish public from private and behave appropriately in public. *Gyoyang* is close in meaning to education, but it is not something one learns in the classroom. Rather, one learns it early on through participation in organized social life. As one goes through various rites of passage, one grows into a wholly "cultivated" social human being.

Once on a very rare occasion, I visited Pyongyang with children from South Korea, expecting that the children from the two Koreas could meet each other and play together. However, once we were in Pyongyang, such meetings showed no sign of taking place. Those of us from the South thought that since meetings between children would be nonpolitical in nature, they could take place without a hitch. However, the North Koreans seemed concerned that their children could be easily influenced, so they were unwilling to let them be exposed to strange children who were beyond their control.

In the meantime, the children from South Korea ended up going to events organized for adults, and they soon became bored and restless. They started chattering, making noise, and running around. Their teachers first tried to calm them, then tried to warn them, but to no avail. When I saw that

Figure 5.3. The rites of passage: (top) the Young Pioneer Initiation Ceremony gives children the first taste of social competition through a process of "selection" and "exclusion"; (bottom) the March of the Thousand-Li Road of Liberation is a rite of passage for children preparing for leadership in youth. Top, source: Uriminjokkiri. Bottom, source: Taeyanggwa Chongchun [The Sun of the youths] (Pyongyang: Geumsong Youth Press, 1999), 162.

the North Koreans were looking at the children with astonished looks on their faces, I said to them apologetically, "Kids, right?" But one of them responded solemnly, "We are good at *gyoyang*. . . . Our children never do that." I could not quite believe what I was hearing. However, recalling the behavior of the children of the North that I had seen, I thought that perhaps he had a point.

The most important symbolic rite of passage that all North Koreans go through is joining the Young Pioneers. It is the first organization that all girls and boys join, with members aged from seven to thirteen. Although everyone is obligated to join, not everyone is admitted at the same time; exemplary students are invited first.* In the process, children experience for the first time the harsh realities of success and failure, selection and exclusion, membership and marginalization. Even very old people proudly tell of the overwhelming emotion they felt when they were selected first among their childhood friends to wear the iconic red scarf. By the same token, many others recalled the painful memories of being excluded from the initial selection and feeling embarrassed as they gazed longingly at classmates with the red scarf on their shoulders.

Competitive rites of passage are part of the political socialization process that all North Koreans must go through, beginning with the Young Pioneers and continuing when they progress to membership in the Socialist Workers' Youth League. True to the slogan of the Young Pioneers, they "cultivate" themselves to be "always prepared" for social life. Then, in the Youth League, as well as in the military, at workplaces, and at universities, people are constantly preparing themselves to become eligible to join the Workers' Party, the highest level of social organization one can join as an adult. Once inside the threshold of an organization, one must compete all over again in order to ascend to a position of power and status.

None of the formal selection processes are open to the public, but it is clear that one's family background (*songbun*) influences the outcome. Still, the ability to properly handle social relations is a crucial prerequisite. The core strategy involves building good relationships with others and being recognized for one's loyalty and ability. In order to achieve these goals, one needs to learn how to self-censor while always being conscious of the eyes of others. Even when one must criticize others, one must know where to draw the line and how to remain sensitive to one's shifting environment.

------

* Basically, it is mandatory to join in the second grade of elementary school. However, the joining process is scheduled three times a year to create a sense of competition. It is said that 30 percent will be admitted on February 16, Kim Jong-Il's birthday; 50 percent on April 15, Kim Il-Sung's birthday; and the rest on June 6, the foundation day of the Young Pioneers. Naturally, the first subscribers in February will be full of pride, while the rest will feel inferior.

Thus, North Korean children from an early age have abundant experience in organized life, which includes, but is not limited to, communal assemblies. South Korean children, on the other hand, grow up in an environment that is tolerant of the pursuit of individual aspirations, while cognitive learning is given priority. If children from these two environments met, how would they interact? Unfortunately—or perhaps fortunately—North Korean adults blocked opportunities for such encounters. They watched the South Korean children from a distance, smirking at them. It seemed that they felt certain that children from the South were not appropriately cultivated.

"Be Careful Not to Be the Object of Gossip"

"Make sure you don't become the talk of the town!" This is a mantra that North Koreans repeat constantly. Parents tell their children this in the morning before they leave home for school. Husbands and wives tell it to each other before leaving home for work. Before going to a communal assembly, it is a pledge that one makes to oneself. That is how much one has to be conscious of other people's eyes, ears, and mouths. Perhaps that is why North Koreans' attitudes toward social life tend to be prudent and serious. In general, they respond using safe clichés that are well within the boundaries of the principles.

However, I was often shocked by what seemed to be a complete shift in the attitudes of some North Koreans once the space had changed from public to private. We are quick to regard such people as two-faced. However, while there may be differences in circumstances and degrees, people in all cultures distinguish between public and private environments.

In fact, there are various cultures in which significant differences in behavior can be seen in public and private domains. The Japanese culture of *tatemae* (the behavior and opinions one displays in public) and *honne* (one's true feelings) is an example that has been studied anthropologically.[21] Benedict interpreted this dual attitude of the Japanese as a means of creating a strict distinction between public and private spheres and knowing how to respond accordingly.[22] In other words, while one is on one's best behavior when in public, displaying cultivated self-control, one may be free to express one's emotions in a natural way in private settings. In such a culture, the ability to segue smoothly between the two spheres is considered a sign of cultivation. In that sense, a Japanese person who is polite and kind in public may become rude and arrogant in private. Of course, the opposite can also be true. The point is that people are culturally trained to make a distinction between the two domains and act accordingly.

In Western cultures, by contrast, especially in America, while individuals are socialized to make a clear distinction between private and public spheres, it is believed that a mature individual should maintain a consistent self-identity as much as possible. Thus, one often sees American public figures casually displaying their individuality, even during solemn official ceremonies. The belief here is that the self cannot be affected by circumstances and roles. This is the self-image that many Westerners believe in and try to live up to.

When the anthropologist David Plath introduces the concept of maturity in Japan, according to which social relations *between* individuals are valued, he points out the bias in Western psychology in which absolute value is accorded to self-actualization *by each* individual.[23] In a culture that values human relations, the various roles required of a person must be performed in line with the boundaries that accompany each role. Sometimes it is necessary to be able to properly perform contradictory roles in order to be culturally "mature." This is the ideal type of human being in societies where meaning in life is pursued through human relations and the performance of one's social roles. In these cultures, role compartmentalization is an ability that one develops in order to overcome the inner conflict arising from reduced consistency.[24]

"You Don't Know Anything about Revolution!"

People living in a collectivist culture tend to live by convention. In the public domain, in particular, they are prone to interact politely and defensively. To those who are used to a culture of individualism, such attitudes can feel inflexible and frustrating. In formal, high-tension situations, such as at official meetings between South and North Koreans, not to mention between the United States and North Korea, conflict is likely to arise due to such cultural differences.

When inter-Korean exchanges were active in the mid-2000s, bringing an increasing number of visitors from South Korea, the North Korean authorities trained new guides, putting large numbers of them to work. The novice guides were as tense as could be, handling every issue of conflict in a defensive manner. What used to be possible for South Koreans in past visits was now completely out of the question. After being met with disappointment and frustration time and time again, such as visiting children's hospitals and orphanages, one staff member from a South Korean NGO finally exploded after a few drinks at dinner.

"You people don't know anything about revolution!" the man yelled as soon as we boarded the bus waiting for us outside the restaurant. "Cheap sons of bitches! I'm never coming back to Pyongyang!" The streets in Pyongyang were dark and silent. No one on the bus dared say a word. The driver pulled over and cut the engine. Everyone remained frozen in silence. Finally, the chief guide quietly gave an order to move ahead, and we were on our way.

Once back at our hotel, representatives from the South stepped forward and called an emergency meeting with the North Korean guides. The guides sat with stiff faces as one of them spoke in a fit of indignation. "We just heard what should never be uttered in Pyongyang, the capital of the revolution. This is so serious that it cannot be discussed here. We must report it to the top. We cannot be responsible for your safe return home." Their tone and continuing threats suggested that they felt truly insulted.

We tried to make excuses and apologize for the staff member's indiscretion, telling the Northern guides that he had once been an ardent activist in South Korea's democracy movement and that he normally didn't drink. "That is why we don't like so-called activists from South Korea," one of them responded. "They think they are big revolutionary heroes!"

An experienced South Korean representative who had been sitting quietly and watching everything unfold now addressed the seething North Korean guide. He talked down to the guide. "So what! Our staff member did not insult the Dear General, did he? You have been such greenhorns at guiding us that it's you who have disgraced Dear General. Isn't that true?" The guides hesitated, seemingly at a loss. The attempt at role reversal seemed to have worked. I chimed in: "This conflict arose because young workers from both North and South tried hard to do their best. Misunderstandings can take place and harsh words can be exchanged when there is passion in one's heart. Let's try to understand each other's hearts rather than their words. Let's forgive and forget, share a few drinks, and talk things over." My intention was to turn this serious political drama into lighthearted play.

The South Korean staff member who had exploded earlier washed his face with cold water and came back. That night, he and the North Korean guides sang together in the hotel karaoke room, arms around each other's shoulders. The North Korean guide who had spoken with bloodcurdling harshness earlier was then a completely different person. I can still remember the unguarded expression on his face as he sang the mournful song, "The Unforgettable One in My Heart."

SURVEILLANCE AND PUNISHMENT

"Don't You Hear the Recording Sound?"

We don't necessarily need to be surveilled, eavesdropped on, or tailed to feel scared. Rather, it is the thought that anyone, anytime, anywhere can become the target of such tactics that is distressing. As one who spent his college years in South Korea under a military dictatorship, I immediately recognized in the face of a young North Korean guide I spoke to one day the everyday terror that comes with living in a surveillance society.

"Don't you hear the recording sound? The recording sound?" The guide sitting next to me abruptly whispered, looking around. He looked terrified. We were in a bus headed for Mount Myohyang from Pyongyang. Fear is contagious, indeed. I shuddered with fear too. What had we just been talking about? I tried to recall. I felt something was amiss, replying to him, "You can hear the sound of a recorder here?" After hesitating for a moment with a flustered face, he blushed, uttering something irrelevant. I grasped the situation immediately. He had made a mistake. We had been talking about the South Korean economy and the free trade agreement with the United States. As I had been speaking, he had responded enthusiastically as if to say he understood.

The guide reminded me of a friend who had asked me desperately, his face white with fear, "Don't you hear the wiretap?" It was at a coffee shop in the 1970s, when South Korea was ruled by a dictatorship. We would be walking together, and he would say, "We're being followed!" and grab my hand. He was a tenderhearted poet who suffered from hallucinations throughout his college years. He was neither a great activist nor a pro-democracy fighter. He was simply an ordinary student suffering from anxiety after having undergone interrogation by police and being thrown in prison.

A middle-aged North Korean refugee woman who had mastered survival strategies while enduring hardships at *jangmadang* told me that money could solve any problem, except when it came to political matters. Then she shook her head and told me how her husband had died because of a "political matter" gone awry. Her husband had always been careful about his conduct because his father had been expelled from Pyongyang for "sectarianism." When the Leader's portrait went missing from the neighborhood in which they lived, her husband was singled out as a suspect because of his bad family background. The authorities dragged him away and interrogated him. When he returned, he was tormented by extreme fear and anxiety. Unable to prove his innocence, he became increasingly depressed. One freezing winter night, he stripped down and poured cold water over himself, crying and repeating the phrase, "Dear Leader! I will cleanse myself!" His delirium worsened, and he died soon thereafter. Tears ran down her face as she told me this harrowing story. Afterward, she sighed, saying, "It was a long time ago. People are probably not so naive nowadays."

"Revolutionization" and "Pardon by the Leader"

Human rights issues in North Korea are serious. The problem is not limited to everyday surveillance. The brutality of the means of punishment is arguably second to none in the world. Those responsible for the slightest challenge to the regime are subjected to horrific punishment. Fear of daily surveillance and punishment is as widespread in the society as it was in the Stalinist Soviet Union or Nazi Germany. However, not all people are watched constantly, and not all people become the direct victims of violence.

Not all of the correctional facilities in North Korea are political prison camps, as they are known in the outside world. Neither do they all engage in the cruel treatment of inmates. There are correctional facilities of various levels for nonpolitical crimes, which outnumber political offenses. First, the Ministry of People's Security (*inminboanbu*), whose function is similar to that of the police in other societies, is in charge of arresting and punishing people engaged in general criminal acts, such as murder, theft, assault, fraud, bribery, and various other violations of law and order. Detention facilities for those found guilty of such crimes include the "collecting point" (*jipgyeolso*), the "labor unit" (*nodongdalyeondae*), and the "correctional facility" (*gyohwaso*). Poor food, hard work, and harsh conditions are the norm at these facilities, and inmates are subjected to violence by prison authorities. At the same time, North Korea has a judicial correctional system that is not particularly different from that of other modern states in quarantining nonpolitical offenders.

What *is* problematic—and the subject of international concern—is the persecution of political prisoners by the State Security Ministry (*gukgaanjeonbowibu*) and the state secret police. Once someone is suspected of a political crime, the arrest, interrogation, court trial, and imprisonment take place without due process. Furthermore, the families of suspects are considered guilty by association. For this reason, the handling of political prisoners in North Korea is widely cited as one of the most serious examples of violations of human rights in the world. Testimonies concerning Yodeok Concentration Camp, the classic concentration camp for political prisoners, have brought to light such concerns.[25]

By international standards, many of the crimes leading to brutal punishment by the state secret police in North Korea are minor offenses. For example, as seen in the case of the lost portrait of the leader, anyone found guilty of damaging photographs, statues, or monuments of the nation's leaders; of deriding revolutionary slogans or political propaganda; of disseminating antigovernment documents or information; or of stealing or damaging national resources is subjected to severe punishment. Regardless of how trifling the offense, those deemed political crimes like those listed above are punished severely. In short, the North Korean regime considers the slightest expression of complaint an ontological threat to itself and inflicts severe punishment to prevent the people from even thinking about voicing grievances against the regime.

At this juncture, it is important to consider the issue of political purges following instances of sectarian conflict and challenges within the elite. Contrary to what is widely believed, in many cases political purges do not end in the deaths of those purged or their complete expulsion from the elite. Punishment for political crimes committed by members of the elite often takes the form of "reeducation," with eventual reinstatement in mind. Thus, after an entire family has been banished, supposedly indefinitely, to the "revolutionary zone" of a concentration camp, its members undergo a self-reform process ("revolutionization") via a "thought reeducation" program. This process involves detainees endlessly repeating confessions, repenting, and demonstrating firm determination to be born again.

These political prisoners write petition after petition to the Leader, taking oaths of allegiance and earnestly expressing their love for, and faith in, the Leader. If they are recognized for their fervently renewed loyalty and "self-reformation," they may receive a "pardon." They are reinstated to their former lives and even have their confiscated property returned to them. Any such restoration measure is not a "right" but a "gift," since no legal grounds are specified, and decisions are made arbitrarily by an invisible power. In other words, for those in the dire situation of seeking a political pardon, the Leader's love and grace are their only hope. A few are pardoned in this manner, thereby motivating other political prisoners to continue their self-reformation and pledges of allegiance while enduring brutal violations of their human rights.

In fact, the elite group in North Korea is composed primarily of the families of anti-Japanese guerilla fighters, the members tied to each other by many degrees of kinship. Hence, most of the minor political crimes they commit are treated as matters involving character flaws, and they are given opportunities to redeem themselves and reaffirm their allegiance. Caution is used in administering extreme punishment within the ruling group so that frustration and resistance do not become collectivized.

"It's Not Over Yet!"

I still shudder whenever I come across ardent testimonies exposing North Korean human rights violations, not because the horrors are bizarre to me but because they are so strikingly similar to what we experienced in South Korea decades ago. South Koreans are all too familiar with horrific systems of surveillance and punishment under a military dictatorship. Personally, I only experienced a small part of it, but countless others, including democracy activists, were tortured severely and had their human rights violated.

South Korea in the 1970s and 1980s was infamous internationally for its human rights violations. The reign of terror and human rights suppression was overt. Tear gas was hurled at street demonstrators, and numerous pro-democracy activists, journalists, workers, and students were illegally arrested. Those suspected of political offenses were taken away in the middle of the night. They were then ruthlessly interrogated, mercilessly tortured, forced to confess, and subjected to perfunctory court proceedings, often long sentences, and some even executed. The brutal torture techniques of the Japanese colonial police that were used on independence activists were employed to oppress democracy activists. Many people lost their lives in the process. Several cases, including the Gwangju massacre, are especially notorious.

Recently, many testimonies document abuses from the period. The victims still suffer pain from the scars of the violence. It was a crime and a terrible state terrorism that devastated the lives of victims and their families. The damage of torture, both physical and psychological, lasts a long time. Nowadays, citizens are relatively well aware of the torture of those times not only through court records but also through novels, movies, and dramas.[26] Most "innocent people," both then and now, may harbor a vague fear of state power without ever having personally experienced the brutality of its violence.

In the summer of 2019, young people from East Asia came to Seoul to study Korean democratization and human rights as represented by the widely known "Candlelight Revolution." After conducting a field study at several memory sites, including human rights museums, an old prison, and a former torture site used in anticommunism investigations, a Japanese woman said that she was terrified by the replica images of Japanese police torturing independence activists during the colonial period. But she was even more surprised to learn that South Korean police had carried out similar torture on their own people in the heart of Seoul up until democratization.

A young man from Taiwan who identified himself as a police officer talked about his impression, saying that he admired Korea's democratization, which had led to the establishment of memorial halls for democracy and human rights. He also mentioned that Taiwan had yet to formally inquire into the truth concerning similar incidents of state violence committed during the Cold War. He then asked, "What punishments did the torture-inflicting police officers receive? Have those who set up and operated such terrible facilities been tried? What about those who gave the orders?" The young Koreans present shook their heads. The man from Taiwan spoke again, "Then it can happen again, any time. It's not over yet!"

State violence is not limited to certain periods and certain countries. I am reminded of George Orwell's *1984*. In the book, the author recounts a vivid torture scene; as a young man, he had witnessed the torture and execution of Burmese independence fighters while serving as an officer of the British Imperial Police Force in colonial Burma.[27] One cannot but think also of those subjected to indefinite detention and torture at the Guantanamo Bay detention camp. The US government has yet to close this detention camp even as it accuses other states of grave human rights violations.

There is an argument that crimes against humanity must be punished without statutory time limitations and regardless of national borders so that the perpetrators cannot get away with their crimes by claiming that they were carried out in response to government orders or by justifying them on the basis of ideological convictions or religious beliefs.[28] This argument by human rights activists is considered by many commentators to be both idealistic and unrealistic, some of them even arguing that the international community is not ready for such measures. However, it seems to me to be the most compelling solution. Even as we speak now, North Korea and more than a few other countries in the world are engaging in the torture of people for political reasons. Torture can be revived in any country. How can we stop it? What must we do to prevent it?

A HISTORY OF TRIALS AND SETBACKS

Kim Jong-Un's declaration that North Korea would build a "civilized socialist state" is an explicit acknowledgment, in the language of socialism, that Pyongyang has updated its objective to that of becoming an economically developmental state. However, the modifier "socialist" is added to indicate a wish to distinguish itself from capitalist developmental states. Based on this distinction, the North Korean ruling power justifies a regime centered around the Supreme Leader and state control of labor and capital.

One may ask why North Korea has only now decided to walk the path of development despite all its neighbors having opted to do so years ago. One could also ask why North Korea started its nuclear weapons program, which continues to hold the country back from development.

In fact, several times in the past, North Korea has signaled its intention to follow a development model similar to the Chinese one, and indeed it made earnest efforts to achieve this. However, each time it tried, it failed, due to pressure and obstructions from within and without. In this section, I review the thirty-year history of North Korea's attempts and setbacks.

Inter-Korean Basic Agreement and the Nuclear Crisis

In October 1991, Kim Il-Sung went to China and inspected industrial facilities in Shanghai and Beijing. He met with Deng Xiaoping, Jiang Zemin, and other state leaders and discussed possibilities for North Korean economic development in light of the Chinese experience. He was particularly keen on learning about the reforms and opening-up policy that had begun with the establishment of special economic zones in Shenzhen and other areas of Guangdong adjacent to Hong Kong. He seemed to have taken heart from the fact that, unlike the Soviet Union and other Eastern Bloc countries whose regimes had collapsed in the wake of liberalization, China had maintained its communist regime after forcibly suppressing its people's explosive demands for democratization at Tiananmen Square and achieved rapid economic growth.

It was partly as a result of this trip that the historic Agreement on Reconciliation, Non-Aggression, and Exchanges and Cooperation between South and North Korea (also referred to as the Inter-Korean Basic Agreement) was signed on December 13, 1991. In the fall of that year, North Korea and South Korea joined the UN simultaneously, the two nations formally recognizing each other as state entities. In February of the following year, the Joint Declaration on the Denuclearization of the Korean Peninsula by the two Korean leaders, Rho Tae-Woo and Kim Il-Sung, went into effect. There was also an agreement that the South would stop partaking in joint military exercises with the United States. All that remained to be completed for the fulfillment of the Basic Agreement was the creation of extensive special economic zones that would link capital, technology, and knowledge from the South with land and labor from the North.

Kim Woo-Choong (1936–2019), chairman of the Daewoo Group in South Korea at the time, had a hand in crafting the economic development plans of Vietnam and other socialist countries in Eastern Europe. Utilizing his experience, he proposed building a large industrial complex in Nampo, a port city near Pyongyang. At the time, the sewing and shoe-manufacturing industries in South Korea were in decline due to increasing labor costs. His plan was to move factories to North Korea and create a joint venture model, as the Chinese were already doing successfully with companies in Hong Kong, Singapore, and Taiwan. In response, North Korea mobilized a massive workforce, constructing a ten-lane highway between Pyongyang and Nampo.

However, Kim Jong-Il, then the successor-in-waiting, is known to have been wary of inter-Korean cooperation on economic development, fearing for the security of the regime "because, unlike in continental China, the distance between North and South Korea is short." In fact, on the day on which the Basic Agreement was signed, Kim Jong-Il formally succeeded Kim Il-Sung as Supreme Commander of the Korean People's Army. Whether it was because North Korea had actually started developing nuclear weapons or because there were external pressures working against the agreement, the so-called North Korean nuclear crisis erupted, and the Basic Agreement became all but a dead letter, putting the kibosh on plans for special economic zones.

Soon North and South Korea were caught in a maelstrom of changing circumstances caused by a litany of developments, including Pyongyang's withdrawal from the International Atomic Energy Agency (IAEA) in June 1994, US threats to attack the Yongbyon nuclear facilities, the failure of North-South economic cooperation plans and the ensuing economic crisis in North Korea, and an agreement to host a summit meeting between President Kim Young-Sam of South Korea and Kim Il-Sung. But in July 1994, a few weeks before their scheduled meeting, Kim Il-Sung died. Soon after that, the Great Famine began.

Expecting the imminent collapse of the North Korean regime, South Korea and the international community ratcheted up their blockades and pressure as hunger engulfed the nation. Faced with the possibility of regime collapse, Kim Jong-Il announced his *songun* (military-first) policy—the first step in declaring de facto military rule. The existential crisis faced by the nation was dubbed the "Arduous March," invoking the memory of Kim Il-Sung's fabled march in the 1930s during the fight against the Japanese imperial military. The message was that the people of North Korea had to unite, as the guerrilla fighters of the Kim Il-Sung era had done, to thwart the imperialist blockade and overcome the economic crisis. While industries came to a standstill and over a million lives were lost to famine, the North Korean regime held out until the twenty-first century, employing an extreme strategy in defending the regime.

My first visit to Pyongyang came at the tail end of the Arduous March. Hardly any cars could be seen moving in the city. I recall seeing people in dark khaki clothes with heavy rucksacks on their backs going to and fro with resolute steps. The scene was so stark that it felt surreal.

Inter-Korean Summit, the Axis of Evil, and the Nuclear Test

The inter-Korean summit of June 2000 brought with it the hope of facilitating inter-Korean cooperation and attracting foreign investment to revive North Korea's economy. Yet, such hopes were dashed. The biggest disappointment came from the breakdown in the colonial reparation talks with Japan over the issue of North Korea's kidnapping of Japanese citizens. The situation grew even bleaker when the Bush administration adopted its hard-line stance against the "axis of evil," citing North Korea's human rights violations, and dialed up the pressure. Ultimately, North Korea went back to its nuclear weapons program, conducting a nuclear test in October 2006.

Whether based on a personal obsession of the Supreme Leader, a group decision by the elite, or the collective will of the people, North Korea has chosen to pursue nuclear arms. It is reasonable to ask what possible outcome the country sees as justifying the selection of such a difficult road. "Comrades, I see the light at the end of the tunnel," Kim Jong-Il reportedly told his top officials on the eve of North Korea's first nuclear test. "The dawn is near."[29]

But, rather than light, nuclear testing would only bring more hardship and suffering. Indeed, North Korea's six nuclear tests and its continuous development of new missiles over the years that followed would only serve to deepen its isolation and suffering as international sanctions intensified and neighboring countries fretted about the possibility of nuclear war. With nuclear weapons as its Maginot Line for defending the regime, North Korea began its preparations for a third power succession.

Once Kim Jong-Il was confident of the regime's security, he turned his attention once again to economic development, embarking on what would be his last overseas trip in May 2011. His itinerary was almost identical to that of Kim Il-Sung some twenty years earlier, a journey made in preparation for North Korean economic reform and opening up before the signing of the Inter-Korean Basic Agreement. As his father had done, Kim Jong-Il toured special economic zones in China and met with the current and future premiers of China to ask for their support and cooperation. Before he died suddenly in December of that year, he reportedly said that in 2012, the one hundredth anniversary of Kim Il-Sung's birth, the door would be wide open for North Korea to become a strong and prosperous nation. What he meant to say to the audience at home and abroad was that because he had successfully defended the sovereignty of the nation, it was now possible for North Korea to make the full-fledged transition to a developing economy.

When Kim Jong-Un came to power after his father's death, he too went through a period in which he feared for the security of the regime amid high tensions within and beyond North Korea's borders. Predicting the early collapse of the hereditary system in North Korea, the international community has strengthened economic blockade and military pressure. Along with US troops stationed in South Korea over seventy years after the armistice, the military buildup of South Korea and Japan and the regular large-scale joint military exercises of these countries threatened the security of North Korea itself. In response to these pressures and insults, Kim Jong-Un responded with menacing military parades and repeated nuclear tests and ballistic missile launches that captured the world's attention.

Yet, even while prioritizing these draconian displays of power, the so-called Young General championed a national goal of creating a "civilized socialist nation." In making public appearances decked out in attire reminiscent of Kim Il-Sung, Kim Jong-Un was making a public statement: I am ready and willing to carry out my historical duty, to fulfill the last wish of my grandfather, the founder of the nation.

It was through the military-first policy laid out by his father that Kim Jong-Un made a display of his "dangerous" presence. Only when he had weathered various politico-military crises was he able to sit down with the heads of South Korea, the United States, China, and Russia between 2018 and 2019 in order to enter negotiations involving the future of his country. The world was watching with bated breath, wondering if he would retreat to *songun* politics or finally succeed in starting down the path of a developing nation, as his grandfather had set out to do some three decades earlier.

NOTES

1. Duk-Sung Cheon, *Songunchongchie Daehan Rihae* [Understanding *songun* politics] (Pyongyang: Pyongyang Chulpansa, 2004), 8–9.

2. Workers' Party of Korea, Kimjongil Seonjip [Anthology of Writings and Speeches by Kim Jong-Il] 14 (Pyongyang: Workers' Party of Korea Publishing House, 2000), 267.

3. Tu-Il Kim, *Songunshidae Wiinui Chongchiwa Norae* [The politics and songs of the Great Man of the *songun* era] (Pyongyang: Munhak Yesul Chulpansa, 2002), 254.

4. Tae-Woo Kim, *Pokgyeok: Migonggunui Gongjungpokgyeok Girogeuro Irgeun Hangukjeonjaeng* [Bombardment: Reading the Korean War through the records of the US Air Force's aerial bombings] (Paju: Changbi, 2013).

5. It is written in Chinese characters, 洋夷侵犯 非戰則和 主和賣國.

6. Video recording of an upper-level kindergarten class in Pyongyang, March 6, 2000.

7. Tu-Il Kim, *Songunshidae*, 253.

8. Duk-Sung Cheon, *Songunchongchie* 7.

9. Duk-Sung Cheon, *Songunchongchie* 8–9.

10. Excerpt from the song "Hyeongmyeongui Sunoebu Gyeolsaongwiharira" (We will defend until death the revolutionary nerve center).

11. See in particular Articles 2, 8, and 10 of the "Ten Principles for the Establishing of the Monolithic Ideology of the Party."

12. Their attempt to protect the emperor system succeeded: Washington preserved not only the emperor system but kept Hirohito on the throne to better control the Japanese. The iconic photo of MacArthur with Hirohito during the occupation is emblematic.

13. An excerpt from the song "Sonyeondanweon Urido Chongpoktan Doerira" (Members of the Youth League, we too will become total bombs) from the song book *Dangshini Eopseumyeon Jogukdo Eopda* (Without you, there is no fatherland either), 1997, 82.

14. Clifford Geertz, *Negara: The Theatre State in Nineteenth-Century Bali* (Princeton, NJ: Princeton University Press, 1980).

15. In return, the United States offered softer terms and actually preserved the emperor on the throne under US military-political hegemony. Cf. Tsuyoshi Hasegawa, *Racing the Enemy: Stalin, Truman, and the Surrender of Japan* (Cambridge, MA: Harvard University Press, 2005).

16. "Hyeongmyeongui Kkotssiaseul Ppuryeogandane" (Spread the seeds of revolution), a song included in *5 [O] Daehyeongmyeong Gageug Noraejip* [Song book of the five greatest revolutionary musicals] (Pyongyang: Munhak Yesul Chulpansa, 2008).

17. Jin Kim, "Gungmini 3 [Sam] Ilman Chamajumyeon . . ." [If our fellow citizens would put up with it for just three days . . .], *Joongang Ilbo*, May 24, 2010.

18. Fyodor Tertitskiy, "The Party's 10 Principles, Then and Now," NK News, December 11, 2014, https://www.nknews.org/2014/12/the-partys-10-principles-then-and-now.

19. NKChisikinyeondae, "Bukhanjumin Saenghwal Chonghwa (Communal assembly of North Koreans)," November 2012, https://youtu.be/wKdOqQSNnsc.

20. Ruth Benedict, *The Chrysanthemum and the Sword: Patterns of Japanese Culture* (Rutland, VT: Tuttle, 1987), 223.

21. Takie Sugiyama Lebra, *Japanese Patterns of Behavior* (Honolulu: University of Hawaii Press, 1979), 110–36.

22. Benedict, *The Chrysanthemum and the Sword*, 145–75.

23. David W. Plath, *Long Engagements: Maturity in Modern Japan* (Stanford, CA: Stanford University Press, 1980).

24. Susan J. Pharr, *Political Women in Japan: The Search for a Place in Political Life* (Berkeley: University of California Press, 1981), 144–47.

25. Chol-Hwan Kang and Pierre Rigoulot, *The Aquariums of Pyongyang: Ten Years in the North Korean Gulag* (New York: Basic Books, 2005).

26. These artistic works, whether movies or novels, contribute to the remembrance and understanding of the atrocities by the regime and the struggle for democracy in South Korea during that period. Famous K-movies such as *1987: When the Day Comes* (2017) and *A Taxi Driver* (2017) are based on true stories of ordinary people who became involved in the democratic movement. The renowned author Kang Han's novel *Human Acts* (2016) explores the impact of the Gwangju massacre on the lives of various characters, including a boy who participated in the resistance.

27. George Orwell, *1984* (London: Secker and Warburg, 1949); *Why I Write* (London: Penguin, 2005).

28. Hannah Arendt, *Eichmann in Jerusalem: A Report on the Banality of Evil* (New York: Viking, 1963).

29. Rodong Sinmun, "Jongron [Editorial]," *Rodong Sinmun*, September 8, 2006.

Epilogue

When North Korea was severely damaged by floods in the summer of 2012, South Korea's conservative government made an exception to its hard-line policy toward North Korea, permitting the provision of humanitarian aid to its northern neighbor. As a procession of trucks loaded with emergency relief supplies from South Korean civic groups rolled into Kaesong near the inter-Korean border, I visited the town in order to attend an inter-Korean working-level meeting being held there. It was shortly after Kim Jong-Il had died and his son, Kim Jong-Un, had inherited power. The North Korean delegation included young members of the elite, descendants of revolutionary families, part of a new generation that was emerging with Kim Jong-Un. One of them told what appeared to be a joke after criticizing the South Korean government's economic blockade policy: "Rumor has it that these days in the South, the people who voted for Lee Myung-Bak as president want to cut off their fingers. Well, they should do better at the coming presidential election." I couldn't stand to hear it, so I said, "At least we can change the president once every five years!" The Southerners burst into laughter. The Northerners chuckled along for a moment before they quickly hardened their faces.

I felt strongly at the time, as I do now, that the decisive turning point in today's South and North Korean societies was the democratization of South Korea. What enabled South Korea to achieve democratization when it had existed under authoritarian political rule until the late 1980s? What was preventing the same from happening in the North, and would those roadblocks change soon? After walking different paths for so long, will it even be possible for the South and the North to communicate and live together in peace? Is unification of the two Koreas possible? Such questions coursed through my mind as I walked past traditional houses in Kaesong that had managed to survive countless rounds of gunfire and bombings during the Korean War.

Before the forced division of the peninsula, Korea was a kindred society even under Japanese rule. After winning World War II, the United States and the Soviet Union, having crushed Japan, occupied the Korean Peninsula and divided it.[1] But the thirty-eighth parallel, the border between the two superpowers, was not merely a straight line on a map. The separation of the peninsula along its trajectory mercilessly divided families, relatives, friends, and neighbors.

The border that turned one nation into two states became the front line of the first major hot war between the Cold War powers. Fighting at the forefront of the respective camps, both South and North Korea were thoroughly destroyed in the conflict until a truce was finally reached in 1953. Yet even now, seventy years later, the war is not over. After the Korean War, polarization between North and South accelerated as the Cold War allies of each regime provided support.

During a long era of armistice and confrontation, authoritarian political structures with absolute power at their centers were established in both North and South Korea. The dictators on each side used the wartime trauma suffered by their people to foster enmity toward the other in the climate of Cold War geopolitics between the superpowers, the United States, the Soviet Union, and China. Despite differences in their systems and ideologies, each argued that a strong government was needed due to the presence of the hostile other. Kim Il-Sung in the North and Park Chung-Hee in the South demonstrated strong leadership during times of hardship and poverty. Both men played leading roles in the rapid industrialization of their respective countries, becoming symbols of two very different nation-states.

North Korea became a model state for the socialist world as the nation that achieved the "Miracle of Chosun" (the first Korean miracle) in the 1960s. South Korea, in turn, achieved the "Miracle of the Han River" (another Korean miracle) in the 1970s, becoming a representative capitalist-development success story. Both sides, the North and the South, were able to build highly efficient nation-states in a short period of time after the war based on the fierce survival strategies of the people and centralized systems of national mobilization.

However, the dictators stoked a sense of crisis to create the conditions justifying their lifelong power, making persecution of political opposition and purges routine. Even in South Korea, which claimed to be a liberal democracy, political oppression and human rights violations continued, and civil rights continued to be suppressed, creating numerous victims. On one page of this history, I too experienced this political oppression as a seventeen-year-old high school student.

On a sunny fall morning in 1972 as I headed to school, I saw a tank parked in front of the gate of Gwanghwamun in Seoul. Its long barrel and machine guns were pointed at the square, and soldiers were toting guns with fixed bayonets. This was the scene that greeted me on the first day of the "October Restoration," the military coup in which Park Chung-Hee made his "Special Presidential Declaration," assuming lifetime dictatorial powers. During the first break, I, a model Boy Scout, asked my friends, "Did you see the tank in front of Gwanghwamun? Isn't it cool?" One of my friends reproachfully replied, "Democracy is dead. What's cool about that?" I suddenly felt abashed. In my head, the words "democracy is dead" kept repeating themselves. At lunch, I began talking to my friends again. The country was put under martial law, and all universities were closed. We decided to make our voices heard even as high school students. We numbered seven in all, meeting up during every break time. We printed up messages opposing the Restoration and distributed them around our school. A few days later, we were arrested, court-martialed, and imprisoned. Amid the chill winds of the Restoration, the infamous Seodaemun Prison was cold, dark, and frightening. This was the swift end to my naive youth.[2]

When Kim Il-Sung died in 1994, his son Kim Jong-Il became the first hereditary successor of power in a socialist country. Upon Kim Jong-Il's death in 2011, power was once again inherited by his son, Kim Jong-Un. Taking the helm of the country at the young age of twenty-seven, Kim Jong-Un exuded an air of charismatic power by mimicking his grandfather's appearance and dress style. In an unfortunate historical parallel, Park Chung-Hee's daughter, Park Geun-Hye, was elected president in South Korea the following year, channeling the ruling image of her father, and even replicating her mother's hairstyle.

Power succession is not solely the concern of dictators; it involves groups that seek to maintain their privileges around the leaders and therefore work desperately to reproduce the existing power system. Power groups in both the North and the South exist and coexist by displaying hostility toward each other. Paik Nak-Chung introduces the concept of the "division system" to describe a symbiotic antagonism designed not to bring about unification but to perpetuate division. Power groups in the North and the South seek to maintain the status quo and enhance their own status.[3] North Korea frequently escalates tensions as elections approach in South Korea, and there have even been incidents in which vested interests in South Korea have requested armed provocation on the part of North Korea via secret negotiations.

South Korean civil society relentlessly resisted the military dictatorship. Following decades of persistent struggle—from the Student Revolution in April 1960 to the Gwangju Democratization Movement in May 1980 and the

June Revolution in 1987—the people finally succeeded in achieving their goal of democracy. Countless students and citizens had been the victims of arrest, torture, and massacre by the military dictatorship. Their brave efforts shattered the chains of autocratic power. The Candlelight Revolution in 2016, which resulted in Park Guen-Hye's impeachment and ultimate arrest, clearly demonstrated that the practice of democracy had already been institutionalized. This was a brilliant achievement of the decades-long democratization movement.

South Korea became the first postcolonial country to realize both industrialization and democratization. In particular, with the realization of democratization, people were able to enjoy freedoms and civil rights that they had never experienced before. Numerous regulations that had been enforced for national security reasons were removed, and the workings of government became more transparent. Unrestricted overseas travel was now permitted, and labor rights and social welfare began to be protected in a practical and tangible manner. Each of these changes required a struggle. Freedom of speech and the press did not come overnight, of course. Even after political democratization, the system that had censored literature, movies, and music was abolished only after years of resistance. Without such a struggle for the democratization of everyday life, BTS's songs and dances would not have seen the light of day. Progressive actors, on the authoritarian power's "blacklist," would not have appeared in the movie *Parasite*, and the K-drama *Crash Landing on You* would have been banned or even punished as benefiting the enemy. Democratization was a long and intense process of change involving the awakening of bodies and minds that had been tamed by power.

South Korea's democratization succeeded in breaking the link of authoritarian power succession, but many vested socioeconomic interests continue to be inherited and reproduced within a neoliberal structure. Competition has intensified in schools and workplaces and spread throughout all areas of life. The community life that existed in earlier times has withered. As Daniel Tudor puts it, it has become "a country that has achieved miracles, a country that has lost joy."[4] In the shadow of the glamorous K-culture's global achievements, there is the dystopian reality illustrated in *Squid Game*. While alienation and depression are common problems faced by people in affluent neoliberal societies, the world's highest suicide rate and lowest birth rate in South Korea demonstrate the difficult survival conditions for isolated individuals.

Today, democratizing North Korea has become an urgent task. Despite repeated predictions of imminent regime collapse over the past thirty years since the famine, the North Korean power system remains strong. Pressure from the outside world and efforts at containment have ironically strengthened the leader-centered dictatorship. By making nuclear weapons and missiles a symbol of "sovereignty," it was possible to strengthen the grip on the regime and its inherited power. In the meantime, however, North Korea became an impoverished country. As its isolation has become prolonged, and as power has become concentrated, corruption has become commonplace.

Yet, even under such a dictatorship, daily life in North Korean society is actually changing rapidly. The informal lives of North Koreans are already connected with the outside world. North Korean foreign currency workers are no longer limited to China and Russia but can be found in places such as Dubai and Poland as well as in various Southeast Asian and African countries. Global apparel brands operate factories in China that employ North Korean workers and operate subcontracted factories in Pyongyang and other major cities in North Korea. Pyongyang citizens secretly watch South Korean dramas and performances by K-pop singers and openly consume foreign products. North Korea has already become an "unconsciously capitalist" society with indirect connections to the global capitalist economic system.[5]

There are people who think of North Korea as an island that is completely closed off and isolated. They argue that if leaflets and shortwave radios are sent from the outside, the people inside will learn about the outside world and then rise up to overthrow the system. But this is nothing but Cold War prejudice. North Korea is already moving to become a global nation. The outside world simply does not recognize or acknowledge that reality.

In order to democratize North Korea, its official relations with the international community must be expanded. The democratization of South Korea was not achieved by civil resistance alone. South Korea had already been profoundly integrated into the global economy and politics. The mass demonstrations in South Korea in 1987 have drawn considerable attention from the international media, especially because it was right before the Seoul Olympic Games in 1988. Pressure and checks on the part of the international community prevented the South Korean authoritarian power from carrying out full-scale military suppression of the kind seen in Myanmar.

It is worth recalling that German reunification became possible in part as a result of exchanges between East and West Germany and cooperation from the international community. Following a similar principle, South Korea and the international community must strengthen exchanges and cooperation in order to have a practical impact on the process of North Korean democratization. The informal changes that can already be observed will only lead to formal institutional changes when the regime's obsession with security is overcome through the establishment of diplomatic ties between North Korea and the United States and its allies.

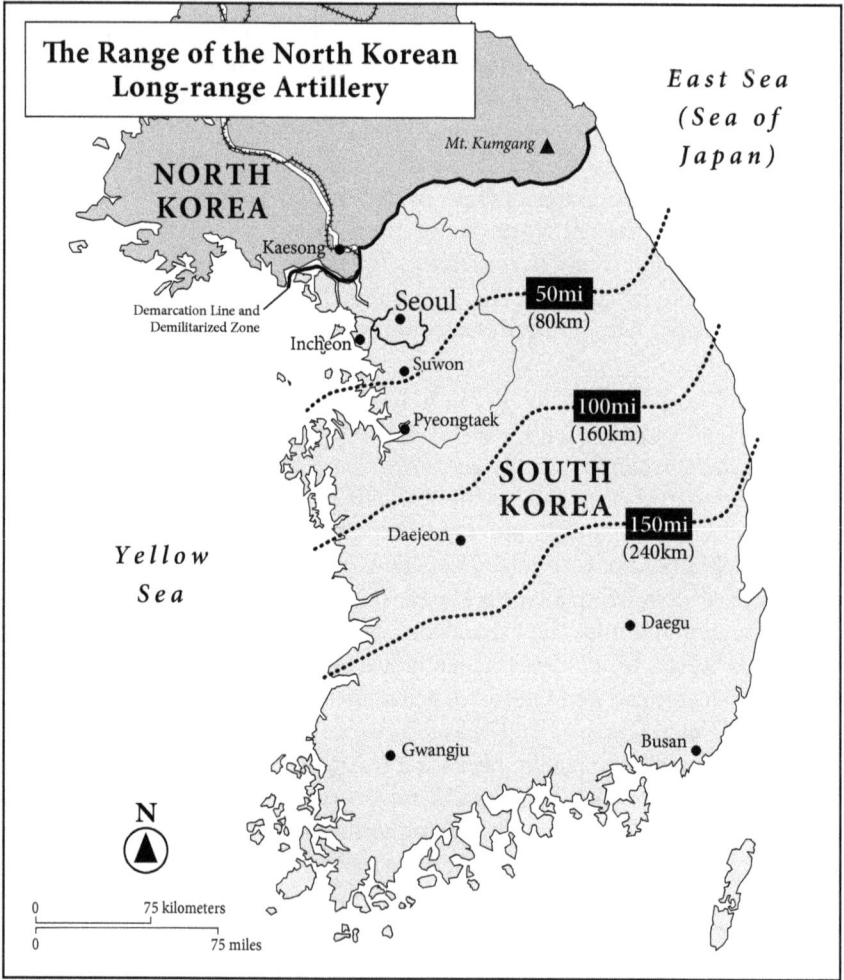

The Range of the North Korean Long-range Artillery

NORTH KOREA

East Sea (Sea of Japan)

Mt. Kumgang ▲

Kaesong

Demarcation Line and Demilitarized Zone

Seoul

50mi (80km)

Incheon

Suwon

Pyeongtaek

100mi (160km)

SOUTH KOREA

150mi (240km)

Daejeon

Yellow Sea

Daegu

Gwangju

Busan

N

0   75 kilometers
0   75 miles

Map 2. The range of North Korean long-range artillery. Byung-Ho Chung

Those with deep hostility toward the North Korean regime think that it should be destroyed through war. Some even argue that regime change is possible through the use of short-term, concentrated attacks. However, within fifty miles of the DMZ, where North Korea's military power is concentrated, lies Seoul and its metropolitan area, home to more than twenty million people, close to half of South Korea's population. If Gangnam in Seoul were Manhattan in New York, it would be comparable to having thousands of North Korean long-range artillery batteries and missiles lined up on Long Island. If modern warfare with its terrifying destructive power were unleashed, millions of human lives could be sacrificed. North Korea's nuclear armament has now gone beyond the rudimentary stage and reached a level where it can use various strategic nuclear weapons, including hydrogen bombs and intercontinental ballistic missiles, in combat. War on the Korean Peninsula could escalate into a hot nuclear war.

Armed conflict on the Korean Peninsula would bring not only devastation to the two Koreas but great damage to the world. Unlike the Korean War seventy years ago, these two countries have become powerhouses that cannot be ignored, albeit in different ways. South Korea is the tenth-largest economic power in the world and the seventh member of the 30-50 Club (which includes rich countries with average per capita incomes exceeding $30,000 and populations exceeding fifty million), and North Korea is the ninth nuclear-armed country in the world. These two nations only seem relatively small because of their geopolitical locations bordering superpowers China, Russia, and Japan. But the destruction of the South Korean economy, which includes key industrial facilities underpinning the global economic system in fields ranging from semiconductors and batteries to electronics and automobiles, would cause irreparable damage to the global economy.

The security crisis on the Korean Peninsula is intensifying first and foremost in the media and in cyberspace. The Global Financial Crisis and the COVID-19 pandemic exacerbated existing social inequality and caused many throughout the world to lose hope for the future. Regimes that fail to improve the living conditions of people in their countries seek to distract attention by creating external enemies and inciting anger toward them. Today, perceptions of North Korea are at their worst, not only in South Korea but in much of the international community. The politics of hate amplifies the crisis. Biased news from mainstream media and fake news on social media seriously intensify tensions. A politician who incites people using aggressive rhetoric is dangerous and irresponsible. The first step to achieving peace will involve overcoming the anachronistic politics of hegemony and war games.

The international community has focused attention on North Korea's leaders and political slogans. However, just as South Korean society is not monolithic, neither is North Korean society. The leader and the soldiers seen in the military parades in Pyongyang are not the only North Koreans. Twenty-six million people with conflicting interests live there: the residents of Pyongyang and those of other regions, party cadres and non-party members, men and women, war generation and famine generation, specialists and engineers, and farmers and laborers in countless occupations. Today, we need to look at North Korea not only as a state but also as a society.

Much time has passed since Korea's division. Most of the first generation that experienced the separation directly have passed away without ever knowing the fate of their loved ones. For them, unification meant reuniting, embracing one another, and repairing broken relationships. However, for most people in South and North Korea, now separated for more than three generations, unification represents the creation of something new rather than a restoration of something that once was.

Both the North and the South have undergone such distinct changes that a return to a homogeneous "past" seems impossible. Unification has to be a process rather than an event. It can only occur when the North and the South address their respective challenges and develop into societies that can accept compromise as the price of ending the long decades of war and division. Solutions to the problems of the two Koreas require that the North embark on the task of democratization in order to establish a less oppressive society, while the South must tackle the task of humanization in order to build a more inclusive society that can accept differences. The international community can facilitate such a process. As we break down the barriers and work closely together, gradually overcoming the boundaries that divide, we can call this "unification."

The unification of the Korean Peninsula can serve as a catalyst for achieving sustainable peace in East Asia and throughout the world. I hope that the North, the South, and the international community will collaborate in order to build peace, averting the potentially catastrophic consequences of an escalating New Cold War conflict that could end in nuclear holocaust. Cultivating peace together, along with overcoming climate and ecological crises, is an imminent task that human society must jointly address.

NOTES

1. Tsuyoshi Hasegawa, *Racing the Enemy: Stalin, Truman, and the Surrender of Japan* (Cambridge, MA: Harvard University Press, 2005).

2. Byung-Ho Chung, "Tanks and BTS Fans in Front of Gwanghwamun," *Hankyoreh*, November 12, 2020, https://english.hani.co.kr/arti/english_edition/english_editorials/969713.html.

3. Nak-Chung Paik, *The Division System in Crisis: Essays on Contemporary Korea* (University of California Press, 2011).

4. Daniel Tudor, *Korea: The Impossible Country* (Rutland, VT: Tuttle, 2012).

5. Hyun Ok Park, *The Capitalist Unconscious: From Korean Unification to Transnational Korea* (New York: Columbia University Press, 2015).

Bibliography

Arendt, Hannah. *Eichmann in Jerusalem: A Report on the Banality of Evil.* New York: Viking, 1963.

———. *The Human Condition.* Chicago: University of Chicago Press, 1958.

Armstrong, Charles K. "'Fraternal Socialism': The International Reconstruction of North Korea, 1953–62." *Cold War History* 5, no. 2 (May 2006): 161–87.

Augustine, Matthew R. "The Limits of Decolonization: American Occupiers and the 'Korean Problem' in Japan, 1945–1948." *International Journal of Korean History* 22, no. 1 (February 2017): 43–75.

Bakhtin, Mikhail. *Rabelais and His World.* Bloomington: Indiana University Press, 1984.

Barthes, Roland. *Empire of Signs.* New York: Hill and Wang, 1982.

Becker, Jasper. *Hungry Ghosts: Mao's Secret Famine.* New York: Henry Holt, 1998.

Benedict, Ruth. *Race: Science and Politics.* New York: Viking, 1964.

———. *The Chrysanthemum and the Sword: Patterns of Japanese Culture.* Rutland, VT: Tuttle, 1987.

Certeau, Michael de. *The Practice of Everyday Life.* Berkeley: University of California Press, 1984.

Chang, U-Jin. *Adeukhi Mon Yennarui Uri Sonjodeurul Chajaseo* [In search of our ancestors from very long ago]. Pyongyang: Social Science Press, 2009.

Cheon, Duk-Sung. *Songunchongchie Daehan Rihae* [Understanding *songun* politics]. Pyongyang: Pyongyang Chulpansa, 2004.

Cho, Hong-Min. "Kim Jong-Unui 'Wurin Wae Meugeul Geuk Upna' Geuggeonghae Nolla" [Kim Jong-un was worried, 'Why don't we have food?']. *Kyunghyang Shinmun*, October 10, 2010. https://www.khan.co.kr/politics/north-korea/article/201010102220305.

Choe, Hak-Nak. "Bukhan Seollarui Sobiwa Seonmul Yeongu: Uimuwa Wibanui Maegaeroseo Sul" [A study on New Year's Day consumption and gifts in North Korea: Alcohol as a medium of duty and transgression]. Symposium proceedings, Korean Society for Cultural Anthropology, Fall 2019.

Choe, Jin-I. *Gukgyeongeul Sebeon Geonneun Yeoja* [The woman who crossed three national borders]. Seoul: Bookhouse, 2005.

Choe, Jin-Seok. *Minjunggwa Geuroteseukeuui Munhwajeongchihak Mihail Baheuchingwa Saengseongui Sayu* [The cultural politics of *minjung* and the grotesque: Mikhail Bakhtin and generative speculation]. Seoul: Grinbi, 2017.

Choi, Gi-Man. *Taeyanggwa Chongchun* [The Sun and the youths]. Pyongyang: Geumsong Youth Press, 1999.

Chosun [Korea], June 2001. *Chosun Nyosong* [North Korean women], April 1989.

Chung, Byung-Ho. "Bukhan Eorini Giawa Hanguk Illyuhagui Gwaje" [Children, the North Korean famine, and the task of Korean anthropology]. *Korean Cultural Anthropology* 32, no. 2 (1999): 155–75.

———. "Bukhan Gigeunui Illyuhakjeong Yeongu" [An anthropological study of the North Korean famine]. *Tongilmunjeyeongu* [Korean journal of unification affairs] 16, no. 1 (2004): 109–40.

———. "Bundanui Teumsaeeseo: Talbuk Nanminui Sarmgwa Ingwon" [In the interstices of North-South division: The lives and human rights of North Korean refugees]. *Dangdaebipyeong* [Contemporary criticism] 16 (2001): 236–55.

———. *Gonangwa Useumui Nara: Inryuhakjaui Bukhan Iyagi* [State of suffering and smiling: An anthropologist's story on North Korea]. Paju: Changbi, 2020.

———. "Hamgyeongdo Aideurege Namhaeui Miyeogeul" [Sea mustard to the children of Hamgyeong Province]. *Hankyoreh*, February 21, 2012. https://www.hani .co.kr/arti/opinion/column/519927.html.

———. *Jinruigaksha Ga Nojoita Kitachosen: Gunan to Hohoemi No Kuni* [North Korea observed by an anthropologist: A state of suffering and smiling]. Tokyo: Seidosha, 2022.

———. "Living Dangerously in Two Worlds: The Risks and Tactics of North Korean Refugee Children in China." *Korea Journal* 43, no. 3 (Fall 2003): 191–211.

———. "Naebongmanhan Hyojaga Eopda" [Nothing beats long johns for filial piety]. *Hankyoreh*, January 27, 2011. https://www.hani.co.kr/arti/opinion/column/460956.html.

———. "Naengjeon Jeongchiwa Bukhan Ijumineui Chimtuseong Chogukka Jeollyak" [Cold War politics and penetrant transnational strategies of North Korean migrants]. *Review of North Korean Studies* 17, no. 1 (2014): 49–100.

———. "North Korea: Beyond Charismatic Politics." *Asia-Pacific Journal: Japan Focus* 16, no. 13 (2018). https://apjjf.org/2018/13/chung.

———. "North Korean Famine and Relief Activities of the South Korean NGOs." In *Food Problems in North Korea: Current Situation and Possibility*, edited by Gill-Chin Lim and Namsoo Chang, 239–56. Seoul: Oruem Publishing House, 2003.

———. "North Korean Refugees as Penetrant Transnational Migrants." *Urban Anthropology and Studies of Cultural Systems and World Economic Development* 43, no. 4 (2014): 329–61.

———. "Preface: Namgwa Buk Aideul Eotteoke Kiulkka?" [How are children raised in the South and the North?]. *Gaettongine Noriteo* [Gaettongi's playground], 2007.

———. "Tanks and BTS Fans in Front of Gwanghwamun." *Hankyoreh*, November 12, 2020. https://english.hani.co.kr/arti/english_edition/english_editorials/969713.html.

Chung, Jean-Kyung. "Bukhansaramdeului Seongyeokhal Teukseonggwa Gachigwan: Talbukja Jaryo" [The gender-role characteristics and values of North Koreans: Data from North Korean refugees]. *Korean Journal of Psychology: General* 21, no. 2 (2002): 163–77.

Collins, Robert. *Marked for Life: Songbun, North Korea's Social Classification System*. Washington, DC: Committee for Human Rights in North Korea, 2012.

Conn, Peter J. *Pearl S. Buck: A Cultural Biography*. Cambridge: Cambridge University Press, 1996.

Cumings, Bruce. *Korea's Place in the Sun: A Modern History*. New York: Norton, 1997.

Demick, Barbara. *Nothing to Envy: Love, Life and Death in North Korea*. London: 4th Estate, 2010.

Douglas, Mary. *Purity and Danger: An Analysis of Concepts of Pollution and Taboo*. London: Routledge, 2002.

EU, UNICEF, and WFP. "Nutritional Survey of the DPRK." November 1998.

Geertz, Clifford. *Negara: The Theatre State in Nineteenth-Century Bali*. Princeton, NJ: Princeton University Press, 1980.

Goffman, Erving. *Stigma: Notes on the Management of Spoiled Identity*. Englewood Cliffs, NJ: Prentice-Hall, 1963.

Gong, Yong-Chul, and Hun-Mo Chung. "3[Sam]-Dae Seseup Jigeum Bukhaneseo Museun Iri Ireonago Inna?" [The third-generation succession—What is happening in North Korea now?]. *KBS Special*. South Korea: KBS-1 TV, June 28, 2009.

"Gongdong Saseol [Joint editorial]." *Rodong Sinmun*, January 1, 2012.

Green, Christopher K., and Stephen J. Epstein. "Now on My Way to Meet Who? South Korean Television, North Korean Refugees, and the Dilemmas of Representation." *Asia-Pacific Journal* 11, no. 2 (2013). https://apjjf.org/2013/11/41/Stephen-Epstein/4007/article.html.

Gyoyukdoseo Chulpansa, ed. *Haebanghu 10 [Sip] Nyeonganui Gonghwaguk Inmin Gyoyukui Baljeon* [The improvement in people's education in the DPRK in the ten-year period after liberation]. Pyongyang: Gyoyukdoseo Chulpansa, 1995.

Han, Kang. *Human Acts*. Translated by Deborah Smith. London: Granta, 2016.

Han, Man-Gil, ed. *Bukhaneseoneun Eotteoke Gyoyukhalkka: Bugnyeokkeseo Salda on 16 [Simnyuk] Inui Saengsaenghan Gyoyuk Cheheomgi* [How do the North Koreans educate? The vivid educational experiences of sixteen people who have lived in the North]. Seoul: Urigyoyuk, 1999.

Harari, Yuval. *Homo Deus: Miraeui Yeoksa* [Homo deus: A brief history of tomorrow]. Translated by Myeong-Ju Kim. Paju: Gimm-Young Publishers, 2017.

Hasegawa, Tsuyoshi. *Racing the Enemy: Stalin, Truman, and the Surrender of Japan*. Cambridge, MA: Harvard University Press, 2005.

Hassig, Ralph C., and Kong-Dan Oh. *The Hidden People of North Korea: Everyday Life in the Hermit Kingdom*. Lanham, MD: Rowman and Littlefield, 2009.

208   *Bibliography*

Hong, Min. "Bukhan Sijang Ilsangsaenghwal Yeongu: Geuroteseukeuwa Bujorigeug 'Sai' Eseo" [A study of daily life at a North Korean market: "Between" the grotesque and the theater of the absurd]. In *Bukhanui Ilsangsaenghwal Segye: Oechimgwa Soksagim* [The world of everyday life in North Korea: Shouts and whispers], edited by Sun-Seon Park and Min Hong, 292–362. Seoul: Haneul, 2010.

Hu, Elise. "South Korea's Newest TV Stars Are North Korean Defectors." NPR, January 31, 2016. https://www.npr.org/sections/parallels/2016/01/31/464798910/south-koreas-newest-tv-stars-are-north-korean-defectors.

Hübinette, Tobias. *Comforting an Orphaned Nation: Representations of International Adoption and Adopted Koreans in Korean Popular Culture.* Stockholm: Stockholm University, 2005.

Huizinga, Johan. *The Autumn of the Middle Ages.* Chicago: University of Chicago Press, 1996.

Humphrey, Caroline. *The Unmaking of Soviet Life: Everyday Economies after Socialism.* Ithaca, NY: Cornell University Press, 2002.

Hunter, Helen-Louise. *Kim Il-song's North Korea.* Westport, CT: Praeger, 1999.

Hwang, Jang-Yup. "Bukhanui Jinsilgwa Heowi" [The truth and falsehood of North Korea]. Institute for Unification Policy, 1998.

Ito, Abito. *Kitachosen No Jinmin No Seikatsu* [The lives of the North Korean people]. Tokyo: Koubundou Publishers, 2017.

Jang, Hoon, dir. *A Taxi Driver.* 137 min. South Korea: Show Box, 2017.

Jang, Joon-Hwan, dir. *1987: When the Day Comes.* 120 min. South Korea: CJ Entertainment, 2017.

Jang, Tae-Han. *Heugin: Geudeureun Nuguinga* [African Americans: Who are they?]. Seoul: Hanguk Gyeongje Sinmunsa (Korea Economic Daily Co.), 1993.

Jeon, Su-Il. *Gwanryo Bupaeron* [Theory on bureaucratic corruption]. Seoul: Seonhaksa, 1999.

Jeon, Yeong-Seon. "Bukanui Daejipdanchejo Yesulgongyeon 'Arirang'ui Jeongchisahoejeok, Munhwayesuljeok Uimi" [The politico-social and literary-artistic significance of the North Korean mass performance "Arirang"]. *Jungso Yeongu* [Sino-Soviet affairs] 26, no. 2 (2002): 131–58.

———. "Kim Jong Un Sidaeui Munhwajeongchi, Jeongchimunhwa" [Cultural politics, political culture in the Kim Jong-Un era]. In *Kim Jong Un Sidaeui Munhwa* [Culture in the Kim Jong-Un era], edited by Yeong-Seon Jeon. Seoul: Haneul Chulpansa, 2015.

Rodong Sinmun, "Jongron [Editorial]." September 8, 2006.

DailyNK, "Jongyeonghanun Kim Jong Un Daejang Dongjiui Widaeseong Gyoyang Jaryo" [Educational material for learning (about) the greatness of Honorable General Comrade Kim Jong-Un]. October 6, 2009.

Joeunbotdul (Good friends). *Bukhansaramdeuli Malhaneun Bukhan Iyagi* [Tales of North Korea told by North Koreans]. Seoul: Jongto, 2000.

Ju, Seong-Ha. *Pyongyang Jabonjuui Baekgwasajeon: Ju Seong-Ha Gijaga Jeonhaneun Jinjja Bukhan Iyagi* [Encyclopedia of Pyongyang capitalism: Real North Korea stories as told by reporter Ju Seong-Ha]. Seoul: Bukdodeum, 2018.

Kang, Chol-Hwan, and Pierre Rigoulot. *The Aquariums of Pyongyang: Ten Years in the North Korean Gulag.* New York: Basic Books, 2005.

Kang, Joon-Mann. *Seouldaeeui Nara* [The country of Seoul National University]. Wonju: Gaemagoweon, 1996.

Kang, Ju-Won. *Amnokgangeun Dareuge Heureunda: Munhwaillyuhakjaui Nuneuro Bon, Gukgyeonggwa Gukjeogeul Neomeo Aungdaung Salgo Osundosun Jinaeneun Saramdeul Iyagi* [The Amnok River flows differently: The story of people quarreling and living in harmony beyond the barriers of national borders and identities, seen through the eyes of a cultural anthropologist]. Seoul: Nulmin, 2016.

———. *Naneun Oneuldo Gukgyeongeul Mandeulgo Heomunda* [Today, I am still making and breaking the border]. Seoul: Geulhangari, 2013.

KBS. "97 Jigeum Bukhan Museun Iri Ireonago Inneunga" [97 what's happening now in North Korea]. South Korea: KBS-1 TV, June 22, 1997.

Kim, Duk-Young. "(Suyogihoek) Mireuchoyu, Naui Nampyeoneun Jojeonghoimnida" [Wednesday feature series: Mircioiu, my husband is Jo Jeong-Ho]. 60 min. South Korea: KBS-1 TV, June 23, 2004.

Kim, Hyo-Ryun. *Taeyangui Pumsokeseo Kotpineun Jaenyeongui Hwawon* [The garden of talents blossoming in the bosom of the Sun]. Pyongyang: Munye Chulpansa, 2018.

Kim, Il-Sung. *Inmin Jeonggwongigwan Ilkundul Apeseo Han Yeonseol* [A speech delivered to the workers of the people's government organs]. Gimilseong Jeojakjip [Anthology of writings by Kim Il-Sung] 33. Pyongyang: Chosun Rodongdang Chulpanbu (Workers' Party of Korea Publishing House), 1987.

Kim, Jaeeun. "The Making and Unmaking of a 'Transborder Nation': South Korea during and after the Cold War." *Theory and Society* 38, no. 2 (March 2009): 133–64.

Kim, Jae-Ung. "Yeonjwajewa Chulsinseongbunui Gyujeongnyeokeul Tonghae Bon Haebang Hu Bukhaneui Gajokjeongchaek" [North Korean family policies after independence seen through the defining power of the guilt-by-association system and family backgrounds]. *Journal of Korean Studies* 187 (2019): 313–41.

Kim, Jin. "Gungmini 3 [Sam] Ilman Chamajumyeon . . ." [If our fellow citizens would put up with it for just three days . . .]. *Joongang Ilbo*, May 24, 2010.

Kim, Min-Kwan. "Choegeun Bukhan Smatupon Iyong Hunhwang Mit Sisajon" [The current condition and implications of the usage of smart phones in North Korea]. In *Weekly KDB Report*. Seoul: Korean Development Bank, 2020.

Kim, Sang-Soon. *Juche Yesului Bitnaneun Hwapok* [Glowing canvases of *juche* art]. Pyongyang: Pyongyang Yesul Jonghap Chulpansa, 2001.

Kim, Sung Kyung. "Bukhan Jeongchichejewa 'Maeumui Seupsok': Juche Sasanggwa Sinso Jedoui Jakdongeul Jungsimeuro" [The North Korean political regime and the "mind convention": With a focus on *juche* ideology and the workings of the sinso institution]. *Hyeondai Bukhan Yeongu* [Review of North Korean studies] 21, no. 2 (2018): 191–231.

———. "Change and Continuity: North Korean Society at a Crossroads." *Global Asia* 16, no. 3 (2021): 50–57.

Kim, Sung-Mo, Sung-Il Tak, and Chul-Man Kim. *Chosunui Jipdanchejo* [Mass games of Korea]. Pyongyang: Oegungmun Chulpansa, 2002.

Kim, Tae-Woo. *Pokgyeok: Migonggunui Gongjungpokgyeok Girogeuro Irgneun Hangukjeonjaeng* [Bombardment: Reading the Korean War through the records of the US Air Force's aerial bombings]. Paju: Changbi, 2013.

Kim, Tu-Il. *Songunshidae Wiinui Chongchiwa Norae* [The politics and songs of the Great Man of the *songun* era]. Pyongyang: Munhak Yesul Chulpansa, 2002.

Kim, Yeon-Gwang. "Good-Bye! Kim Il-Sung." *Weolgan Chosun* [Chosun monthly], December 2005.

Kwon, Heonik. "'Seeking Good Luck' in North Korea." *Asia-Pacific Journal: Japan Focus* 20, no. 9 (2022). https://apjjf.org/2022/9/Kwon.html.

Kwon, Heonik, and Byung-Ho Chung. *North Korea: Beyond Charismatic Politics.* Lanham, MD: Rowman and Littlefield, 2012.

Kwon, Hyeon-Suk. *Rumaniaui Yeonin* [Lovers in Romania]. Seoul: Minumsa, 2001.

Lankov, Andrei. *The Real North Korea: Life and Politics in the Failed Stalinist Utopia.* Oxford: Oxford University Press, 2013.

Lautze, Sue. *The Famine in North Korea: Humanitarian Responses in Communist Nations.* Medford, MA: Feinstein International Famine Center, Tufts University, 1997.

Lebra, Takie Sugiyama. *Japanese Patterns of Behavior.* Honolulu: University of Hawaii Press, 1979.

Lee, Gi-Beom. *Namgwa Buk Aideuregen Cheoljomangi Eopda: Lee Gi-Beom Gyosuui Maheunahopbeon Bangbuggi* [The children of the North and South do not have a barbed wire fence between them: A travelogue of Prof. Lee Gi-Beom's forty-nine visits to North Korea]. Paju: Bori Publisher, 2018.

Lee, Richard Borshay. "Eating Christmas in the Kalahari." *Natural History,* December 1969.

Lee, Young-Jong. "Kim Jong-Un Jeonsaegye debwuinal," *JoongAang Ilbo,* October 11, 2010.

Maruyama, Masao. *Thought and Behavior in Modern Japanese Politics.* Edited by Ivan Morris. New York: Oxford University Press, 1969.

Medical Aid for Children. "Bukhan Yeoseongeui Imsin Mit Chulsangwa Geongange Gwanhan Bogoseo" [A report on pregnancy, childbirth, and health among North Korean women]. Seoul: Medical Aid for Children (an NGO based in Seoul), 2005.

Min, Young-Kyu. "Kim Jong-Un 'Beteunam Gyeongjebaljeone Gipeun Insang, Gyeongheom Gongyu Huimang" [Kim Jong-Un 'impressed by Vietnam's economic development, hopes to share experience']. *Yonhap News,* March 2, 2019. https://www.yna.co.kr/view/AKR20190302037200084.

Morris-Suzuki, Tessa. "Exodus to North Korea Revisited: Japan, North Korea, and ICRC in the 'Repatriation' of Ethnic Koreans from Japan." *Asia-Pacific Journal: Japan Focus* 9, no. 22 (2011). https://apjjf.org/2011/9/22/Tessa-Morris-Suzuki/3541/article.html.

———. *Exodus to North Korea: Shadows from Japan's Cold War.* Lanham, MD: Rowman and Littlefield, 2007.

Munhak Yesul Chulpansa. *5 [O] Daehyeongmyeonggageung Noraejip* [Song book of the five greatest revolutionary musicals]. Pyongyang: Munhak Yesul Chulpansa, 2008.

Myers, B. R. *The Cleanest Race: How North Koreans See Themselves and Why It Matters.* London: Melville House, 2010.

"Najajin Babsang" [The lowered meal table]. *Chongnyon Munhak* [Youth literature], December 2003, 26. Pyongyang: Munhak Yesul Jonghap Chulpansa.

Natsios, Andrew S. *The Great North Korean Famine: Famine, Politics, and Foreign Policy.* Washington, DC: Institute of Peace Press, 2001.

NKChisikinyeondae. "Bukhanjumin Saenghwal Chonghwa (Communal assembly of North Koreans)." November 2012. https://youtu.be/wKdOqQSNnsc.

Noland, Marcus, Sherman Robinson, and Tao Wang. "Famine in North Korea: Causes and Cures," *Economic Development and Cultural Change* 49, no. 4 (2001): 741–767.

Oh, Hyeon-Cheol. *Songun Ryeongjanggwa Sarangui Segye [Songun* Leader General and the world of love]. Pyongyang: Pyongyang Publishing House, 2005.

Oh, So-Won. *Hadaka No Kitachosen* [Naked North Korea]. Tokyo: Shinchoshinsho, 2013.

Orwell, George. *1984.* London: Secker and Warburg, 1949.

———. *Why I Write.* London: Penguin, 2005.

Oxford Poverty and Human Development Initiative (OPHI). "Bhutan's Gross National Happiness Index." https://ophi.org.uk/policy/bhutan-gnh-index.

Park, Han-Shik, and Guk-Jin Kang. *Seoneul Neomeo Saenggak Hada: Namgwa Bugeul Galanonneun 12 [Yeoldu] Gaji Pyeongyeone Gwanhayeo* [Thinking beyond the lines: Regarding twelve prejudices dividing North and South Korea]. Seoul: Buki Publisher, 2018.

Park, Kyung Ae. "Women and Revolution in North Korea." *Pacific Affairs* 65, no. 4 (1992): 527–45.

Park, Hyun Ok. *The Capitalist Unconscious: From Korean Unification to Transnational Korea.* New York: Columbia University Press, 2015.

Paterniti, Michael. "The Flight of the Fluttering Swallows." *New York Times Magazine*, April 27, 2003, 46.

Pharr, Susan J. *Political Women in Japan: The Search for a Place in Political Life.* Berkeley: University of California Press, 1981.

Plath, David W. *Long Engagements: Maturity in Modern Japan.* Stanford, CA: Stanford University Press, 1980.

Pyongyang Chulpansa. *Minjokui Oboi [The father of the nation].* Pyongyang: Pyongyang Chulpansa, 2012.

Robinson, Joan. "Korean Miracle." *Monthly Review* 16, no. 9 (January 1965): 541–49.

Robinson, W. Courtland, Myung Ken Lee, Kenneth Hill, and Gilbert Burnham. "Famine, Mortality, and Migration: A Study of North Korean Migration in China." In *Forced Migration and Mortality*, edited by Holly E. Reed and Charles B. Keely, 69–85. Washington, DC: National Academy Press, 2001. https://www.ncbi.nlm.nih.gov/books/NBK223341.

Ryang, Sonia. "Japan, North Korea, and the Biopolitics of Repatriation." *Asia-Pacific Journal: Japan Focus* 21, no. 6 (2023). https://apjjf.org/2023/6/Ryang.html.
———. "The North Korean Homeland of Koreans in Japan." In *Koreans in Japan: Critical Voices from the Margin,* edited by Sonia Ryang, 42–64. London: Routledge, 2000.
———. "The Rise and Fall of Chongryun—from Chōsenjin to Zainichi and Beyond." *Asia-Pacific Journal: Japan Focus* 14, no. 15 (2016). https://apjjf.org/2016/15/Ryang.html.
Ryom, Hyong-Mi. "Aireul Kiumyeo" [Raising a child]. *Chosun Munhak* [Korean literature], November 2002.
Sanger, David E. "U.S. Nuclear Talks with North Korea Break Down in Hours." *New York Times,* October 5, 2019.
Scott, James. *Weapons of the Weak: Everyday Forms of Peasant Resistance.* New Haven, CT: Yale University Press, 1985.
Seok, Yungi. *Konaneui Haenggun* [The Arduous March]. Pyongyang: Munye Chulpansa, 1991.
Shin, Sang-Gyun. *Bokbadeun Sessangdungideul* [Blessed are the triplets]. Pyongyang: Geumsong Chongnyon Chulpansa, 1993.
Rodong Sinmun. "Widaehan Kim Jong Il Dongjiui Ryongjonenun" [To the memory of the Great Comrade, Kim Jong-Il]. December 30, 2011.
Smith, Hazel. *Hungry for Peace: International Security, Humanitarian Assistance, and Social Change in North Korea.* Washington, DC: US Institute of Peace Press, 2005.
Song, Ki-Chan. "Jongcheseongui Jongchieseo Jongcheseongui Kwanriro" [From identity politics to identity management: The ethnic education of the *Chosun hakkyo* and the identities of Zainichi-Koreans]. *Korean Cultural Anthropology* 51, no. 3 (2018): 207–78.
Song, Seung-Hwan, and Yeong-Su Weon. *(Wiinirhwae Pikkin) Useumui Segye* [The world of smiles (as observed in anecdotes of the Great Man)]. Pyongyang: Pyongyang Chulpansa, 2003.
Tertitskiy, Fyodor. "The Party's 10 Principles, Then and Now." NK News, December 11, 2014. https://www.nknews.org/2014/12/the-partys-10-principles-then-and-now.
Tudor, Daniel. *Korea: The Impossible Country.* Rutland, VT: Tuttle, 2012.
Tudor, Daniel, and James Pearson. *North Korea Confidential: Private Markets, Fashion Trends, Prison Camps, Dissenters and Defectors.* 2nd ed. Clarendon, VT: Tuttle, 2020.
Uriminjok Sorodopgi Bulkyo Undong Bonbu (Korean Buddhist sharing movement). *Bukhansigryangnanui Siltae (Jaryojip)* [Reality of the North Korean food shortage]. Seoul: Joeunbotdul, 1998.
Wada, Haruki. *Kitachosen: Yugekitaikokka Kara Seikigunkokka e* [North Korea: From guerilla state to regular army state]. Tokyo: Iwanami Shuppan, 1998.
Woo-Cumings, Meredith. *The Developmental State.* London: Cornell University Press, 1999.
Workers' Party of Korea. Kimjongil Seonjip [Anthology of writings and speeches by Kim Jong-Il] 14. Pyongyang: Workers' Party of Korea Publishing House, 2000.

Yi, Myeong-Ja. "Kim Jong-Il Tongchi Sigi Gajok Mellodeurama Yeongu: Bukhan Geundaeseongui Byeonhwareul Jungsimeuro" [A study on family melodramas during the reign of Kim Jong-Il: With a focus on changes in modernity in North Korea]. PhD diss., Dongguk University, 2005.

Zhu, Billy. "Dansume!" [In a single breath!]. YouTube video, 06:29. March 10, 2013. https://www.youtube.com/watch?v=SSbYc0ojjo8.

Index

9 781538 193846